Don't Thank the Messenger

Is your glass half full?

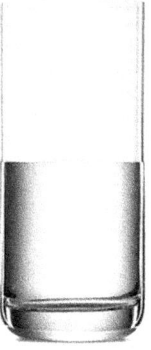

"...with God all things are possible."

Matthew 19:26

Don't Thank the Messenger

A true telling of divine communications

and supernatural encounters

JJ Jorgensen

Don't Thank the Messenger
Published by
Jorgensen Enterprises, LLC, New Jersey

Distributed by Ingram Publisher Services LLC, Tennessee

ISBN: 978-1-7346266-2-9

© 2019 James Jorgensen

All rights reserved. This book or parts thereof may not be reproduced in any form, stored in any retrieval system, or transmitted in any form by any means—electronic, mechanical, photocopy, recording, or otherwise—without prior written permission of the author, except as provided by United States of America copyright law.

For permission requests, write to the author via email to publisher@jor-ent.com.

NOTE: Some names were altered for security and privacy reasons.

DEDICATION

For my Heavenly Father, Blessed Mother, and their Awesome Son; and,

For Lisa, my wonderful wife and partner in all things; and,

For my best man and honorable son, Matthew James; and,

For my family, be they by blood, marriage, or spirit; and,

For Mom, who is always missed, but never far from here; and,

To all those that influenced my life, here and on the other side,

Thank you.

Table of Contents

Prologue .... Page 1
Chapter 1 – Jumping in Feet First .... Page 3
Chapter 2 – Then Science Gets Involved .... Page 10
Chapter 3 – The Good, the Bad and the Hug .... Page 17
Chapter 4 – A Next Day Delivery Prayer Coming Up .... Page 22
Chapter 5 – Lenny's Father Wanted a Sandwich .... Page 31
Chapter 6 – A Secretary No More .... Page 39
Chapter 7 – Change is a Constant Thing .... Page 48
Chapter 8 – A Guy Named Joe .... Page 53
Chapter 9 – A Coney Islander Dancing in Danbury .... Page 66
Chapter 10 – On The King's Birthday .... Page 76
Chapter 11 – You Have to Go Home Now .... Page 84
Chapter 12 – Good Luck Parking the Car .... Page 93
Chapter 13 – Watching Time Fly .... Page 99
Chapter 14 – The Signs are also the Message .... Page 106
Chapter 15 – Four Bananas for a Penny .... Page 114
Chapter 16 – You Could Call it Governmental Theft .... Page 122
Chapter 17 – The Astonishing Biblical Invasion .... Page 129
Chapter 18 – The Trouble with Nanny .... Page 138
Chapter 19 – The Superhuman Troublemaker .... Page 148
Chapter 20 – All Scratched Up with Nowhere to Go .... Page 156
Chapter 21 – The Doubly Sad November .... Page 160
Chapter 22 – Bullies and Teachers Remembered .... Page 168
Chapter 23 – Stations of a Small Boy's Cross .... Page 176
Chapter 24 – He Said Nephi One, Seven .... Page 186
Chapter 25 – The Rainy Day Sales Call .... Page 193
Chapter 26 – The Night Della Got Her Groove On .... Page 199
Chapter 27 – Child Welfare Man to the Rescue .... Page 206
Chapter 28 – The Spell and the Wildcat .... Page 212
Chapter 29 – A Night out of Coney Island History .... Page 219
Chapter 30 – The Tingler on Chiller Theater .... Page 230
Chapter 31 – The Three Knocks .... Page 238
Chapter 32 – What Could Have Possessed Her .... Page 248

Table of Contents (*continued*)

Chapter 33 – Follow the Light .... Page 257
Chapter 34 – Here Comes Mr. Big Nose .... Page 263
Chapter 35 – Loud Noises and Holy Water .... Page 268
Chapter 36 – And Then There Was Me .... Page 276
Chapter 37 – Sometimes Trouble Follows You .... Page 285
Chapter 38 – There Goes Trouble .... Page 292
Chapter 39 – Run From Your Life .... Page 297
Chapter 40 – Dancing in the Dark .... Page 304
Chapter 41 – Detour on the Way Home .... Page 315
Chapter 42 - Does She get a Phone Call or Not .... Page 321
Chapter 43 – There was Always the Fall Guy .... Page 328
Chapter 44 – A Rolex Watch and Armani Suit .... Page 334
Chapter 45 – A Life Interrupted .... Page 338
Chapter 46 – What is Blue and Stops the Clock .... Page 345
Chapter 47 – Mikey Didn't Like It .... Page 349
Chapter 48 – Catching the Red Eye .... Page 358
Chapter 49 – You Are Not Welcome Here .... Page 366
Chapter 50 – A Quirky Connection to Waldron .... Page 373
Chapter 51 – The First of the Unwanted Visions .... Page 383
Chapter 52 – Submerging the Car in My Pajamas .... Page 397
Chapter 53 – The Miracle of the Causeway .... Page 404
Chapter 54 – The Room Was Full of People .... Page 410
Chapter 55 – That's what Stocky Means .... Page 418
Chapter 56 – Fun Filled Time in the Recovery Room .... Page 424
Chapter 57 – Our Spooky New England Adventure .... Page 432
Chapter 58 – I Didn't Think They Could do That .... Page 443
Chapter 59 – The Christmas Bird .... Page 454
Chapter 60 – A Gentleman Walked Forward .... Page 462
Chapter 61 – Dancing Across the Bedroom Floor .... Page 473
Chapter 62 – Her Hand Was Held with Love .... Page 483
Epilog .... Page 488
Acknowledgments .... Page i

PROLOGUE

Have you ever been to an after-hours party? It's that wild party that takes place after the nightclub closes. Well, imagine going to an *after-life* party.

I did, more than once. On each occasion, I entered the party as the unexpected escort of one recently deceased person. We'd walk into the most amazing venue, where my eyes embraced breathtaking beauty. Each time this phenomenon occurred, I felt like an uninvited guest, a surprise witness to a welcome home party on a scale so grand, it just had to be magical. The environment is bright and pure and feels as welcoming as a fine summer day.

During what could have been a few seconds here on Earth, I went to the other side of the veil, and saw where families and friends reunite. The reception for the newly arrived is unimaginably energized, stunning, and magnificent. So many smiling faces. Those gathered for the reception are beyond euphoric, they're super-happy.

Yet, these are all mortal terms, because in truth, no words can describe the beauty and joy experienced on the other side, in what I have come to call the Bright Room.

You might ask how I obtained a backstage pass to such a glorious celebration. I think it was because I was born dead.

CHAPTER 1
JUMPING IN FEET FIRST

1960s

According to my mother and grandmother, my life started on the other side of the veil. Finding the way here is tough enough for anyone, and according to my mother, God bless her soul, mine was a very difficult entrance.

At the time of my arrival, she was in Cumberland Hospital, which sits in the Fort Greene section of Brooklyn, New York.

Mom said she twisted in pain during her labor with me, because I was trying to jump out feet first (I did try to make it up to her later in her life). She also said that although her labor during my birth had been awful, one of my younger sisters was even worse, as she took thirty-six hours from labor to birth, in spite of being premature. Glad I wasn't the worst one in the bunch. Sorry Sis.

During my backward delivery I was strangled by the umbilical cord, the very source of nourishment in the womb. According to my mother and grandmother, who had been present at the auspicious occasion of my arrival, I came out blue and cold. Apparently, I was quickly resuscitated.

Mom said her OB doctor was a Philippine-American person. She explained that when the OB doctor got into the emergency room where I was being delivered, she flipped my mom upside down on the bed, pushed me back in, turned me around, and pulled me out. Mom said the doctor cut the cord and immediately began to resuscitate me. Eventually I started bawling.

It must have been a terribly frightening experience for my mother and grandmother, because they both thought I was a goner. Mom had already lost one son at birth, a couple of years before me. His was a stillbirth. For some reason, yet to be determined, God didn't see fit to leave me all blue and frosty.

By the way, if you ever discuss genetic memory, let me share something. I'm in my fifties now, and I still choke and cough almost every night, for just a few minutes after I lay down. I believe I cough for no reason at all. Might sound weird, but I think my throat remembers day one.

Weird occurs often in my life. For example, in or around the beginning of almost every year I experience premonitions. These visions are discussed later in the book.

In really unexpected places random messages have been delivered through me for people around me. They could be about anything, like jobs, health, things lost, and more. Such messages have come from the other side for decades, and I believe it started at birth.

Sometimes I hear or see people that have passed on. You could say I see ghosts or spirits. No, I'm not a medium, at least not by choice. When such interactions occur, it happens in no organized manner, or on a schedule. It just happens. I can't make it happen. I don't want to either. There are a lot of scary things in the world that are unexplainable, and I am not looking to accidentally invite them.

Those unsavory things had to come from somewhere. Thank

the Lord that I never saw that other place where the scary things come from. People talk about that place, and although I haven't seen it firsthand that doesn't mean I don't think it exists.

When I suddenly hear the unseen things it's a little unnerving. Spirits often give me messages to pass on to loved ones or friends at the most random moments: A New Year's Eve party, business conference, or barber shop. Anywhere.

Unexpected information is uploaded into my mind directly, hopefully from a divine source. Such information would leave me knowing something, without knowing why I knew it. And no, I never see lottery numbers appear, not ever, not once, and I refuse to ask for them (again).

I listen intently to the quiet voice that occasionally gives me guidance. I believe it's my guardian angel. It's feels sort of like heeding your instincts, following your gut, with a voice. Please note that if your guardian angel gives you helpful advice, be sure to listen. The few times I didn't listen, I endured consequences; one was really painful.

My life has been greatly affected by spiritual guidance. Once when I was a little boy an angle saved me from bullies. There is a whole chapter about that experience in here.

You might be surprised by this, but I have faced some supernatural horrors, and fought them off, or at least tried. I fight with faith and courage in spite of hairs raised, or chilly goosebumps running all over my skin. Having courage and being scared can go hand in hand.

On certain occasions, I helped bless or cleanse a home. Cleansing a friend's house is an interesting experience, at least for me. Cleansing refers to the removal of something unwelcome, by the power of faith. I do bless and cleanse our own home, every so often.

Among the weird experiences I have had is something called remote viewing. On rare occasions, I can see through the eyes of other people, usually family, regardless of where they are, and that is as awkward as it sounds.

The "veil" is a term used to describe the unseen divide between this life and the next. Based on the wide range of paranormal incidents I've had I believe the veil to be quite thin. There are moments when it must be so thin that any human being can experience the unusual or some kind of phenomenon. I'm sure many of you reading this felt something strange or inexplicable in your life. You might have felt déjà vu or had a dream that seemed very real.

Have you ever felt like a loved one that passed had just visited you in some unique way? Loved ones that have left us can visit in numerous forms or through varied medium.

At the most uncanny moment a ray of sunshine can break through, a butterfly, dragonfly, or cardinal may appear. A touching song can play when least expected, but right on time. These are all carriers of spiritual outreach.

Adults humans are typically limited in sensing the other side. Various resources espouse that small children and pets can be highly sensitive to spiritual activity.

I believe it's because they do not have the mortal stamp of cynicism, so their inner eyes are still open, affording them a better view.

With great humility, I have had the honor of helping a number of souls find their way into peace, into the Light. I believe some were drawn to me looking for help, where others were just in the same place I was.

Later I will share an event that took place in Washington, DC, that was perhaps the most profound occurrence I ever had with regard to helping souls cross over.

However, I know there are many souls that are still here when they should've gone home. Why? I can't answer that, because I don't know. I'm not a preacher, and this is not a lecture. Sometimes a soul just can't find the way home.

CHAPTER 2
THEN SCIENCE GETS INVOLVED

Present

These real-life events will not be told in chronological order, so I decided to provide the most relevant decade at the beginning of each chapter. *Present* means this decade. I hope providing this proves helpful in reflecting each historic period. Ultimately it's up to you to decide how you feel about the experiences I'll share.

Before we proceed, let's consider that not all things can be explained. Science would agree that this is true in the micro and macro aspects of the universe. Regarding the micro, macro, and quantum physics in general, I understand very little. If interested, I'd suggest reading a book related to the subject: Fritjof Capra's "The Tao of Physics" (2010).

Capra's work offers a glimpse into the comparative nature of physics and eastern mysticism. There is much to learn about the interconnectivity of life, and I felt Capra's book to be illuminating. Capra speaks to certain historic experiments that were performed by scientists studying the speed and passage of sub-atomic particles.

These scientists used a machine called a particle acceleration chamber to study the interactions of said sub-atomic particles in motion. Why they did this is not of concern.

One of the observations from this *micro-study* has relevance to this telling. The scientists realized they could observe sub-atomic interactions, but they couldn't identify the medium upon which the particles travelled. In other words, the experiments represented that all particles are not independent, and that all matter is connected (Capra, 2010, pg. 138).

Think about it. What does light travel on? I'd say that an unsolvable mystery was found in the micro-verse.

An unrelated observation had to do with space. Astronomers were using powerful telescopes to look at specific activity in the far reaches of space. While observing this *macro-verse*, they came to a similar conclusion as did the micro scientists - they couldn't identify things. Approximately 80% of the mass of the universe is made up of a material that scientists cannot directly observe. It's known as "dark matter". Dark matter does not emit light or energy, yet it is believed to hold the universe together (Space.com, Redd, 2019).

Scientists agreed that they could not identify the void or inky blackness of space or qualify what kind of medium it was that allowed stars and planets to move upon it. Another oddity that was identified over a period of years is that some of the vast blackness appears to be moving on its own. How and on what medium is excruciatingly unknown.

So, be it micro or macro, not all things of this universe can be seen, nor all questions answered.

We still ask questions. One might ask, what is it that holds the soul and body intact to begin with? Why is there life at all? This telling is not a study of quantum physics or the final word on spirituality.

Therefore, I have no answers to those questions. I have more questions.

Why is life here on Earth such a pickle for so many of us? Maybe that pickle thing is the reason lost souls get stuck here. Perhaps some of us depart the physical form, but still have our fingers in a hypothetical pickle jar somewhere.

My loved ones must not have pickle jars, as they all seem to be rare visitors, live or dead. My friends visit me, both live and dead. In fact, a dear departed friend, Everett, visited me while my wife and I attended a spiritualist church in Northern New Jersey. We attended the ceremony on Christmas morning of 2017.

Part of the service included an open mic for the mediums on the dais, or something like that. As this segment proceeded, a given medium stood up, and began to speak to the congregation. The medium was saying that she had a visitor, a sweet man, a good guy. She mentioned boiled onions and buttermilk, that he was a smoker and he wore glasses. He was giving her specific information which she shared with the group. She said he was naming someone, James or Jimmy. He also mentioned a New York City connection.

While this medium was talking to the congregation in general, another medium from the dais asked if anyone understood or related to what was being shared. I did.

Lisa knew that I did, but we stayed quiet. The details were pretty awesome. It seemed apparent that Everett was there to reach out to me. Oh, I had no doubt it was he that came through the medium speaking that Christmas morning. Why am I so sure it was Everett?

The information provided by the medium was too specific and highly focused. It was as though my memories and experiences with Everett were exposed. It was uncanny how the person speaking through the medium described things only Everett would know to say to me, so it had to be him.

The medium was an utterly unknown person to me. In fact, I was one in an audience of many, at a place we only visited that one time. The medium said that their spiritual visitor was providing incomplete sentences and random words, and a place. Then she shared the words in no formal order,

"Brooklyn, two partners in crime, dancing fool, better words, and baseball hat, Sinatra's music, and strongly urged that someone finish what they started."

Everett often called me and my friend John two partners in crime. I was from Brooklyn, and definitely a dancing fool. The reference to "better words" most likely meant speaking without the Brooklyn accent, which Everett had helped me with.

He also spoke of Sinatra's music, and enjoying a good time. I was always singing the Chairman's best.

The medium said he was showing her a newspaper article, some kind of memorabilia. I was used as model for store advertisements where Everett and I worked. According the lady speaking, the gist of the message was about finishing what I started. It seemed Everett was there to remind me to finish writing this book, and probably finish my other literary projects. The specific medium didn't know me from a hole in the wall, and never directly engaged me.

For me, life is about engaging others. I like to talk with people and love to laugh with people. Of course, I know that life is not always a laughing matter. I learned that from Everett when I was a young man working beside him in Danbury. He had a tough life, yet he was an amazing soul.

My wife and I sat there in that spiritualist church knowing something profound had resulted from us attending. On the way home we laughed about the quirky life we share. We laugh often. I like to laugh.

Please don't think my life is seen through rose-colored glasses. Like all of you, there are days that I'd like to just sleep-in, hug my pillow, and skip it.

CHAPTER 3

THE GOOD, THE BAD AND THE HUG

Present

Apart from the paranormal experiences I have had, my share of ill-disposed human interactions was not lacking. In my younger years I was stabbed, thrown through a window, and shot at (FYI, they missed). These were all separate events.

Once I was "taken for a ride" (i.e., kidnapped at gunpoint). I escaped, but it was a freaky circumstance to say the least. More on that later. Don't feel bad about any of this, I never felt like a victim. In fact, my sentiment is just the opposite; I always felt like a survivor, a very blessed one. I've experienced the good, the bad, and the unusual, but honestly, the good has always outweighed the bad, at least as far as I can tell.

How much good is there? Well, there have been times when I've heard the voice of angels and felt the Heavenly presence of glorious beings, including the Holy Spirit. In those moments when the Holy Spirit visited me, it felt nothing short of wonderful. Saying *wonderful* is insufficient to describe the feeling one gets when hugged by the Holy Spirit.

To explain my encounter with the Holy Spirit, I'd say it's like a sudden onset of warm chills, combined with an electrical sensation, and goosebumps, pretty much everywhere. When this phenomenon occurs, my whole self feels incredibly tingly, and sometimes it makes me cry, but not a sad cry.

The *hug* happens suddenly and unexpectedly and can happen while listening to music, during mundane events like driving, walking, doing dishes, or watching a movie. It's a spontaneous combustion of amazement and love.

I don't know what else to call the phenomenon, so I refer to it as a hug from the Holy Spirit.

I believe that God's love can be communicated through any medium. I know God is there, and He listens and gets involved. I feel that sometimes we mortals don't seek Him or trust Him enough. Think about it, we don't trust each other much in these so-called politically correct, restless times.

For me, having faith without doubt is essential, but it's also important to be a good person. Be nice, and try to show kindness, even when challenged. I'm no saint in any of this, but I consistently try.

Sometimes I just talk to God. I think it's great to have a simple conversation with Him, the kind where *we* both actually listen.

For those that feel my saying "Him" is placing a sexist perspective on things, forget that. I say Him as a matter of personal feeling, and not from understanding. Note that I truly understand very little, nanoscopic at best, when it comes to the Divine. There is more to it than I can know. I am not important enough in the scheme of things to question the presence of God.

Not in any sense of my mortal understanding could I define who, what, or where God is. I believe God is real, He is here, and we are not alone. We share our existence with far more than our eyes can see or our hands can touch.

Every day we see and experience amazing things: rainbows, the birth of puppies and kittens, new treatments or cures for illness, or full recovery from traumatic injury. I'd say these examples are all miracles. Miracles and faith are an important part of my life and have always been.

How many videos have you seen where different animals get along, and even demonstrate warmth and love for each other, but you thought it was impossible?

I have faith that life can overcome any obstacle, and love and peace can come to any species in so many ways we couldn't count it. Sure, my faith has grown after experiencing heavenly interventions, but fundamentally, it was from the knowledge that more exists in this life than just the clothes on my back and the air that I breathe.

God has been good to me. I feel connected with the universe and believe much of life is felt and experienced in the essence of our being, our soul.

Faith is a fundamental component for my life. Please, let me share something fascinating: every prayer I have ever prayed has been answered. Every single prayer, since I was a boy. Sometimes I say special prayers to help someone, and combine the prayers with fasting. Almost always, I pass on helpful information or see a healing occur. I thank God for his answers. Me, I'm just a messenger.

Some of the prayers I have prayed were answered immediately, sometimes on the very next day, like a special delivery.

CHAPTER 4
A NEXT DAY DELIVERY PRAYER COMING UP

2000s

In 2007, my wife Lisa was going through a really tough time trying to find a job. Responding to advertised job opportunities, she sent her resume to tons of companies.

Lisa had been looking for two years and had almost zero responses. She was lucky to have a solid freelance gig, where she art directed and graphically designed the entire layout of a 48-page newspaper called the *Angelic News*.

Lisa provided total creative direction throughout the paper for the *Angelic News*, and she also provided them with as-needed art for advertisers.

The problem was that this one gig was the gist of her creative director freelancing; it was her largest, stable client. Unfortunately, some event drastically hampered the newspaper's funding structure, which left her without a large stable client.

Without bias, let me share that Lisa is an amazing artist, and she can work in just about any medium, and create just about anything. Her design skills and talents won numerous awards.

In fact, she earned high accolades early in her career. While working at the *Baltimore Magazine*, she was honored with a Print's Regional Design Annual Award of Design Excellence, and she earned the Society of Newspaper Design Award of Excellence, working for brand-recognized publications. She won other awards as well during the time she was building the foundation of a solid creative art career.

There are paintings in our home that Lisa created during her undergrad work at the School of Visual Arts in New York City. I have them in prime visible positions and never hesitate to point them out to visitors. Lisa earned a Bachelor's in Fine Arts at the age of twenty- one and has two Masters. She is smart, creative, and just plain adorable. (I hope she'll keep me!)

Unfortunately, talented as she is, there was no foreseeing the downfall of the economy and the collapse of the dot coms. It resulted in a long period of unemployment for her.

After a year and yet another, she was on the verge of despairing about finding full-time work, which brings us to one next day prayer delivery.

At that time, Lisa did take a part-time job at the public library in town, which was my idea. She spent so much time there, I thought she might as well apply for part-time work.

It was a good idea, but part-time work at a public library didn't match up to the education and effort Lisa had invested so much into achieving. She was hoping for another art director opportunity like the one before the dot com bubble popped.

One afternoon I came home from work to find she had been crying. Seems Lisa had mailed out about thirty resumes over the previous three weeks, and nothing was happening. In her own words, she felt unemployable, that her achievements and resume were worthless. She said nobody would ever hire her. Her confidence was shaken to the core.

You see, Lisa had gone through some really difficult emotional times earlier in her life, and the seeds of that sadness were still inside, tucked deep within. I felt bad for her, and I knew she needed help. I gave her a suggestion. It was morning time, and I was about to have breakfast. We ate a light fare of yogurt and toast. During that time, I was praying for an answer, and it came. I suggested to Lisa that she had to find faith.

I promised her that if she could just try to have faith, one-hundred percent faith, with no doubt, then she would get her prayers answered the very next day, special delivery.

She took a little time to deliberate what that meant and finally agreed it was a good idea. She was nervous about it, as the concept was very new to her.

I prayed with her and asked the Lord to show kindness and to help teach her that faith without doubt can actually make things happen. Faith is a power, not just a belief mechanism. It's the power of His love. We prayed together and ended the prayer in Jesus name. I began a fast. In the prayer, I asked the Lord to give Lisa an answer tomorrow. Not days later, not a week later, or a month later, but the next day.

I prayed without doubt, and I knew my Heavenly Father would come through for her. Trusting in God is so important. Jesus said, 'With God all things are possible' (Matthew 19:26). I love God.

A reinforcement of human faith comes when one sees results. The next day came, and I broke the fast with prayer. We both had things to do. I had a job to go to, so I did. I worked for the town we live in, doing specification writing for the procurement office. I was happy to have the job, especially as it was a mile from home, and I could serve the town in some good way. It was the best commute I had since unemployment.

I expected to hear from Lisa at some point during the day, but she didn't call, and we didn't talk till later. When I came home, I found her in a happy state of shock. She told me that not one, but two Fortune 500 companies called her during the day.

She explained that one woman went out of her way to tell Lisa how amazing she felt her resume was. She told Lisa she was very impressed and invited her for an interview. That first company was JP Morgan Chase, a very prestigious organization indeed.

Of course, I was thrilled to see how happy she was and couldn't help but remind her that I always knew her resume was great. Not that I had to have an "I told you so" moment, but yeah, I did. The recruiter from the other company that called made similar remarks about the resume she had submitted. That second company was KPMG, a highly respected auditing and accounting firm, which still thrives in the top four of the field.

Lisa was thrilled! KPMG was very interested in meeting with her but needed to set the time and place down in an email. It was forthcoming that same day but had not arrived yet.

Therefore, Lisa had two positive resume responses, which was obviously something very new. She also had great feedback on her resume.

So, one might say, "big deal", how is this a miracle, or next day delivery? This is where faith plays a part, and the evidence presented substantiates the belief.

Both of the companies invited her for an interview, and both chose the same day. One wanted to meet in the morning and the other in the afternoon. Not enough evidence?

Well, this little miracle includes the fact that both interviews were in the same building and meeting on the same day. Both interviews were to be held on different floors of the same building, 345 Park Avenue. Coincidence? I think not.

I believe the strength of real faith was demonstrated for Lisa. In addition to the resume responses, during that same week a full-time position was opening at the Public Library where she was working part-time. At my urging she applied for that as well.

Our prayers were answered the very next day. Faith without doubt can make the most amazing things happen, and sometimes help make the simplest things look amazing.

When something that profound occurs, the feeling that comes with it is just awesome. It's emotional, happy, teary, goose-bumpy, and filled with sheer amazement.

Lisa had a lot to consider, so we used an Excel spreadsheet to illustrate mathematically the best course of action for her. Surprisingly, the best choice was to accept the full-time job at the Public Library. The commute was a mile one way, about five minutes. She could come home for lunch, as I did most of the time.

She would not have to incur travel costs, lose a bunch of hours commuting each day, and she'd have little to no dry-cleaning bills. Moreover, food in the City was expensive compared to lunch at home. Ultimately, she had to choose for herself, and she chose the library. Today she is the Young Adult Librarian, working mostly with tweens and teens. She has had countless opportunities to apply her art training, talents, and skills for the benefit of the library and its community.

The kids love having her there, which I witness firsthand. She has the right heart for the job, a kind, thoughtful, and creatively generous heart. So, was it a miracle? Well, Lisa has been at the library now for over a dozen years. It is the longest running job she ever held, and to this day, she's still happy going to work.

I'm happy for her. In her lifetime, on more than one occasion she saw that faith mattered. She learned that next day delivery of prayer is real, especially when you have faith without doubt, and ask in His name.

CHAPTER 5

LENNY'S FATHER WANTED A SANDWICH

2010s

A same day prayer delivery took place on the job. At the time, I was working for the County of Essex, as the county's Director of Purchasing and Qualified Purchasing Agent, which is a governing body appointed role.

I worked there for a little over five years. One of my direct reports was a guy named Lenny.

Lenny was an interesting character. He had a Masters in Finance, and an unusual knack for memorizing numbers, statutes, and laws by numeric reference. His quirky personality was often magnetic but not always for the right people. He had a magnanimous heart. In spite of his idiosyncrasies, most everyone that worked with him genuinely liked him. However, Lenny was actually a very sad fellow.

Earlier in his life, Lenny lost his younger brother and mom, not at the same time, but close enough. He told me that each was a traumatic loss for him. I didn't know him when they had passed. The feeling he had about their loss was expressed in his words, and sometimes his behaviors. Lenny missed them. He still had his father around, but he was often worried about the old man. He felt that he was going to die and leave him alone. It didn't happen until a few years after I worked with Lenny, but it came to pass that his father became ill.

It affected Lenny immensely. He was a little surly at times and became messy, as if he wasn't paying attention to anything. His mind was at home, worried. On top of this, Lenny wasn't well himself.

He had trouble with his eyes; I think it was because he was diabetic. A few times, he couldn't come to work because he couldn't see well enough to drive. It was difficult for Lenny.

It was tough for the office, too. Lenny was basically my number one assistant with the title Principal Buyer, but he couldn't do the job when he couldn't see.

His long-time colleague Chris was kind enough to drive Lenny to work and back home on a fairly frequent basis. Chris and I are good friends, so I can tell you that he does have that way about him. He felt sorry for Lenny and didn't want him to feel abandoned. Eventually, Lenny would be well enough to return on his own and get back to the task at hand, though he struggled with his sight and overall health. He really helped me appreciate how blessed I was.

Sometimes Lenny would pass out at his desk or nod off. It wasn't his fault. He wasn't well. I always cut him slack on that and tried to be an understanding boss.

What Lenny did that drove me nuts was talk over me when I was trying to explain something or answer a question. You couldn't get a word in. He was unrelenting. After so many efforts to get him to stop talking I'd lose it. Chris, would laugh out loud every time I would say,

"Lenny, you got two ears and one mouth! Why are your lips still moving!"

I'd usually have to press on, and talk louder, because he couldn't stop. I'd have to say things like,

"I still see your lips moving, Lenny. Shush"!

We almost made a game of it. The back and forth exchange lasted the whole five plus years I was there.

We made good memories all of us, me, Lenny, Chris, and the gang. I cared for all of them. Still do. They are always in my prayers. In Essex County, I learned that being a boss means being a protector, mentor, and ally.

The boss should be someone you can trust, someone that strives to make your life better, and helps you advance. I tried.

At one point, Lenny's father slipped into a coma. He hadn't been coherent for a week or more. I was sitting at my desk when I heard Lenny get a phone call from someone. It was easy for me to hear the staff, because my office was right next to the team's workspace, and my door was almost always open. The call sounded bad. Len was loud and upset.

He came into my office, visibly shaken. He told me that the hospital where his father was staying wanted to send him to hospice. He got up and walked back to his desk, muttering something incoherent. We knew what hospice meant. I prayed for him and asked God for mercy.

Lenny came back into my office. I got up and closed the door. He sat in the chair next to my desk, and quietly sobbed. He was heartbroken. I felt awful for him. He was crying, and he said through sniffles and tears,

"I wish I had another chance to tell my father I love him. We didn't get a chance to talk, not for the last two weeks." He cried more. I felt worse.

Then I heard that little voice inside. I listened carefully to what was being said. It was always a friendly, often authoritative, little voice. Then I smiled and gave Lenny a hug, well more like I shook him a bit, and said,

"Snap out it. I have some news for you."

He looked up at me through moist eyes, with a quizzical expression written upon his face. I told him what I was told.

"Lenny, you have to go to the hospital and see your father. You will get time to speak with each other, and everything will work out. Before you go to the hospital, you might want to get your dad his favorite sandwich because he is going to ask you for one. But most importantly, you guys will have time together, okay?"

He shook his head. He asked me if I was just trying to cheer him up.

"Lenny, I know this", I said, "I don't know why I know it, but I know it. Go see your father, and don't forget the sandwich."

He said thanks and indicated that he felt a little better. Moving slowly, he gave me a little hug and left for the day. Around ten that night my cell phone rang. It was Lenny.

He was very excited and sounded a little out of breath when he spoke.

"I don't know how you did that, but thanks! My dad was awake when I got to the hospital, and he did ask for a sandwich, he wanted tuna salad." He sounded overjoyed.

"How did you do that? How did you know?"

I laughed a little and said,

"Lenny, I didn't do anything. Don't thank me. Thank God."

I was feeling pretty thankful to God myself. Lenny said he would give thanks and then said goodnight. His father's health stayed stable. They had almost three more months together before Lenny's father passed. He was sad once again after his dad was gone.

I know the months following his dad's death were pretty tough on Lenny. In addition, I left the Purchasing Director job at Essex County, basically to do the same job for another county.

It was tough leaving him, Chris, and the others behind, but career paths can change and mine did. I later learned from our mutual friends that Lenny's health had deteriorated, and he was unable to go to work. I lost touch with him for a while but kept him in my prayers.

I saw Lenny on September 13, 2018, at a quarterly meeting for our professional association, Chapter 7 of the NIGP, where I served as President for eight years.

During a break in moderating, I approached Lenny and told him I was glad to see him. He said he came to the meeting because he had missed so many meetings over the last year, due to his being sick.

It was good to see him that day. It's my belief that Lenny is very happy now. He is with his brother, mother, and father, because he too left us and crossed over, just a few days after I saw him. Looking back, I always felt sorry for Lenny; his losses were so deep.

Nowadays, I feel relief for him. In faith, I know he is safe and well and at peace with his family. God bless him.

CHAPTER 6

A SECRETARY NO MORE

1990s

Another memorable next day delivery took place in 1995, also work related. At that time, I was married to Martha, my son's mother. We had married in December of 1991, and Matthew was born to us in July 1993.

During 1995, Martha was working in the information technology section of Wunder Bank, the world-renowned private bank. She loved the company, quite understandably, as they provided helpful tools for families, including a children's center for as-needed day care.

Wunder Bank was once a client of my own when I worked in the temporary employment market. I always felt they exemplified thoughtful employment. From what I read they still rank way up at the top of the list for best companies to get hired by.

Nevertheless, even the best places have people in them, and people have freedom of choice. Martha had a supervisor that chose to be difficult to work with.

In 1994, on a cold February 17th, I slipped on black ice from the very top of the stairs of the brownstone we lived in. The building was located in the Carol Gardens section of Brooklyn.

The slip was furiously fast, and it catapulted me high into the air, then slammed me down hard. I hit my lower back on the curb some eight feet away, crushing and damaging lumbar disks and fracturing my cervical spine. The pain was 11 out of 10. This event had a long-term affect.

The accident occurred while Martha was working at Wunder Bank. I had been badly injured. In the days that followed, we thought I was possibly crippled for life. At the time, I guess her boss knew that, and when an advancement opportunity was presented, he wouldn't allow her to apply for it, as it would move her out of his of department. He wasn't nice about it.

In my opinion, her boss was rotten for not letting her take a chance on the promotion. His outright denying her the opportunity was contrary to the organization's culture of internal development. Martha didn't tell me all the details of this interaction she had, but I imagine the supervisor saying that she was going to have to remain in his department until he left it.

She came home to our apartment that evening in tears and explained that the supervisor refused to let her apply for yet another promotion opportunity.

He must have used some awful words, as she was really upset. She seemed utterly frustrated and despairing. We had supper. After we ate, I hobbled into the kitchen, propped myself up on one leg and a crutch, and did the dishes. I wanted to help.

While washing dishes I prayed for a next day delivery, for some salvation for her. I prayed for delivery from her enemy and the difficult circumstances she was facing.

She needed help tomorrow, not later. Immediately upon my closing the prayer in Jesus name, a voice came into my head. It spoke very clearly and with impressive detail.

"Tell her that tomorrow she will hear of a new job. It will no longer be secretarial, the pay will be around $50,000 per year, it'll be located in midtown Manhattan, not downtown, with a possible commute or relocation to Connecticut, and she will have an office of her own and an assistant."

No joke! That's what it said. This friendly adult male voice said all that verbatim, clear as a bell, and with authority. I stood in the kitchen thinking about what I had just heard.

With trepidation, I immediately relayed the message to her, as accurately as possible.

The message was received by her with extreme skepticism. Martha thought I was just trying to cheer her up. She understandably didn't have the greatest amount of faith at that moment, especially with me injured as I was.

The next day she went to the company's human resource office, intent on applying for the other job and maybe officially complaining about her boss. Before she could tell the human resource professional anything, the woman closed the door and told Martha something instead. She asked her to keep the discussion in confidence.

She told Martha that she was leaving the firm that week, in fact the next day. She was starting a new job with greater responsibility at a top accounting firm.

She continued by saying that she knew Martha had a good reputation for detail and a solid work ethic. She then asked her if she would be interested in going with her to take on the role of Communications Coordinator.

The woman explained that the Communications Coordinator job she sought to fill was not secretarial and paid around $50,000 a year. She further explained that the job was not located downtown, but was instead in midtown, and that Martha would have to consider commuting or relocating to Connecticut.

Apparently, Wilton, Connecticut was home to the main headquarters of this new firm. Of course, she would have her own office and an assistant. She offered Martha the job right there on the spot, and Martha took it.

She called me immediately after that discussion with the human resources professional. She wanted to share what she experienced but was too excited. I said let's talk at home.

Later, she recounted the events.

"I almost fell right off the chair when she spoke" she chuckled.

She restated the entire dialog to me and noted how incredible it was that the woman repeated exactly what I said the night before.

Then she said,

"How could you know exactly what she was going to say?"

I couldn't know. That was the truth of it.

Subsequently, Martha took the job at the mid-town office of Audit & Accounting, a highly respected accounting and auditing firm. She did get an office with a window view and an assistant in the building on 50th and Broadway. Her salary was slightly over fifty thousand a year, just like the little voice said.

That voice that I have heard, every so often was interesting, accurate, and compelling. It always spoke with positive purpose. Hey, don't judge the whole "voices" thing. I don't choose the experience, it just happens.

Martha enjoyed working for the highly reputable Audit & Accounting, but that new job she took in mid-town Manhattan turned out to be a bigger nightmare than the prior one in similar respects. In the new job, her boss treated her like an administrative Bob Cratchit. The woman was extremely demanding and often erratic. Martha would get frantic phone calls at all hours from her boss. A few calls were after 11:30 pm and Martha was still expected to be in at 7:30 am the next day.

It became really tough, and she often expressed how much she wanted to go back to the other financial institution. I prayed for her to have peace. I felt a little responsible but could only turn to God for help.

Another message came with an unexpected surprise for us. All of us were driving on the FDR, headed to the West Side Highway towards Audit & Accounting to drop Martha off for work.

Our son Matthew was looking out the window and saw the old neighborhood where the Wunder Bank office building was. That was the one with a childcare center, which he remembered fondly. It was a safe and friendly place. He popped a question to us from his car seat.

"When can I go to the Children's Center again?" he asked innocently.

His mom just sniffled. The last time Matt was at the Children's Center in Wunder Bank was quite a while back. He was almost four at this time, and the place was still fresh in his mind. I drove and prayed for them both. In my head a voice spoke, one that was very familiar.

"Let her know that tomorrow she will be called for a chance to go back to Wunder Bank, and her new job will bring her into the CEO and Chairman's office."

I repeated what I heard, verbatim. She snapped that I should stop pretending to be some kind of psychic and didn't speak to me during the rest of the ride to her office.

The next day while Martha was at work in mid-town, she got a call from a Wunder Bank HR person. Someone there was interested in having her work for them in the communications office. Since it was on the same floor, the job might involve interaction with the office of the Chairman and CEO.

"Would you be interested?" the caller asked.

Martha went back to Wunder Bank the following weeks and has been there since, for over twenty years.

Although I may have helped introduce her to Wunder Bank during my time in the human capital marketplace, I have to say that she worked very hard and climbed up the ladder on her own. Martha is a shining example of the term *solid work ethic*. She has my utmost respect for that.

CHAPTER 7
CHANGE IS A CONSTANT THING

2000s

In a few years, after certain other minor miracles affected our lives, it all proved to be insufficient for our marriage to last. It wasn't all a bed of roses for anyone, as my disability sometimes resulted in depression and crankiness.

In spite of the positive parts of life where the divine had assisted us, Martha appeared to lose her interest in being with me. It happens.

She made her intention clear on September 10, 2002, the night before the anniversary of the 911 tragedy. She expressed clearly that she wanted a divorce, that she no longer wanted to be married to me, and wasn't willing to pursue life the way things were. At the time, I was terribly heartbroken.

The writing was on the wall for a couple of years. At some point during the autumn of 2000, I had begun living in the guest room of our house, on the lower floor. Since that time, I slept apart from Martha.

Why did I move down to the guest room? Because my legs twitched and jumped at night in my sleep. I believe this phenomenon stemmed from the injury to my spine.

I think the twitching was because I was healing, but that restless leg thing was sometimes so erratic it would wake me, or I'd fall out of bed. Healing process or not, the movements disturbed her sleep more than my own, and she had to get up and go to work pretty early.

I tried to help. In the morning, I'd make the bed while she showered and had coffee and breakfast ready before she left.

I'd go out and warm the car in winter. It was the least I could do at the time.

Before I moved downstairs, we tried to make it work, but ultimately, I relocated down to the guest room. I understood the need for restful sleep, but it was lonely down there. I should have seen the red flag that was being raised albeit so slowly.

Subsequent to her declaration of divorce, my time in the basement became stressful. I had nowhere to go, and it was painfully obvious I couldn't afford the house on my own, being disabled and unemployed for so long.

My heart was despairing, as I was again being forced from home with no power to stop it. I vividly remember that last night, the one before I utterly gave up.

I went upstairs to say goodnight to Matthew and her. I quietly pleaded with her one last time to keep the family together.

She was resolved about it and said,

"I wish you could find somebody that would love you, the same way you love."

I remember saying back to her,

"Be careful what you wish for."

For me, we ended on that night. I was alone and stayed downstairs trying to find my own way, keeping my son close to me while I still could. He was my reason for breathing.

Divorce is a hard thing to experience for all parties but especially for children. Up to that point, I'd been with Matthew nearly 24 hours a day almost eight years straight; I couldn't comprehend leaving him. I was sure he was greatly upset that I might be leaving, having overheard his parents trying to talk things through.

Unfortunately, I couldn't afford to buy Martha out of the house. What money I had was invested in the house with other portions of my funds invested in my education at NYU. The last of my savings was used to pay off credit card bills. The divorce, just like the marriage, was a life-altering, learning event.

Matthew ultimately learned that his dad had to move away, and I felt helpless as to what to say or do to make it better. To leave my son just about killed me; it was the most painful thing I ever did in my entire life. It was harder than saying goodbye to my mother when she died in 1997.

After I moved, I cried almost every night. I prayed often, and the pain eventually subsided. God had something else in mind for me at the time of the breakup. I prayed and prayed and believed that God had a plan, and I was determined to follow it.

CHAPTER 8
A GUY NAMED JOE

1990s

Let me tell you about another determined guy, a fellow named Joe that I met on my way to school. On numerous occasions I have shared the story about this guy I met on a Manhattan bound F-train.

I was on my way to New York University. The math class I had that day was in the mid-town campus on 42nd Street. I entered the subway system from the Carroll Street stop in the Carroll Gardens section of Brooklyn. I hobbled onto the train platform, book bag on shoulder and cane held tight, then waited to board the F train going from Brooklyn to Manhattan.

At the time, my expectation was simply one of conveyance and study with no plans to chat with strangers. However, one conversation was apparently unavoidable. No matter how often I tell this story I find myself just a bit more amazed. Honestly, how many people do you personally know that might have been "remote-controlled" by another human being? On that particular day I was.

I began going back to school approximately three and a half years after my back injury and surgery. During the first two years, I was frequently unable to walk without lots of help. Sometimes I couldn't feel both legs. Other times I just felt needles and pins. Pain was always there like a constant companion, the kind that won't shut up when you really need quiet.

In the fourth and fifth year I needed to walk with a cane due to the fact that my legs were still wobbly, and occasionally one leg would go blank or numb, which felt like suddenly stepping in a deep hole. I couldn't explain it any better than that.

I feel blessed these days, as I have so much of my legs back that I can amble about as needed. I can even dance again, thank the Lord.

Back then, and only occasionally, one leg or the other would suddenly "disappear."

At least that's what it felt like to me, like a disappearing leg trick, performed by some kooky magician. It was a real pain in the ass, as that was where I'd usually try to land when the leg phasing happened. When I fell, I always thought it probably looked like a comedic pratfall.

For some silly reason that only He knows, my falling often happened when I was smiling at or saying hello to a neighbor or passerby. They would see me collapse and crash like a planned pratfall and crack up laughing, except when blood splattered (happened once).

Don't feel too bad; I laughed too. It was just as funny to me. What can I say? Perhaps I had too much Three Stooges as a kid.

I digress. There I was on my way to New York University. I began taking courses there to learn to be a webmaster since it was a growing industry and I wouldn't need legs to do it. I ended up staying in NYU long enough to earn an Associate's Degree in Business Computer Applications. I was happily pursuing a higher education in my late thirties.

NOTE: I earned my Associate's Degree at age 40, my Bachelor's Degree at age 50, and my Masters of Science in Management at age 57 (The moral: it's never too late to learn).

On my way to NYU, I slowly moved along President Street to the Carroll Street subway station. I enjoyed looking at all the classic brownstones and smelling the small patches of recently cut grass, and the scent of bread baking from the Italian pastry and bread bakeries that dotted the neighborhood. Although I had physical discomfort to one degree or another, my olfactory senses and my desire for delicious food were still going strong.

I entered the subway on Smith Street and began my subway commute to NYU. My neighborhood stop was the Carroll Street F train station, and it usually took about twenty minutes to get to mid-town from there. On the way to the train, I was thinking about the classes I was going to attend, one of which was math computations.

I had a hard time with advanced mathematics. I don't think my troubles with math were due to my being a math moron (or maybe because I was), but I had trouble with abstract math concepts that I didn't think applied in my life. Comically, I was dead wrong; my life needed complex math in more ways than one. There I was on the way to school, carrying my algebra book in my knapsack.

I intended to study during the subway ride to school. The F train was pretty much on time back then, and I remember I wasn't waiting too long to board.

I stood waiting on the platform for only a couple of minutes when the F train pulled in. Before I got on the train, out of habit I began looking at the people around me. To my left about ten feet away were two ladies in their mid-twenties, probably Goth, as they were dressed in black, and further away was a guy in a business suit. To my right, more than twenty feet away was a group of teenagers on their way to the Village.

I guessed Village because I heard one say something about Bleecker Street when I shuffled past them earlier.

When the train arrived and we boarded, the Goth ladies got in the same car as me, but the suit and the kids went into different cars. After boarding, I looked around again, still in my NYC survival mode but saw no potential threats and settled into my seat. I've had some particularly interesting encounters on the subway. I survived two genuinely negative subway-riding incidents in years past, which left me wary.

Basically, I paid attention to the people sharing a subway car with me.

Growing up in Coney Island or just growing up in New York, most folks are alert for trouble, though by His grace, in spite of riding subways night and day for years, I stayed safe.

I made sure no danger was present before becoming engrossed in algebra. I remember thinking that I was happy to have made it all the way to the subway without falling down, and I opened the algebra book as the train was leaving the platform.

Studying would occupy me on the ride into Manhattan. I had a way to go before reaching the midtown campus of NYU, which was located on 42nd Street, between Fifth and Sixth avenues. A few minutes into the ride I heard a strange man speak to me. He said,

"You have to tell them Joe is okay."

I caught the *J* and *O* sound but wasn't immediately sure if it was Joe or John. After some thought, I realized it sounded much more like Joe. The man sounded young and certainly spoke English clearly. There was a young guy sitting across from me listening to headphones. I looked at him and asked,

"Did you say something?"

Of course, he didn't hear me because he had headphones on. I decided to ignore the incident and go back to studying. Maybe it was someone playing on the PA system. I felt the steady rocking of the train as it zipped along in the tunnel and dug back into the math. The train was just about to enter Jay Street and Borough Hall when the voice came into my head again, and it was more serious and quite urgent. The guy said,

"You have to tell them I am okay."

Did I mention that his voice came into my head, and very clearly? My head was fine before entering the subway.

I immediately started to get a headache. Brief panic surged, and I thought I might need a CT-scan or something. Maybe the whole episode was a stroke coming on. Only a few minutes had passed since the train departed Carroll Street; if need be, I could have gone back home. Arriving at the Jay Street station, my head began to hurt worse than before.

For some reason, my attention was being drawn to the two women to my left, the ones that boarded the train on the same platform as me, all dressed in black and dark grey. They were sitting in one of those seats by the window that face forward, on the opposite side from where I sat. Something was literally making me look at them, turning my head in their direction; the craning of my neck was not voluntary. My head really hurt, and it was steadily getting worse. The guy in my head spoke again, this time he sounded really pissed.

"You have to tell them. If you don't go and tell them that I'm okay, I'm going to make your head hurt worse than this."

Suddenly the pain level of my headache increased threefold beyond the migraine level. That was enough for me. After my back injury, pain was something I understood and didn't want any more of.

Motivated, I closed the book and zipped it up in the knapsack. I was up on my feet, dragging my left leg a bit while leaning on the cane. I cautiously approached the two women. I could see that the one sitting next to the window had been visibly upset. Her eyes looked red and watery as though she had just been crying.

The look on the young lady's face painted a bleak picture, and God only knew the things she might have been thinking. I immediately felt sorry for her but didn't know why.

The two of them looked like twenty-somethings all dressed in black, but I think the one on the outside seat had on a dark grey or blue knee length skirt.

That outside girl frowned at me as I approached.

"Hi," I said, and then continued uneasily.

"I don't know how to ask you this without sounding a bit nutty. I've had some weird stuff happen in my life, but this is truly strange, probably the strangest thing that ever happened to me. Anyway, do either of you know a guy named Joe or John"?

Frown-face looked like she was quickly making the jump from annoyed to angry. Maybe I interrupted something between them. She was definitely the tougher of the two.

She gave me the dirtiest look available and asked me why I wanted to know, so I told her.

"There's a guy in my head named Joe or John, but I think it's Joe. He said if I didn't tell you that he is okay he would make my headache worse than it is, and it's really bad right now."

The girl by the window erupted in tears. She looked completely freaked out. Tears literally burst from her eyes like a lawn sprinkler. I turned to move away, mumbling apologies, saying I never meant to upset anyone. People in scattered seats looked at me as though I was some kind of pervert. The other girl, the tough one, grabbed my wrist like a vice. She almost made me fall over.

"Don't go," she stammered, "why did you say that?"

She was suddenly frantic and had my wrist in a grip Zena would envy. Her friend was looking up at me through these tear-filled eyes, almost breathless with sobs.

I did the best I could to explain again about the voice and the headache.

I reiterated that Joe just wanted me to say he was okay, that he was really intent on my telling them that, and that he was making my head hurt pretty badly to motivate me. The grip loosened and the girl told me why they were both so upset.

"We just came from a funeral in Carroll Gardens. It was for her cousin, Joe."

She tilted her head at the sobbing young lady next to the window and continued,

"He was her best friend."

She put her arm around the window-seat girl, who smiled bravely through more sniffling, and lots of water works. Lips quivered and they both began crying in earnest, this time quietly and painfully. Window-seat girl was obviously heartbroken. I felt so bad for her.

She must have been very close to Joe. I realized when I first approached the two of them that she looked despondent, and now I knew why. They were not Goth; they were coming from Joe's funeral.

Maybe Joe thought she was considering something stupid, and

so he reached out through me, the one living radio station on the train that would play his tune and deliver his message. I brought it to them live with one mean headache as postage. The train approached the West 4th Street station in Manhattan. I decided I would exit there and go across the platform to take the express to 42nd Street. It was arriving across the subway platform just behind us.

I apologized and said that I hoped they would be okay. They were both just smiling and crying. As I walked away, I heard the two of them exclaiming things to each other.

"Oh, my God, he is alright, Joe is alright."

"Thank you, God. Thank you. I cannot believe what just happened."

"That is so like Joe to do something like that, so like him."

When I crossed the platform, I looked back. The F Train doors were closing, and the sad window-seat girl was looking at me through the glass, her right hand held flat against the window, her head nodding. Her lips moved, mouthing the words "Thank you."

Simultaneously, in my head, Joe said,

"Thank you."

Just like that, my headache disappeared.

I never asked the names of those two young ladies, but if either of you read this, please feel free to contact me. I hope that what Joe did those years ago put your lives on a brighter path. I assure you that you will see him again. Joe, God bless you. Maybe your intervention that afternoon prevented something terrible from happening.

Joe was not the first or the last spirit to enter into my life. In his case, I was just a messenger or maybe a stage puppet, dancing to an urgent tune that others couldn't hear, even others Joe had loved in life.

CHAPTER 9

A CONEY ISLANDER DANCING IN DANBURY

1980s

In July 1980 when I got off the plane at JFK airport, my brother-in-law Blackie was waiting to meet me. He was married to my older sister Loretta, and he and I had been great pals before I left for Vermont. He was my only big brother.

I had been away for almost a year. After accepting the Honorable Discharge, I visited some Air Force friends stationed in California at the Presidio in Monterey. I wanted to see them before going home to Brooklyn.

At JFK, I walked down the gangway with my duffle bag over my arm and saw Blackie wave to me. He said he was shocked to see how skinny I was. I explained that I had too many parties, too little food, and barely any sleep. In spite of my gaunt look, he was happy to see me. I was happy to be home. I didn't stay gaunt for very long. In fact, that was the last time I was below 190 pounds that I can recall. Hey, I'm a stocky kind of guy.

We drove back to Coney Island where I tried to go home. Within a couple of weeks, I got a job and found an apartment of my own. It was in Brooklyn on Avenue W and West 6th, basically around the corner from L&B Spumoni Gardens. They have the best Sicilian pizza in the world, at least to me. This new life was short-lived. The steps I took to try and go home just didn't work out. I had taken my last bite out of the Big Apple and had to make changes.

My apartment life ended in six months, and I moved back in with my mother and brother in Coney Island. During this time, I reconnected with a few friends that I knew before going away. One was Billy. We had become good friends while working together at McDonald's in Brighton Beach.

We had gone out to a couple of clubs in Brooklyn and once or twice in the City. I think we made a good tag team. I liked Billy a lot, and he proved to be a good friend.

Billy was lean, and nearly six-foot-tall. He was a sharp-looking Latino, with a dapper mustache, and dark eyes. I was almost as tall, at five-ten, blondish, and somewhat thick muscled, but not that big. My eyes are hazel with a flicker of blue or amber, depending on the light. We looked a bit like Crocket and Tubbs some might say. We resumed our friendship when I came home.

Sometime in June of 1981 he invited me to go to Connecticut to party with a friend of his that was a DJ in a club called the Cuckoo's Nest. We took a train from Grand Central to Bethel, Connecticut, dressed like two guys that walked off the set of Saturday Night Fever.

We walked right into this redneck, shit-kicker bar next to the train station and used a pay phone to call Frankie G., who was Billy's friend. It took him about an hour to come get us. We endured dirty looks from the regulars and drank two cokes while waiting, saving our money for later.

When Frankie showed up, he was all smiles and genuinely impressed me as a man who knew how to enjoy life. I liked him from the start. At the Cuckoo's Nest I met some of the other folks that would pepper the canvas of my life while living in Connecticut, guys like Harry, Gordon, Mark, and Johnny.

On that first night, Frankie G and I found an interesting connection. Whenever he played the right tunes, I could dance like a maniac. Music gave me energy. I'd jump, twirl, slide, do a half split, jump back up and touch my toes, and gosh knows what other goofy dance tricks. I could literally dance all night long. It was a ton of fun for me. The eighties were filled with high energy dance tunes like Donna Summer's *I feel Love*, or Cerrone's *Supernature*. During songs like Patrick Hernandez's *Born to Be Alive*, and Spark's *Beat the Clock*, I could move like crazy.

On one of my visits there, Frankie, Billy, and I watched as MTV launched. It was a few days before Frankie G's birthday, which was August 6. We went out club hopping afterwards, ending up at the Cuckoo's Nest, even though Frankie was off that night. We owned the night.

The Nest had a decent sized dance floor, all stainless steel. It had the requisite disco ball above it and mirrored walls. The DJ booth was setup off to one corner, accessible to the crowd for requests to be made. The bar was a square configuration, and when you entered the club you walked right into the bar area, dance floor to the right rear portion of the club. A small coat-check room was off to one side of the entrance as you walked in.

Half-sober Cuckoo's Nest patrons would watch me do front flips, handsprings, and backflips on the dance floor. They actually applauded. Man did that blow my head up. Frankie and Billy loved every minute of it because they were the ones that brought me there.

We spent hours dancing and drinking and dancing some more. It was a blast. At night's end we went to the Diner across the road, where we ate and joked almost to dawn.

That first night in Connecticut, Billy and I stayed over at Frankie's grandmother's house in Bethel. We got in around three-thirty in the morning, as quiet as we could. I slept on the couch. I woke up early after about four hours. I was still excited about all the fun I had and was ravenously hungry, so I quietly prowled into the kitchen at seven-thirty expecting to find nobody awake. It was a Sunday after all.

That was when I met Frankie's grandmother, Aurelia A. She was a darling. She toasted some English muffins and made scrambled eggs for me. I fell in love with her. She was the grandmother I always wanted. If she was adopting, I was moving.

Well, Grandma didn't quite adopt me, but I learned that she did take on boarders. I visited there a few more times, and she and I really took a liking to each other. She was originally from Bangor, Maine and circumstantially settled down in Bethel, Connecticut. She was the cutest little old lady at just about five nothing and ninety pounds (if soaked).

She was almost always smiling, with her granny-like, wire-framed glasses and little bun of a hairdo. I recall that she may have been in her late seventies of age when we met for the first time in the summer of 1981. I remember telling her I had been honorably discharged from the US Air Force, an Airman First Class. She understood that I had travelled the country a bit and I liked living in other places like Connecticut.

Grandma told me some amazing stories about her life. She had a couple of tragic losses early on, but you'd never know it to speak with her. She had the demeanor of a woman that overcame all obstacles with faith and will power. I loved to hear first-hand her stories about the Great War and her U.S.O. work.

Grandma was also a Latter Day Saint or Mormon. During the entire time I lived there, she never expounded about her religion to me, never once tried to compel me to join a church or do anything more than say grace when we all ate together, which I took pleasure in. She was an amazingly good cook. Her beef stews, chicken pot pies, and all her baked goods, like chocolate chip cookies, were just delicious. And, oh, that chocolate cake! It was a real pleasure to be there with her.

Come late September 1981, I officially moved from Brooklyn to Bethel. The timing was good for me, but it wasn't good for my mom and siblings. My mom was still recovering from brain aneurysm surgery she had in earlier that year. She was doing okay and had help from my sisters and brother-in-law. I know it was hard for her and my siblings for me to move away again, but I just couldn't stay there in Brooklyn anymore.

The few friends in Brooklyn that I was closely connected to had also moved on to other things, expanding their lives beyond the grind. I needed to grow up, and as far as I could tell, that also meant growing away. I needed to make a life.

Grandma A. welcomed me right away. She easily saw into the heart of that twenty-one-year-old city kid, who was thrilled to actually mow a lawn, smell the flowers, and listen to the sound of trains passing in the night.

One of my favorite things to do with Grandma was load up the recycling into her 1969 Oldsmobile Toronado and sit in the passenger seat while she drove down to collection place. Grandma drove at a snail's pace. It was a surreal feeling, as if I was living in the 1950s. This little old lady was something special.

When I moved up to Bethel, the room Frankie and I shared had two twin beds, two chests with five drawers each, and one-night table that separated the beds, and one closet. In spite of how that sounds, the two sides of that room could not have appeared more different or separate if there had been a wall between them.

My side of the room looked like a military barrack: bed made with hospital corners, and my clothes and goods neatly folded and color coded. Frankie's side of the room was the nightmare of Felix Unger.

To his credit, he occasionally represented himself a little better than Oscar Madison, but not often enough for a real Felix like I was. Still, we became fast friends and chose to be brothers in spirit. That's still how I see him, as a brother.

During the entire time I lived with him, he worked as a DJ. He spun records in more than one club, but my fun-filled favorite was always the Cuckoo's Nest, located in Brookfield, Connecticut.

Thursday's, located in Danbury, was another club I had fond memories of. Thursday's had a fifty-cent shot night, which was greatly enjoyed by wild things like I was at the time.

My having the chance to stay in Grandma's little house on Grassy Plain Street was one of life's warmest acts of kindness towards me. It was peaceful there. I was living there when the Danbury News

Times posted a press release announcing that three young men had been accepted onto the Bethel Police Department, me being one of them. I felt that was cool. I was happy there with her and Frankie, and the other boarders that came and went.

Looking back, I realize that Billy knew how much I loved dancing, especially as he'd seen me show off in a couple of Brooklyn discos. He also knew I had gone through some troubles with mob guys in Brooklyn, so I guess he thought I might like the change of atmosphere from Brooklyn to Connecticut.

I'm really glad he talked me into that first Connecticut trip. I miss the guy. Billy was taken from us by sickness far too young, a long time ago. He will never be forgotten. God bless his soul. I look forward to seeing him again someday.

CHAPTER 10
ON THE KING'S BIRTHDAY

1980s

I took a few jobs in Connecticut, while waiting for a call from the NYPD. I had taken the NYPD test earlier that year and did very well on it. I was put on a three-year waiting list to eventually be called up. While in Bethel I worked part-time for Joseph O. at his Getty Station. It was walking distance from Grandma's place. She recommended me to him. He was one of the nicest guys ever.

Joe trusted Grandma unreservedly, and so he took me under his wing. He taught me how to change oil, replace brake pads, and a number of other practical auto mechanic skills. Pumping gas was fun because the customers there were friendly and pleasant to talk to.

One of my other favorite Connecticut jobs was in Danbury at a prestigious men's haberdashery called Feinson's. That was where I met the wonderful Feinson family. They have my everlasting gratitude, as they gave me chance to begin some of the most important changes in my life.

In Feinson's I met Everett, a life-changing mentor and friend. He was like the general manager of the store and had been a fixture there serving the Feinson family for decades. I also met John at Feinson's, and he and I had our own share of laughs and memories. John proved to be a good friend. Everett often referred to us as *partners-in-crime*.

The two of us would try to duck Everett to avoid any dirty work, like stocking the shoe department or cleaning the bathroom. He'd always find us and tell us what work was needed. Sometimes we did it just to get him to chase after us. Adolescent humor at its best. It's important for me to explain my feeling about Everett. He was a mentor, as I stated, but not an intentional one. It was my impression that the guy genuinely cared about people.

He was a veteran and devout Catholic. His posture was firmly upright, and he never appeared less than dapper. Most folks that met him at work assumed he was rich or super lucky, as he always carried himself as though the world was his oyster. The truth was very different.

His life was tough. After he returned from military service, illness and sight loss plagued his loved ones. But meeting Everett, you'd never know it. He was the supportive structure, the rock of their family. Faith kept him going. He had great faith.

I've met a lot of people in my life that believed in something, and Everett truly believed in God. The Father, the Son, and the Holy Ghost. It showed on his face. No matter who came into the store, folks immediately liked him. I did.

Everett was highly instrumental in helping me improve my diction from a Brooklyn Italian inflection to a somewhat polished, colloquial English. He teased me that I sounded exactly like *Vinny Barbarino* on *Welcome Back Kotter*.

He also said that my speech inflections were not acceptable for a reputable establishment such as Feinson's. I needed to speak like a true gentleman. He helped me improve my vernacular with suggestions of movies to watch. VCRs were a thing then. Classic movies that starred David Niven, Ronald Coleman, Errol Flynn and Cary Grant were my homework assignments.

Everett challenged me to mimic their voices at work, as he had heard me easily mimic cartoon characters, Elvis Presley, and John Wayne. So, I studied. It took me a few weeks to really delve into the classic movies he had suggested. English gentlemen starred in most of them, and I enjoyed them all very much. Derring-do, swashbuckling, detectives, and comedy were among the instructional materials I used. I especially loved David Niven and Cary Grant in *The Bishop's Wife*. What a classic!

After a lot of practicing and a little bit of vocal mischief, I showed up for work one morning at Feinson's and from door opening to store closing, I spoke with a proper British accent.

I drove Everett nuts with accents after that, especially when it was near Saint Patrick's Day. I held onto a genuine-sounding Gaelic brogue for a whole day. My playing with accents was always in the spirit of good fun. I had a blast with it, but it changed my articulation ability overall and proved useful in the future during public speaking events when proper diction was salient.

Everett got sick. He didn't talk about it and didn't show it at work. It was unknown until he was clearly not able to come to work. Afterward, I helped shovel his walkway when it snowed and got groceries for him a couple of times.

Unfortunately, I was on the move and relocated to Florida for a period. I learned from friends in Danbury that Everett got so sick he had to be hospitalized. While I was away, he left for the other side. I like to believe he is happy up there in Heaven and is reunited with his family.

I will be ever grateful to him for the influence he had on my life, the way he demonstrated faith. He said he trusted God all the way. He stood tall, smiled often, and held his own in the presence of anyone.

✳✳✳

One of the other jobs I held in Connecticut was assistant manager for Roy Rogers, located in Brookfield. Working at Roy's I met a girl named Lauren. Hazel eyes, auburn hair, chiseled features, tall, and lithe. Just breathtaking.

We had a whirlwind romance. Lauren had a sense of humor and sexy laugh that just made my hair stand up with interest. We two kids were romantically insane together. In the glorious year of 1983, she and I eloped, albeit in front of her parents. It was a first for us both.

It was my impression that her mom was not comfortable with her daughter's choice. Part of the reason her mom may not have liked me was my voice. In those days, I still sounded like *Vinny Barbarino*, and her family was educated and proper, for the most part. Lauren's father was a really nice guy, genuinely likable. Lauren was a lot like her father.

There I was, married at the tender age of twenty-three to a beautiful woman, four years younger. It was too good to be true, and ultimately, it was. The fact is, we were too young, and I was way too rough around the edges for Lauren, well, definitely too rough around the edges for her mom. Okay, I was just too rough around the edges period.

Looking back, I can understand what her mother must have felt. The marriage ended just shy of a year. Lauren and I both made the mistake of rushing the relationship, and we were both sorry for that. We were married by a Justice of the Peace on July 30, 1983 and divorced on January 8, 1985, which happened to be Elvis Presley's birthday.

Why did it have to be the King of Rock and Roll's birthday? Funny thing, when Matthew's mom and I divorced in 2004, in New Jersey, it was also on January 8th. I love Elvis, as I'm a huge fan of the guy's vocals and movie presence, so understandably, I was all shook up by the universal joke of twice divorcing on his birthday. How freaking weird is that?

After Lauren and I divorced, we saw each other for a period of months, dating on the sly. I once hid in one of Lauren's bedroom closets for about an hour because her mom unexpectedly showed up at her apartment. She didn't want her mom to know I was there (and I didn't blame her). I vividly remember the last night we were together.

It was approximately three months after the divorce, and I was at Lauren's apartment. It was late and I had to leave, as we both had work the next day. We hugged. It was that hug. It was the one that says goodbye for keeps. My heart ached.

I lifted up her face and kissed her softly on the lips. She asked me why I did it, and I said,

"Because I love you."

I meant it. I just didn't know what to do with it. I always hoped that Lauren's life turned out great. She was genuinely nice, and I believe she deserved a good life, so I hope and pray she really had one. They say hindsight is 20-20 but looking at my present, I know the right decision was made. Saying that now doesn't excuse the aftermath of then. After Lauren and I divorced on Elvis Presley's birthday, I moved back in with Frankie and Grandma. Then I got drunk. Often. Not a little drunk, a whole lot of drunk.

It was the kind of drunk that lasted for months, all the way to late August of 1985. During that time, I felt lost. I recall I just wanted to go home, go back to Brooklyn, but I couldn't. The saying goes that you can never go back home.

CHAPTER 11
YOU HAVE TO GO HOME NOW

2000s

We are where we are supposed to be. During my lifetime I really doubted I'd ever get love right. But I was blessed. I have had the good fortune to finally meet someone when I was actually ready to meet her. Since June 2005, Lisa has been Matt's step-mom and my wife. Matthew and I were both blessed when Lisa entered our lives. I believe she was a gift from the Divine.

Regardless of all the troubles I had before I met Lisa, I wanted to make as good a life for my son and me as I could. I realized a long time ago that nobody else can make your life good - only you can do that. Sometimes knowing what's in your heart helps, and listening to that soft-spoken inner voice is imperative, at least in my opinion it is. One thing for sure, it's easier to know what you don't want.

I knew I didn't want to make decisions without guidance from above. I didn't want to get into another imbalanced relationship or get involved with anyone not trustworthy enough to be around my son. I didn't want to be alone either.

I prayed for a true partner. I truly believe Lisa was guided to me, and me to her in answer to both our prayers. Well, everything happens for a reason, so Lisa was there at just the right moment. Hers is the soft voice that calms my soul. However, not all voices are soft, or calming

As a preface, in the autumn 2007 I underwent an operation on my right knee a few months before the events in this chapter. The surgery repaired a torn meniscus on both sides of the knee, so running home, uphill, was out of the question (even a few months later).

On March 2, 2008, I left my Lisa sleeping on the futon in the front room of our little house. It was the part of our house that faces

Elmwood Terrace. We were remodeling the rear portion of the house, including having the kitchen and main bathroom expanded and modernized.

It really needed it. Because of the construction mess, we had to live in the front three rooms, sealed off from the back half of the house, even from the kitchen. We set up a small makeshift kitchen with our microwave and a tabletop electric range. These small appliances were in the rooms in which we were sleeping.

Lisa had taken an antihistamine late the night before to relieve an allergic reaction she was having from the construction dust all around us.

However, even with the allergy medicine and the fact that her hearing was poor in her right ear, I knew if I stayed in the confined space we were sharing I'd wake her up by accident. I felt the proverbial bull in a china shop, so I decided to go for a walk outside. It was about six-thirty in the morning.

I walked around the house to check out the new siding that had been installed. All seemed okay, and nothing was amiss. I chose to go for a walk across the Packanack Lake dam and get coffee from the deli on the western side of the lake. The lake was calm and still covered with ice for the most part.

My breath was steaming in front of me on one of the nicest mornings of the last few weeks. The sky was a crisp and brilliant blue. I was on the dam by myself, about two-thirds across, when a man's voice said,

"You have to go home now."

Just like that, somebody spoke to me. Aloud.

Clear, authoritative, and loud enough to identify as a person talking out loud behind me. I jumped and looked. I was alone on the dam. Going home, I was a mess, as anyone would be if someone unseen told them they had to go home.

I thought the voice was familiar but couldn't place it. The hair on my neck and arms stood straight out all the way home. I might as well have been hit by lightning.

Regardless of my fright, I knew I had to get home. The urgency of those words compelled me. I was walking along the top of the dam on my way to the coffee shop on the other side of Packanack Lake when that disembodied someone spoke aloud.

The dam was a flat, steady walking path, and facing the direction of home, the lake, mostly ice, was on my left, Packanack Lake's tennis courts on my right. The sun was up, and the snow reflected it brightly. I could not go fast enough, and it didn't help that the street I came down earlier was uphill all the way back home. I walked as briskly as I could, heading back to our little home on the corner of Elmwood and Pine.

I got to our block and was horrified to see smoke issuing from the roof on the back half of our house.

I called 911 and spoke to the dispatcher as I entered the back door of the house. I heard the battery-powered smoke alarms inside the front and figured that Lisa had to be up and getting dressed to get out. Inside the back, I got near the utility room and saw that the furnace was on fire.

I told the dispatcher what was going on, and that it was a gas furnace. He said to get everyone out of the house. I said I was on it. I had to go back out the way I came in; I hobbled quickly to the front door and keyed it open.

When I entered the front door, I found Lisa still asleep with the alarm blaring. I thought she'd be ready to leave, but my wife was not moving.

She was sound asleep in a room full of smoke. Flames were crawling on a wall about fifteen feet away from her. She didn't hear the smoke alarm. This had to be due to poor hearing in her right ear and the antihistamine she had taken.

I went to her and shook her awake. I had to shout over the fire alarm.

"Honey, you have to get dressed! There's a fire and help is coming."

She was groggy, but got up and dressed quickly enough, coughing the whole time. We were outside in a minute.

Fire trucks, police cruisers, and an ambulance arrived, just a few seconds after we exited the house. I knew some of the firefighters, as I worked with them on the purchase of their fire apparatus. That was part of my job as the town's specification writer in the purchasing office. Many of them had become my friends. I watched as friends went storming into our house to fight the fire that tried to steal my wife away.

Then I remembered the bird. Lisa looked at me, as we must have had the same idea, our little white cockatiel, Fuji, was still inside, so I darted towards the door. I was brought up short by a police officer and a firefighter, when they saw where I was headed. I told the firefighter to please grab the birdcage inside the front door and bring it out. One of the other firefighters did. He handed me the cage, and I took it over to Lisa.

She took Fuji and went across the street into the home our neighbor, Irene. Fuji had been a rescued bird, now she was twice rescued.

Fuji was an albino or white-feathered, cockatiel that Lisa talked me into adopting; she became our beloved pet. To be honest Lisa talked me into Fuji by calling me at the office and asking me to stop and pick something up on my way home to have lunch.

She was standing outside the public library where she worked with what looked like a small cage with a curtain on it. She just said,

"Please take this home, babe." So, I did.

Here it was the second day of March and very cold out. It was too cold for the bird and the wife. They needed shelter, and our neighbor Irene provided such. I was grateful.

My friend Stu, Chief of the Wayne Memorial First Aid Squad, came and stood by me. Suddenly I went to my knee besides Stu. He grabbed my arm and said,

"Jimmy, are you okay?"

I looked up at him and told him I was fine, but our friends were in my house fighting a natural gas fire that I thought could explode. I told Stu I was praying for them. I was asking God to keep them safe while they did what many other men would never think of doing: stay in danger and fight a hazardous fire to save another man's home.

During the firefight, Company-5 Fire Chief Johnny stood at my side for a few minutes. I told him about the voice that said you gotta go home now.

He told me that if I had ignored that voice my wife would have died from smoke inhalation before my first sip of coffee. She could have died if that voice hadn't directed me.

That first night after the fire, we stayed in a hotel courtesy of the American Red Cross. We discussed the events of the day. Both of us were definitely in shock. Due to fire, water, and smoke damage, Lisa and I were out of our home for the next eight months during cleanup and repairs. The insurance company put us up in an apartment located nearby. We stayed in that apartment for about six months. I'll never forget that day. It's been over ten years since those unforgettable words were spoken so very clearly to me.

"You have to go home now."

CHAPTER 12
GOOD LUCK PARKING THE CAR

Present

2008 was not the first time I heard voices from people I couldn't see, but it was one of the most important times in my life. Losing Lisa would have meant a permanently broken heart for me. Lisa is my soul mate. I love her more deeply, spiritually, emotionally, and intellectually, than any woman I ever loved.

That experience led to some life altering changes. Lisa and I were put in an apartment nearby while the fire damage was repaired. In the first couple of days, while cleaning fire debris, feeling really angry, and frustrated, I threw my back out pretty badly. I wasn't thinking right and was careless lifting things the wrong way. My spine went into a terrible spasm and literally warped. I ended up on the floor writhing in agony. In the following days I was able to get some relief with pain medicine.

While lying on the floor, I did what could be called an introspective look into my physiological problem. I explained to Lisa that I believed my spine was compressed, and I needed to decompress it. While she was on her laptop, I asked her to search for spinal decompression.

Lisa found a device called the DRX9000. It seemed to be an advanced form of spinal traction that had stellar reviews. She searched further, and we realized there was such a machine in our own town, in Wayne. The chiropractic center was called NJ Spinal Care, run by Dr. Wolf. He and his staff proved to be just awesome. He evaluated my MRI, which was performed after our first consultation.

My back was badly bent over the day of my first DRX treatment. After 28 minutes on the device, I stood up straight, at least for a while. The Doctor had prescribed a series of treatments on the

DRX with subsequent adjustments performed by a handheld device. I was also placed into physical therapy with folks that worked in the same office complex.

I seriously hurt my back in 1994 and lived with pain the entire time from 1994 through 2008, although in varying levels. In about four weeks (after the 12th treatment), I woke one morning and thought something was weird. It was. I had no pain. It was the first time since before the accident in 1994 that I experienced such relief. I have been going back for over 10 years to maintain the relief and for as-needed adjustments.

There was no little voice that told me about spinal decompression-that was just logic. When we met, I told Lisa about the voices and events of my early life, and she didn't judge. She was very open-minded to things existential and spiritual. She didn't think I was crazy.

My family and close friends don't believe I'm actually crazy at least no crazier than the rest of the world around us, but I admit saying that I hear voices sounds crazy.

With God as my witness, I am not one of those nuts you hear or read about in the media. Apparently, I'm something else, an anomaly of sorts.

Another unexplainable part of being me is what I refer to as *knowing*. Sometimes I know something but don't know why I know it. I just know it. It's as if the knowledge is suddenly in my memory, part of the things I know for fact. It sounds weird, to me anyway.

An example of this happened when my brother-in-law Joel was about to lose a job he held for a long time. He was understandably concerned about when he'd be able to find and start a new job. I had one of those peculiar intuitions where I knew something but didn't know why I knew it. I told him not to worry, that he'd only have about 30 days between jobs. I suggested he use the 30 days to relax. Within a day or two, he was given a new opportunity in his field, subsequently accepting the offer. The job started almost 30 days from that day.

Another fellow, my cousin-in-law Sobun, was trying to land a job at a respectable hospital. When he was discussing the interview process with us, I suddenly knew he had the job already. I told him so.

I said I knew but didn't know why I knew. Within a day or two, he was advised that he was hired.

The same thing has happened to me regarding my own job hunting. Lisa would be worried, but I knew the job offer was forthcoming. Twice I knew the job was mine, days before the first interview. Of course, that didn't happen every time, and I can't do this on purpose.

I am not an intentional medium. My days are usually mundane, same as most folks. I get up, wash, eat, dress, and go to work. Pretty normal and boring. I just have some quirkiness is all. One of the coolest side effects of my so-called quirkiness occurs when I have to park in the city.

Sometimes I drive from New Jersey into New York City. I typically go in with my wife or with other family members. Parking a car anywhere in the city can be a nightmare unless you don't mind paying for it. I'm kind of stingy that way and would rather be patient and look for a free parking spot. The quirky part is that nine out of ten times I will get a vision or message indicating where to look for a parking spot.

Sometimes the clues are colors, letters, or numbers, and yes, I almost always get a spot within a couple of minutes after receiving the clue. Sometimes faster than a minute. The clues I am given, those letters, numbers or colors, always become evident at or near that parking spot. I think it's cool and my wife thinks it's helpful.

Knowing things, without understanding how I know, has helped me to maintain a level of confidence in the face of some drastic challenges, whether they come in the form of employment, health, or safety issues.

I understand if you're skeptical about this or with my interacting with spirits, ghosts, and other things that go bump in the night. This whole story may be hard to grasp as truth, but it is truth. So help me God, this is all truth.

CHAPTER 13
WATCHING TIME FLY

2000s

Another peculiar example of my weirdness is what I refer to as friendly spiritual interaction. This is with spirits I occasionally discover or that discover me. In the latter half of 2018, I worked at Ramapo College, where each building had automatic doors, respective of the Americans with Disabilities Act of 1990 (ADA) I would imagine. Each automatic door had pads that must be pressed upon in order to be opened.

On more than one occasion I walked out of the office area towards the front doors or walked into the building, never intending to use the automatic doors, yet the automatic door would activate and open up with nobody anywhere near. I'd just say thanks and pass through. I didn't see any harm in it, but I didn't ask for it either.

Over the years, at various jobs my colleagues and I had a variety of inexplicable events around us, from doors moving to papers being pushed or thrown off a desk, to the sound of incorporeal voices, and even seeing people walk around and suddenly disappear. Sometimes the hand dryer in the rest room would activate with nobody there.

When I worked at Essex County, a number of odd events occurred that defied explanation. Sometimes in the office we'd hear heavy crashes just outside in the hallway, only to learn that glass-framed pictures were violently flung from one wall to the opposite wall. One night I had to stay over. I was stuck there because of a snowstorm.

While brushing my teeth around eleven that night, I heard heavy footsteps running outside the men's room, and the runner was banging on the walls. I bolted out to see who it was, and there was nobody there. I finished brushing, then locked myself in my office.

My office had two doors, the outer door had a combination pad and the inner door required a key. Later that night, around one in the morning, something tried to enter my locked office. It startled me to hear the keypad outside being messed with and then hear the outer door open.

Someone or something then started turning the inner doorknob, trying to open it. I went to the inner door, which I had locked, and was about to open it, when the hair on my arms and neck stood straight out. I was scared. I prayed aloud for help and whatever was outside stopped trying to get in.

It might have been me. I think I'm a magnet for this sort of activity. I was at Trader Joe's in our town recently, and one of the staff was amazed when he saw an orange go flying off the stack towards my head. I ducked the fruity projectile and laughed saying,

"You missed."

The employee was speechless, but he agreed that he did see the orange get tossed at me.

Some of these events are just whimsical. Some are wild to see. One time, my son, my father-in-law, and I were waiting for my wife and her mom to come out of the old Costco store in Wayne, New Jersey. We were in the hallway between Costco and Sports Authority, and all of us were looking in the Sports Authority window.

It was around Christmas time and the place was busy. By a column in the middle of the room there was a round table with sports watches neatly stacked on it.

As we stood looking in and talking about sports equipment, we all witnessed that same table flip high into the air, showering watches all over the floor. Literally, time went flying. There was nobody near the table when it happened. Nobody visible.

Curious, my son and I went in and asked the clerk cleaning the mess up if stuff like that happened before. He said yes, that and more. Once, there was a man standing behind his colleague in the office when there was only the two of them in the store. His colleague called his handheld talkie to say,

"I see you behind me, stop playing around."

The clerk said he answered on his own handheld. He told the other guy that he was outside on the sales floor, that he better be careful. The colleague turned around and saw nobody there and ran down to the floor to see his co-worker. They were both scared silly about the incident, the guy said.

My wife and I had seen things flying off shelves in that old Costco warehouse. Not too long after that table-watch flying incident, Sports Authority moved out of the building and, soon after, so did Costco.

Another time, Lisa and I went shopping at the old Pathmark supermarket in Woodland Park, New Jersey. As we were walking through the bread area, we both clearly saw a loaf of bread jump in the air off the shelf to land on the floor. The shelf was about waist high, and there was nothing near it. There was no person or animal.

Another creepy experience happened at a home and office furniture store, called Wall Storage and More. It was in Fairfield, New Jersey. We were looking for a wooden television stand, sort of half a wall unit. The moment we were ten feet inside the store I felt weirded out. Something felt off or wrong about the place. Another strange thing were the employees. Maybe it was late in the day, but they all seemed so listless as to be nearly lifeless.

In the back room on one side of the place, there were clearance items. Lisa wanted to go look. I told her I'd wait where I was and look at the oak wall units. She went over there and came back in three minutes or less. She looked white as a sheet, visibly shaken. I asked her if she felt something troubling on that side of the store, and she said yes. She said it felt downright scary over there. I told her I had sensed something off in that area but didn't want to freak her out too much.

She was ticked off and said I should have warned her. Next time I knew better. We beat feet and got out of that place never to return. It eventually went out of business. These are the kind of quirky things I run into all too often. Many events were positive in nature. A few folks have mentioned that certain events in my life were such good ones that they felt inspired by them. Some liked hearing about angels and miracles. Some enjoyed my sharing experiences of ghosts and other supernatural manifestations, so long as it didn't happen to them.

Sometimes it did happen to them, in good ways or bad ones. His or her unique experiences are no fault of mine. There are many stories about ghosts and things that go bump in the night. One such is the book, "It Was a Dark and Creepy Night" by Joshua P. Warren. In his book, Mr. Warren collected a number of scary supernatural stories based on true life occurrences.

Another incredible collection of true tales comes from the author Hans Holzer, who collected a vast series of real-life instances in "Ghosts, True Encounters with the World Beyond." His published collection has over 750 pages of tales that might make some readers feel jittery. There is a section in Mr. Holzer's book with photos of unexplained phenomena. Having had some ghostly experiences of my own, I believed they were very likely real. Let's face it: at some point we all have one of those dark and creepy nights.

CHAPTER 14
THE SIGNS ARE ALSO MESSAGES

Present

Living a paranormal life is hard enough, but the struggles I've had with the living were often more troubling. I've had difficult encounters with gangsters, thugs, muggers, thieves, and crooked politicians.

Though I am not a saint by many measures, I believe I am a person of honor and integrity. As such, I find myself in adversarial positions with the aforementioned bad guys on a frequent basis.

Incidents with the perceived bad segment of humanity affected me and my family, as well as friends, and colleagues. I am not going to delve too deeply into these particular experiences among the living.

A smidgen of my personal history is required in order for the more spiritual aspect of my life journey to make sense, so there are things written herein to help clarify the where, when and why, and it allows you to get an idea as to what kind of man I am. The substance of this weird autobiography is to share a missive from the other side, which I feel compelled to do.

Perhaps some or all of this information will prove inspiring to a few of you. Inspiring people is a good feeling; it is something that makes this effort worthwhile. Good or bad, it should no longer surprise you that these unexplainable things happen in life. A great number of people experience such phenomena, people from all religious points of view.

I'm grateful to God for all the events in my life, inexplicable or otherwise. It's also true that without His help I would certainly be dead now. My Heavenly Father got me through very dodgy circumstances.

I love God, and not only because prayers have been answered. I love him as a son loves a father. He has allowed me to live a somewhat charismatic life through some very interesting decades, the sixties to today. No matter the obstacles.

I believe the events, media, and music of the times have all been used to carry a message. Messages find their way to me via music playing on a radio, in writing, or even on the back of a truck, a license plate number, or in a movie that I felt compelled to watch. *Are these messages, or just amazing coincidences?*

I don't believe in coincidences; I say they're messages. One could say they are small miracles.

Countless people have had miraculous experiences that they could not explain but knew in their heart's what the answer was. The stories we hear, whether via social media, television, or literature, come from a myriad of faiths and walks-of-life.

A number of published works exist that expound real-life supernatural incidents.

One source of writing that shouldn't go overlooked is called the Bible. There are parables and stories accounted there, and many therein identify messages or signs. The bible to me is the record of mankind's spiritual history.

There was something important I learned young: pay attention to the signs. Signs are also messages.

A helpful anthology that provides a good example is "Real Messages from Heaven", by Faye Aldridge. This is a collection of true-life stories about miracles and angels. From the accounts therein, I am convinced that my experiences are not at all uncommon.

I'm sure that in the past week, hundreds, if not thousands of people, have felt there was a message provided by a loved one, be it via butterfly, dragonfly, song, poem, random comment, or a rainbow. Whatever it was, they saw it as s sign and knew it was a real message.

Perhaps you've heard of mediums, such as the renowned John Edwards. He's got more guts than I do. Same thing is true of Theresa Caputo, the Long Island Medium. My wife and I loved watching her on TLC. Her results were often uncanny, and she's fun to watch.

FYI, my opinion of Ms. Caputo or Mr. Edwards is just that, an opinion. I do not know them and make no representations as to their achievements. I just like their personalities.

My sharing this telling with you is not based on a given religion or specific religious beliefs. Historically, I have been Catholic, Mormon, Presbyterian, and more, but religion is not the gist of this discussion, as it exists on its own merits, created by human or divine involvement, as we may each believe.

Religious practices are not in question with me. I love going to church, when I go. I think any service that allows people to commune with God, maintain a positive tradition, and act in a way that is spiritually supportive for a community is worthwhile.

I am not a fan of any religion that states it is the final doctrine, that without it one cannot achieve entrance into Heaven. For myself, I have already proven that to be false.

Based on my own experiences, good people get into Heaven or at least get into the Bright Room where their welcome home reception is held. Spiritual, natural, and universal are the foundations of my belief system.

For me everything is connected, and Holy Spirit is the name I give to all the positive energy in the universe. In *Star Wars* speak, one could say the Holy Spirit is the Force, or maybe faith is. I believe in

God the Father, the Blessed Mother, their Son, my Lord Jesus, and the Holy Spirit. I also believe in saints and angels.

Does that mean I recognize the forces of darkness? Yes, I do. There is an enemy to the Light and to humankind. I strive against such and pray for help when that enemy becomes apparent. Some of the manifestations of the enemy are frightening, be they in human guise or malicious shadows.

It is ludicrous to think that in a world filled with billions of lives, all with freedom of choice, we'd be free of chaos or malevolence. It's people that choose when to do wrong, when to cause innocent lives to suffer. They have a choice.

Is it possible they are of the darkness and controlled by the true enemy? Perhaps. Sounds fantastic, but if miracles for good exist, then so must evil curses and demonic possessions. Based on this hypothesis, it is possible that they have somehow lost their free will. I don't know for sure. For me, there is no doubt that the enemy of Light exists here on Earth.

What do we understand of good and evil? Good could appear to range from something benign or harmless to something or someone helpful. Love is good, but it can also be a source of pain. What does that mean? Is it evil? No, not love. Love is good, but it can get abused.

I believe that evil takes many forms. The easy forms to spot are anger, hatred, and various prejudices like racism. There is also envy, greed, and all the behaviors that lead the powerful and affluent down a path of self-destruction. I try to avoid these things; I don't seek the negative.

I see strange things often enough, and very clearly at times. Strange stuff is part of my quirky day-to-day routine, even at work, all of it woven into the fabric of my life. The variety of experiences I've had has opened my eyes to certain beliefs.

For example, if one starts each day with love in one's heart and adds a sprinkle of enjoyment regarding nature and the people around them, one should be able to find a fulfilling path throughout the day. I believe most people would rather choose peace and kindness over hatred and rage if they were mindful enough. I have met some that didn't want peace, which seemed basically evil, and there are some I never met personally but may have walked past and felt a chill for no logical reason. It's my belief they are tainted souls. I call them goblins.

There are many folks that I have encountered and felt an awesome connection to. Some of them seemed like old friends or family even thought we had just met. I refer to these people as *kindred spirits*. I believe that when we meet kindred spirits, we are meeting souls that may have known us from the other side of the veil. They are the ones you know in your heart are good people, the kind you can trust.

My advice is to ignore the cruel in your life and focus on making cherished memories, be they of family, friends, pets, or events. Those memories are the treasures worth keeping, as they hold such great magic. They can affect the human soul, both in sharing and in recalling. Even a penny is worth holding onto in life, if it was given to you with love and friendship.

CHAPTER 15

FOUR BANANAS FOR A PENNY

1960s

During the early sixties' times were pretty tough on us. We were living in a Coney Island bungalow that my mom and step-dad bought in 1962. I didn't refer to him as Step-dad until the summer of 1975. Before that summer, he was just Dad. I was led to believe he was my father and so I called him Dad. Subsequent to my 1975 paternal enlightenment, I referred to him as *step-dad*, since that made better sense to me, and that is how he is referenced herein.

Back in the 1960s, that little bungalow by the beach was great all summer but ridiculously cold in winter. During those years, my mom cried too much. She was perpetually sad. Her name Dolores actually meant sorrows, so I guess it fit. Her nick name was Della, which most people used. I remember that she smoked a lot of cigarettes, drank a ton of coffee, and cried often when I was a little boy. There were a lot of laughs here and there but not enough in my earliest days. The day to day seemed tougher for my mom when I was a small boy.

Step-dad also smoked often, but he drank booze all the time. He would come home from working at some factory in Staten Island, start drinking, and then start cursing at mom. She made me pee in his beer a couple of times. He drank it, and each time Mom and I waited for a few minutes before we broke out laughing. He never seemed to catch on.

It was good to laugh, but like I said, life wasn't always funny. Sometimes we were really hungry. We frequently had no money for food, because my *step-dad* didn't always come home, sometimes for weeks and almost never on payday. Nanny, my mom's mom, helped out once in a while.

She gave me ten cents each week on Friday. I would use it to buy myself a Chocolate Cow at Sam's Grocery, which was down on Mermaid Avenue. Chocolate Cow was a delicious chocolate drink in a dark brown can. It just went down smooth. I vaguely remember the funny looking cow on the can.

Sam's grocery store was on Mermaid Avenue and 19th Street, across from the public library. Our little bungalow was on 28th Street between Surf and Mermaid Avenues. It's amazing how fast it all changed, but in 1964 a little boy in Coney Island could walk safely from his home to Sam's Grocery and back, all by himself. My safety was never in question.

Today letting a four-year-old walk away from home is considered unsafe, and in many states a punishable crime, possibly leading to the parent's arrest. Back then, every time I bought a Chocolate Cow, I got one penny back.

Sam the grocer offered me a candy for the penny, so I took it. It was a cherry-flavored gummy fish. What would the penny do for

Nanny anyway? Therefore, I always got the penny fish, except this one particular time.

Summer was hot and I was thirsty, so that Friday afternoon a Chocolate Cow and a cool swim was the best bet. Another cool swim was predominantly on my four-year-old mind. I drank the Cow on the spot at Sam's and raced back home to ask Mom if I could go back to the beach for another swim. Even though I did swim earlier, I figured I could go some more before supper. I was almost to our block when I realized I still had the penny.

What would Nanny do? She would know I had always kept the penny. She was likely to get mad about it, and her face when she was angry was absolutely terrifying.

Spittle came out of her mouth and her eyes bulged. She looked like a raving lunatic, spitting and hissing, whenever she got angry. It was not the event a little kid wanted to experience. At the corner of our block, I stopped walking and just swallowed the penny. I figured that was the right idea. Who'd find it?

I started walking down the street to our house. The houses were all small shacks, but a few looked really nice. The boardwalk was right at the end of the street, and so was the beach.

The smells of summer were an uninterrupted delight as the air was filled with the fragrance of salty-sea air, Nathan's foods, residential barbecues, and the local bakeries. Bus fumes did interrupt it once in a while but not often enough to be a problem.

Our house was a red colored wooden bungalow with a dirty white door and gray roof. *Step-dad* never painted anything. He did kick the door off the frame once. He was such a raging drunk, screaming his head off half the time. One of the times, he was really working my mom over, and Mom screamed to the neighbor through the window. The neighbor called the police. *Step-dad* just took off.

He didn't show up for almost a year after that night. Because she was badly hurt, my Mom went to the hospital. Nanny watched baby Diane and me. She didn't like to hear Diane cry, so she closed the door. I went inside the room to stay with Diane and fell asleep in the crib with her. I still hadn't mentioned the penny I ate. Mom came home the next day. She had learned she was to have another baby, but it didn't make her happy.

I told Mom my stomach was hurting. My mother just puffed her cigarette and looked at her own mother. Nanny said it was probably my nerves. She said I was just a jumpy little kid. I told Mom I had a secret. She bent down to hear it, and I whispered to her that I ate a penny.

She slapped me. Then she hugged me. My nose was bleeding, and Nanny grabbed me by the hair and pulled me from my mother. She put a cold cloth on my face and asked my mother what I said. She asked me where I got the penny.

I was too afraid to say the truth. I told her that *Step-dad* dropped it. I didn't mean to eat it. I only wanted to keep it safe.

My mom got really scared and said I might need my stomach pumped, so I sat down and pumped on it. Nothing happened. Nanny left and came back in a few minutes with a bunch of bananas. She made me eat three of them right away and then tried for a fourth. I told her no more. I was crying because there were too many bananas and she said I had to eat them all. I ate two more, and she made me drink a half cup of olive oil. It's amazing I didn't die on the spot.

Nanny told my mom not too worry; the penny would come out. Sure, I thought; it'll probably come out when I died from the bananas and oil. When I had gotten slapped, I thought that there would be no other punishment. Little did I know. She set me on the toilet and told me not to get off it until she said so. Mom smoked cigarettes and walked back and forth with Diane in her arms and a baby in her belly. She was a nervous wreck.

Somebody knocked on the door and Nanny closed the bathroom door with me on the toilet. I was left there alone, feet dangling, with the smell of bananas still gratefully clinging to my nose. When Nanny closed the door, she said no matter what happens in the bowl, I had better not flush it.

What could actually happen, I thought? Could I poop out a whole banana? Would I turn into a toilet monkey? Strange thoughts flashed through my head while even stranger noises were beginning in my stomach. Something was about to blow. Through the bathroom door, I heard voices. A girl was crying, and Mom was also crying, differently than she had been earlier. They both sounded really sad, and then the girl started screaming that she wanted to go back.

Someone banged on the bathroom door and my stomach fell into the toilet, all of my stomach. I was sure that I lost something important. I yelled for my grandmother.

Then I screamed for her. She opened the door and made me wipe and throw the paper in a bag. Then to my utter shock, she put her left-hand right into the nasty banana cream pie I created. She fished around in the toilet for a minute or so, and when she finally came up, it was with the penny in hand.

"Holy shit", I said aloud, to be immediately slapped again.

CHAPTER 16
YOU COULD CALL IT GOVERNMENTAL THEFT
1960s

After I washed up, I saw that my oldest sister Loretta was back home. She had been dropped off at our front door by my aunt or someone else. She was my oldest sister, and at nine she towered over me. I don't think she was happy to see me. I remember she cried until she fell asleep that night, so I guess she wasn't thrilled to be back in the old bungalow.

I personally didn't cry anymore that day. I probably dreamt that I was climbing trees and eating bananas.

I never kept the penny after that day. Nanny got the change when I made it back from the store. For some reason she refused to give Loretta a dime.

I learned, after a bit of time, that when Grandpa and Nanny split up, Loretta had a chance to stay and live with Grandpa, then with her step-grandmother after Grandpa died. He was my mother's father and had a new wife named Annette. *Step-dad* once told me that Grandpa threw Nanny out because she was a wild Irish broad and that Grandpa needed to marry an Italian lady so he could get into the mafia.

It was true that a woman named Annette became grandpa's new wife, and she was Italian. Later in life I did verify the information herein. One funny thing I learned was that my grandfather forgot to divorce my grandmother before marrying Annette. He was a bigamist. Can you see the potential for dysfunction in this blood line?

Grandpa was so very Italian; his family descended from Calabria and Naples, but I learned a lot later through some fascinating genetic forensic sciences that he was also part Greek. Mom used to say he was from *off the boat,* but I know he was born in New York City. I never met Grandpa, he died the year before I was born, but

Loretta said he was fun. She said Annette was no better than Nanny was; they were both tough and very serious about stuff.

Loretta must have liked visiting Grandpa's big house on Clarendon Road in the Flatbush section of Brooklyn. It seems Gramps was pretty rich. Loretta had nice clothes that she kept in the old bungalow, but I was too small to remember all the stuff she had. She had a lot of frilly girl's stuff that moved to our basement apartment after the city took the bungalow away.

Since Grandpa was dead and Annette no longer wanted to see her, Loretta had to put up with us all of the time.

As I said, Loretta ended up not getting a dime from Nanny. My Chocolate Cow adventures ended, because I didn't get the dime anymore either. Not long after Loretta's return from her winter break, we had to move.

Nanny explained to us that our bungalow was being stolen by New York City. When I grew up, I learned that this type of governmental theft of your home was called *Eminent Domain*.

It was around February of 1964 when we moved out of the bungalow. The city bought the bungalow for a pittance through

Eminent Domain. Mom found an apartment on the corner of West 30th and Mermaid for us. It was a small three-bedroom apartment in the basement of a two-family wooden home. We were the third family.

Even though it was much smaller than the bungalow, I ended up having my own room, which seemed practical since I was the only boy.

The summer of 1964 promised to be hot because the winter had been pretty cold, at least that was what Nanny said would be the case. She promised me that when summer came she and I could see a movie in one of the air-conditioned theaters, maybe once a week. I think the matinee ticket was a buck back then. She kept the promise and did so off and on for a couple of years thereafter. I took a lot of what my grandmother said seriously. She always seemed to know stuff, and it was eerie that she knew what she did.

She knew Sonny Liston was going to get beat by a new boxer named Cassius Clay before the fight ever happened. She swore it would be so, and it was. At the time, I had no idea who either boxer was, but I did hear her tell it to her boyfriend Jack.

My sister Diane was a little bigger in 1964; she was almost year old when we moved. Mom's tummy was still kind of small, even though the stork was coming with yet another member of the family in August.

Here we were with no money and dear old *Step-dad* missing in action. Mom was having a hard time getting financial help.

She went to the welfare office on Skimmerhorn Street in downtown Brooklyn and she was told she had to get a job, pregnant or not. She told my grandmother the woman at the welfare office said she was white and even pregnant white women could find work. After she lit another cigarette, Mom told Nanny that she tried to explain to the woman that she had small children at home and that her husband had abandoned her. The woman at the welfare said the oldest kid could watch the smaller kids. The oldest kid, Loretta, was only ten.

As time passed and Mom tried, she just couldn't get a day job because it was obvious she going to give birth in a number of months. The only job she knew well enough was working as a barmaid, but that meant nights and she wouldn't leave Loretta with her little kids at night and Nanny was non-committal about helping any more than she did.

My mom had no real education; she was a high school dropout. I recall her saying time and again, when I was little, to never drop out of school. Never give up, and never quit school. It had to be pretty hard for my mom, with no job and no money and the last of the cash from the bungalow sale almost gone after buying furniture for the apartment. She eventually got welfare, and she thanked the Lord for it at church.

Boom! Boom! Boom! The sound of explosions and construction were appealing to a little boy like me, but not at all interesting to my Mom. A huge chunk of Surf Avenue in Coney Island was being blown-up and bulldozed. The work was started near the end of winter. I remember walking by with my grandmother to see the block where our old bungalow used to be. The whole block had been flattened; it looked like a snow-covered meteor crash site from a monster movie.

All the bungalows were being torn down only a month after we moved out. This was part of a wonderful New York City plan to build big apartment buildings.

They were euphemistically being called "projects." The weather was turning cold again. The air smelled like snow. March was going out very lion-like.

CHAPTER 17

THE ASTONISHING BIBLICAL INVASION

1960s

While bulldozers and dynamite were being used to flatten the former homes of some unhappy denizens, another group of Coney Island citizens were really pissed off. Seems they also had to move to new places and were not happy about it. They had lived in this given part of Coney Island for a long, long time and were never forced to move away before. These particular neighbors were absolutely furious and something seriously unexpected was about to happen, they were going to protest!

On a peculiarly cold night in the earliest week of April of 1964, a whole army of protestors marched from the demolition site. They must have been pretty upset. Unfortunately, most of the marchers came straight to our block.

They were angry and had nothing but bad intentions. This was not going to be a friendly demonstration. In fact, it would prove to be downright biblical in nature. They were on the attack!

We had gone to bed hungry that night, maybe for the best. After a cold bath, we all climbed into bed to try and sleep.

As I said, I had a room to myself. After being asleep for some hours in my dark windowless little room, I woke to the sound of screaming. It was a scream of pure terror. The scream that woke me was followed by a lot more screams.

I heard my mom screaming. I was afraid. I didn't even move because I was too scared. Then I heard Loretta screaming and also heard baby Diane crying. Doors were slammed. More screaming and more doors were slammed and then it got real quiet. Suddenly I heard a man cursing and shouting outside the door. I remember trembling and praying for God to keep us safe and if need be, together in heaven.

It had to be late at night because I had been asleep for a long time before the screaming started. My eyes felt crusty. I was shaking badly when I began to hear a strange new sound, a sort of a scratching or whispering. No, it was both. It was a horrific sound.

Clearly, something was slowly creeping about inside my room, whispering hideously. The scratching and whispering sounds were all around me.

It began to feel like the room was moving. What was in the room with me? The room was pitch-black so I couldn't see anything. The hissing and scratching noise became louder. So very creepy. I was terrified. I tried to say an "Our Father" and couldn't finish it. The sound increased and I recall that something touched my face. Then, it was moving and squirming on my head.

I screamed for my mom. Nobody came. I yelled louder. The blanket was moving on my legs. Something was touching my feet and my pajama pants. I remember my neck started itching and chills began as the hair on my neck rose. I panicked and screamed and screamed.

"Mommy! Mommy! Mommy!"

I screamed as loud as I could. The door to my room exploded open and the light was suddenly switched on. I heard somebody exclaim.

"Shit!"

It was Sal the landlord from upstairs. Then my eyes adjusted to the light.

"Oh, shit!" I

whispered.

Roaches and water bugs were squirming all over. They covered the ceiling and coated the floor and walls of my room. I mean, they completely covered the whole freaking room. Thousands or perhaps millions of roaches were moving in mass. All you could see was the flow of disgusting bugs. There were roaches on my bed, my pajamas, and in my hair.

Sal grabbed me up from the blankets and shook me really hard. He smacked the bugs off my head and ran as he carried me outside in my pajamas. Mom was there, and Loretta was holding Diane. Mom was as white as a sheet. She was shaking and holding her stomach.

Loretta was shivering from the cold air, and I quickly joined her in the shivering; it was brisk out there.

Landlord Sal stood looking at the house, and he was screaming at the top of his lungs.

"Mother flutters! You rock-sucking, freaking, disgusting roaches!"

Okay, what he said was far worse than that, but you get the picture.

His wife asked him to calm down, but his voice went out to the whole world. He was really furious at those roaches, as they moved all through the house, covering the walls and floors.

The air turned blue with the litany of foul words Sal hurled at them. I felt a bit sick and threw up all over myself. I was a teeth chattering, puking mess. Did I mention there were millions of roaches and water bugs right in our building? It was a biblical infestation if there ever was. Mom was crying and shaking really hard from the cold.

A neighbor lady took baby Diane from Loretta and wrapped her and mom in blankets. Sal took off in his truck. He came back in minutes and carried two big metal cans out of the truck.

He ran into the house with the two cans. He came back out empty-handed and got two more cans from the back of his truck and dumped gasoline all around the walls of the house.

It was cold and really windy. The fire started with a whoosh. Crackling loudly, intense flames were jumping up the walls and reaching for the stars and for the neighbors' homes. The silent screams of millions of insects went up in smoke.

We all stood there in shock. Mom was frantic with the realization that we had just lost all of our things. Every so often, a pop or boom would occur, glass shattered, and occasionally a bunch of burning roaches burst into the street for Sal to stomp on. His hair was all frizzy and wild; his eyes looked like car headlights. His tears flowed like tap water.

Suddenly, the windows all blew out, and we jumped back screaming. I was starting to shiver again. The smoke started to smell funny, almost like burnt hot dogs. My stomach began to hurt, and I threw up again. The house was blazing, and the neighbor's house began to catch. Our house burned down to the ground before the fire department ever showed up. The woman that gave Mom a blanket wrapped a large towel around me. I remember shaking terribly.

Everything was gone. Mom just stood there in shock. After a few minutes of watching the firefighters put out the fire, we began walking. The sun was hours away from rising, and we had no place to go. We went to my Nanny's apartment on West Thirty-Sixth Street, off Mermaid Avenue. We walked the six and a half blocks along Mermaid Avenue. It was the middle of the night, and we had no coats just borrowed blankets. I was barefoot.

At Nanny's apartment, Mom pounded on the outside glass door after ringing the bell. I remember my Mom yelling frantically at her mother's window,

"Please open the f#@king door, Ma!"

Nanny didn't open it. I don't know why, but she didn't open it. The neighbors ignored the noise that my mom made. We had walked six blocks in the freezing cold. We were all crying, cold, and exhausted.

We began to walk aimlessly or, perhaps more to the point, hopelessly. We walked fifteen blocks towards Seventeenth Street and went into the church.

In those days, the church was not locked at night. Our Lady of Solace, or OLS, was the Catholic parish on West 17th Street where we attended Sunday mass. It was on the corner of West 17th and Mermaid Avenue. That night and the next it became our refuge. We slept there in the pews by the Sacred Heart of Jesus and close to Saint Jude. Saint Jude is the saint of hopeless causes. Jude is my middle name.

Although born on the blue side, I wasn't always a hopeless cause. Someone upstairs had to have looked out for me. Every so often this helpful spirit, one that I sometimes referred to as "the little voice", would guide me or tell me of events to come. Once in a while, I wondered if it had been St. Jude. Could've been.

With the help of our parish priest, my mom, sisters, and I had moved into an apartment on the same block as the church: West 17th Street.

Thanks to the incredibly gross memories of the bonfire of the roaches, we all had restless sleep for a lot of nights to come. Thank God for the help we were given by the Monsignor.

As far as I understood it, Our Lady of Solace was another name for the Blessed Mother. For the new apartment Mom found a statue of the Blessed Mother's face. Using a borrowed ladder, she put the statue in a corner nook above the table in the kitchen. It was very high up on the wall.

Holy Mary has always played an important part in our lives and, coincidentally, this church on our block was a shrine dedicated to her. Our Lady of Solace was like a citadel of spiritual strength for most of the Coney Island Catholics.

Something that made sense to me back then, and still does today, comes from the Ten Commandments: Honor thy Father and thy Mother. To me, it means our Heavenly Father and Blessed Mother. I believe it also means we should honor our earthly parents, too.

CHAPTER 18
THE TROUBLE WITH NANNY

1970s

Around July of 1975, my family moved to Brighton Beach, Brooklyn. I recall it was a hot summer that year. We left our last apartment in Coney Island in a bit of a hurry (you'll find out why later on). The years 1975 to 1979 were what I refer to as my Brighton Beach years. During this period, we had a four-room apartment that was a half-block away from the boardwalk. The beach was straight up from the front door, Bay 6 to be exact.

It took us a while to get used to the rumble of the Q and D trains as they passed just outside our building on the elevated track. The two-bedroom apartment we shared was in the rear left of the building, on the corner of Brighton Beach Avenue and Brighton 1st Street.

The apartment was situated above a liquor store and Andre's Pizzeria and Restaurant. There were other apartments on our floor, lived in by other tenants. There was an elderly lady, a thirty-something couple, and a dentist's office.

When you went down the narrow stairway through the glass door at the bottom and out in front of the building, you would find an elevated NYC subway line.

It was the entrance to the Ocean Parkway stop for the D and Q trains. The stairs to the station were halfway up the block. The boardwalk was just across the street also about a half-block walk.

Like I said, our apartment was upstairs from Andre's Pizzeria and right down the block, very near the subway steps, was Rocco's Pizza. As you can imagine, we ate a lot of pizza. On our block, we also had a Carvel, a bar called the Club 101, and a genuine Jewish Deli.

There was a drugstore on the Ocean Parkway corner. It was a busy thoroughfare.

The year 1976 was Brighton in the Pre-Russian immigration era. Little Odessa had just begun to sprout, as the seeds of Russian immigration were taking root.

In fact, I remember reading that a majority of all the Russians that migrated to the United States in the late seventies and early eighties made their start in Brighton Beach, Brooklyn. I believe several movies were made about this; one being titled "Little Odessa."

Nanny, my maternal grandmother, rented a three-room apartment in the building adjacent to ours.

We could literally go from one of our bedroom windows into her living room window by climbing across or by dropping down three feet to the roof and then climbing up into her window. We used the roof often, treating it like a terrace or a patio. Nope, Nanny never did any of the climbing.

For the first few months in our Brighton Beach apartment, it was nice to be there. However, I had to work six days a week during that first summer. I had a job working for a contracting company. Most of the time I installed fences, but a few times I was assigned to drop hot tar on potholes. It was a brutal summer but coming home in the late afternoon and going for a swim across the street made it tolerable. I loved swimming almost as much as I loved dancing. Those were *the* summer sports of my life in Brooklyn.

During that stifling summer the crew I was on spent long weeks in Far Rockaway. We put up wood-framed, steel-wired perimeter fences around demolition sites. We'd dig holes using a jack hammer when necessary, but mostly we'd apply a heavy bar and hole digger. Next, we cemented wooden posts in place. Fence wire would be nailed onto the frame afterward.

Although I was only sixteen I had been working this way each summer for four years. I was used to doing tough physical labor, and we worked hard all day. There were plenty of beaches in the Rockaways, but work kept me from them, except this one time.

One day it was so hot that me and the two guys I was working with just walked down to the beach straight into the water fully dressed. Eric, one of my two co-workers, was a really nice person, originally from Haiti. He laughed so hard when we walked into the ocean. It was infectious. We actually walked in with our clothes, shoes, hammer holder, tools, and a nail apron filled with nails. We got soaked neck deep and it felt great. By the time we walked the few blocks back to the job site, we were dry again. It was *that* hot.

Once I got home I would change into swim trunks and walk across the street to the beach, typically barefoot. I'd cross under the elevated subway and practically step onto the boardwalk. In a New York minute I was swimming in the cool Atlantic Ocean.

The Atlantic Ocean had permeated the air I breathed each day since I was a toddler, tempting me to go in and swim farther out or just float and relax.

The night carried the ocean's scent, and it was like a sweet tranquilizer: the cool breeze and the smell of salt sea which often helped me find sleep. When there was a lull in the normal cacophony of Brooklyn, such as in between subway cars passing by, you could hear the surf gently rolling in and out. It quieted my soul. I really enjoyed God's ocean.

One warm autumn night during our first September in Brighton Beach, my mom asked me to go through the window into Nanny's apartment to see if she was okay. Something my grandmother said had upset my mom. I told Mom that after I finished my homework I'd climb in through the window.

This climbing into Nanny's window had been a frequent occurrence, and I was quite a nimble climber at age 16. I usually enjoyed time with my grandmother, though there was a period of time not long before when we were not close.

During most of my teens, we were okay with one another. Nanny and I often played Rummy 500 together or shared tea and toast, usually with a shmear of peanut butter. After I finished my homework, I got my clothes and stuff ready for the next day. It has been a lifelong habit of mine, this prepping of my next day duds. Once done, I went out the window from mom's bedroom and climbed up into the window of Nanny's living room. I was in a good mood and hoped nothing would spoil it.

Mom said Nanny had been troubled by something. She didn't make it very clear but hinted that when her mother complained to her that morning something seemed a bit different. I figured Nanny just needed company. I planned to sit with her for a while. We'd enjoy some Rummy 500 during the Lawrence Welk show. When I climbed through her window, I found Lawrence Welk standing in front of his orchestra as the music played from her black and white Zenith.

I sat on her couch for a rest. Nanny made me some Irish tea with milk. Lawrence was smiling on TV when suddenly the painting of a sailboat scene that hung above the television began to shake. That was a painting she bought from Woolworth's Five-and-Dime in downtown Brooklyn on a day she and I had walked all the way there and back.

Nanny looked at me intensely and said,

"You see that?"

As it jiggled, I heard the subway train passing outside along the elevated track. I chuckled a bit and explained the circumstances.

"Nanny that painting is shaking like that because the D train just passed."

Being less than seventy-five feet away from an elevated train track, it was absolutely natural for knick-knacks to shake and hanging pictures to slip off a nail. I had been working in construction since age twelve, and although I was no engineer, I felt like I was pretty knowledgeable about driving nails and hanging things on nails. Thanks to the frequent use of a jackhammer on the job, I knew what vibrations could do.

It made sense that the train being so close would shake the picture. It didn't help much to be smart about elevated train vibrations when dealing with a senior citizen that was sure the entire world was haunted.

Nanny looked upset. She grimaced and cringed as though ducking a punch when she looked at me.

"No, Jimmy", she said. "You're wrong. It's here."

Suddenly the twelve-by-eighteen-inch picture screamed across the room and crashed over my head into the opposite wall of Nanny's small Brighton Beach living room. In a flash, I dove out the open living room window onto the lower roof, scraped a knee, and climbed up into my mom's bedroom. My day was no longer calm.

Safe in our apartment, I found my Mom waiting for me. She was sitting at the foot of her bed smoking a Benson & Hedges cigarette, dressed in her usual flowered, five-dollar house dress. She blew smoke away from me and asked what was going on with Nanny.

"Well, what the hell happened? What's wrong with my mother?"

She wanted answers, but I was winded from moving so fast, and my right knee hurt from the scrape that came from jumping out of Nanny's window. I shook my head trying to catch my breath. Then said it plainly,

"Nanny is screwed!"

I told her what occurred.

"No bullshit, Ma! The frigging picture flew across the room and smashed into the wall over my head."

She blew more smoke out of the side of her face and said nothing. She grunted, got up, and went to the kitchen to make a cup of instant coffee. I heard her grumbling in the kitchen,

"More f*#king ghosts."

Mom had experienced enough ghosts over the years. Now it was 1976. Charlie's Angels took over my little brother's life (he loved Jaclyn Smith). My three favorite shows were Wild, Wild West, It Takes a Thief, and Bonanza. They were all enjoying second lives in syndication on TV. It was great to have all three shows on back-to-back, at least for me.

In that same summer, a really big Earthquake hit Asia, and some nut job named Son of Sam was shooting innocent people throughout New York. A groovy, funky sound was coming to us from Wild Cherry, and Rocky Balboa was on his way to a championship called the Oscars.

Believe it or not, gasoline was almost 70 cents a gallon back then. The world was real, and technology and progress were picking up speed. The pop world was not yet heavily focused on superheroes, monsters, faith or the supernatural. But the supernatural did play a part in the lives of our family members.

CHAPTER 19
THE SUPERHUMAN TROUBLEMAKER

1970s

An unexplainable incident occurred in the summer of 1978. I was working in demolition that year, along with a crew that took buildings down floor by floor, dropping the load inside the structure, ultimately to load the debris on dump trucks and cart it away. I also worked the blacktop truck that summer, shoveling ridiculously hot tar off the back of a truck, during what felt like a 200-degree day.

I was on my way home one day, taking the D train, one of my favorite New York City subway lines. I was going from DeKalb

Avenue to the Ocean Parkway stop in Brighton Beach. I recall that when the subway cleared the tunnels the day looked pretty bright. It was my intention to change real quick and run down to the beach for a swim. As I came down the subway exit stairs, I noticed a few police cars with flashing lights, parked right outside the entrance to my grandmother's apartment building. A couple of officers came out of the doorway looking really confused or at least concerned. I ignored the whole scene and went up into our apartment.

While I was changing out of my dirty work clothes, I heard people in the outer hallway. My mom was in the apartment with Patrick, and my sisters were outside (if I knew my sisters, they were probably out smoking cigarettes somewhere). I changed into my swim trunks and a tee shirt, and went into the kitchen for some milk, and maybe a quick peanut butter and jelly, my all-time favorite sandwich.

Mom came into the kitchen, cigarette hanging out of her mouth, housedress intact, and slippers on. She said something weird was going on in Nanny's apartment. Mom said she heard Nanny cursing up a storm.

She asked if I could go and look. I told her she should, but she said her feet were hurting. I'd seen them crunch up like fists from arthritis, so out of respect I said I would go look. Just then someone knocked.

My brother opened the door. It was the police, and they wanted to speak to me. Apparently, Nanny was blaming me for something that took place about an hour before I got home from work. I told the officers that I would go with them next door to her apartment. When we walked in, Nanny looked angry with me. I had no idea why, at least not that particular day.

A couple of weeks before Nanny came to the door of our apartment with a bad temper on. My brother, who had done nothing to her, was slapped just after opening the door. She hit him hard in the face and called him a grease ball.

Mom was not in the house. Since I was going on eighteen and an adult by circumstance, I was not willing to let her hurt my brother anymore. I grabbed Nanny by her arm and guided her to the front door. I opened it and gently pushed her out. I told her to stay out till Mom was home. She turned into a spitting mad, five-foot-two, green-eyed, white-haired, Tasmanian devil, but she couldn't do anything other than spit and curse at me. I had seen enough of her hatred for my little brother and just wasn't having it that day. Don't judge; I did not hurt Nanny, not even a little. I just guided her out the front door with authority. Believe me she deserved it.

Flash forward a couple of weeks and the cops are walking me into her apartment, and there she was looking pissed, pointing her finger at me.

"He did it. He did this thing!"

She was vehement. Her face was contorted with righteous indignation. I asked the police officer nearest me, just what had happened. He took me into Nanny's bedroom. Her single bed was near the window.

This particular window faced a small atrium space with nothing at the bottom but concrete and on all four sides there were the apartment windows, each with the same view. It was a view of nothing but the other tenants. There was a clear break in the window glass, but it was odd. It looked like a large U shape. The glass was broken far too neatly with little to no jagged edges. I looked at the cop and said,

"What did that?"

He pointed at the bed. There in the pillow at the head of the bed was a huge dent, as though something heavy had pushed into the pillow. On closer look, the pillow was clearly broken, having been penetrated by a large metal U shape, which was now embedded in the mattress. I was confused and had no idea what the thing was. I looked at the heavier of the two cops and mouthed the words, "what the heck". He pointed up and said I should go up on the roof. I did.

On the roof was a full-blown mystery. On all the adjoining buildings, tar paper was put down with plenty of tar. Below the layers of tar and roofing paper were anchor bolts or seam clamps between the adjacent buildings. They were u-shaped metal items, probably made of cast iron, perhaps used to hold the buildings together. One such U-shaped bolt was missing.

Clearly, it had erupted up from and through the tar paper, to go somewhere else. The rupture looked like a volcanic explosion. The foot-wide U-bolt was propelled like a rocket. It burst up through the lining, tar paper, and several inches of tar, to go where?

Apparently, it rocketed into the atrium space and blasted high-speed through Nanny's window to land inside the room. It was moving so fast it cut the window glass like a laser and then deeply embedded itself into the mattress, having first passed through the pillows on the bed.

"Holy shit," I muttered to the cop. "She thinks I did this?"

The big guy shook his head and stated,

"Son, no matter what that old lady says, you couldn't have done this. No human being could have done this; you'd have to be superhuman."

We went back down to the apartment. I learned that Nanny had been napping, had just sat up in the bed, and bent down to put her slippers on when the U-bolt roof meteor blasted through her window and into the space where her head had been just seconds before. She was blaming me. She actually thought I did it.

"Look at his muscles. He's really very strong, stronger than he looks. He did this!"

One of the officers asked me where I had been about an hour before. I told him I had just finished working and took the D train home. I was probably still in the truck, getting dropped off at DeKalb Avenue an hour ago. He told my grandmother I was innocent, and that it was impossible for me to have done such a thing, especially as I was not even in the neighborhood at the time.

She pressed the issue, but his colleague stressed that no human being could have removed that U bolt without a lot of tools and noise, and further that no person or hand-held device would have enough power to generate the velocity required to penetrate the glass so cleanly, and then thrust ten pounds of metal deep into a mattress. It had to be some kind of gas issue, what with the heat outside.

Perhaps something in the tar was building pressure due to the hot summer, and that caused the eruption. There was no other explanation, the officer stated. The cops wrapped things up. Later my brother-in-law Blackie put cardboard over the broken window and left in a hurry. Nanny creeped him out, he used to tell me. I told Nanny I was sorry for her shocking event but stood my ground on innocence. She was not so sure. She told me that she knew I was mad at her, and that the anger within me did this thing. I told her I was not mad at her, and that she needed to drink some tea and relax.

Later on, I told my mom to go to Guardian Angel parish and ask the priest to come and bless Nanny's apartment. Something was just plain wrong there. What had transpired was well beyond bizarre.

Even now, decades later, I can clearly remember those certain events. That day made a permanent impression of the strange doings in our lives. As to my grandmother's peculiarity, sometimes it was very scary, and sometimes just weird.

The Guardian Angel parish priest did come and bless Nanny's apartment but made no promises as to outcome. The best he could do was to pray for her safety and for all things to be under the care of our Lord. I wasn't there when he visited her apartment, but Mom was and she said he looked uncomfortable when Nanny told him the story about the U-bolt, and the picture that flew across the room a year or so before.

I couldn't believe that she thought I threw that U-bolt at her. Something did but not me. We all got over it eventually. The days, weeks, and months passed, without so much as a scratch on Nanny's glass.

CHAPTER 20
ALL SCRATCHED UP WITH NOWHERE TO GO
1970s

My brother-in-law Blackie was someone I looked up to as a kid. I loved hanging out with him.

During 1975, I contracted Swine Flu and suffered with high fevers, chills, and nausea, which lasted a couple of months. It was Blackie who drove me to the emergency room when Mom felt it was really necessary. Once, the emergency room doctor soaked me in a tub filled with ice and rubbing alcohol to get my temperature down.

I was sick so long that I lost too much time at school and had to do the tenth grade all over. When I got better, I worked the rest of the time in construction, often with Blackie. He was a good guy. He told me that he was spooked by Nanny and her strange ways. One day he shared a story with me that I believe justified his discomfort with his grandmother-in-law.

Loretta and Blackie had five sons: Bernard, Jr., John, Paul, Joey, and Tommy. Bernard, Sr. was Blackie's real name. One day Paul got hurt, and Blackie had to take him to the hospital.

From what I recall, Paulie may have ridden his bike into a parked truck and accidently broke his arm. I wasn't there. At the time I was living in Connecticut.

Blackie explained to me that he took Paul to the emergency room of Coney Island Hospital. After triage, they were told to sit and wait. Blackie sat by the back wall with Paulie, hoping to get his son's arm fixed up as soon as possible. According to his father, Paulie was a trooper. He was not crying or complaining, just waiting. Paulie was pretty young then, maybe five or six. While sitting in the back, reading a magazine he found Blackie heard some woman at the triage desk exclaim she had been raped by the devil. He thought the voice was familiar. When he looked up, the woman was lifting her sweater to show the nurse two rows of what looked like three-pronged, long bloody scratch marks. They were huge scratches. He didn't think people could actually do that to themselves, so maybe someone had hurt the old woman. Her voice sounded familiar. It was Nanny.

She was hysterical and sticking to the story that she was just attacked by a devil. Clearly, she was injured, and blood was oozing from the scratches through her blouse. Blackie was nervous. He said he sat there by the back wall and prayed that Nanny didn't see him. Just as he thought it, she turned her head and looked right at him.

He told me later,

"Jimmy, I just shit. I got up, walked out, and took Paulie straight to Methodist hospital."

Whether or not Nanny was raped or attacked by a devil is not something I would consider for discussion at this point.

I have implied earlier that she did engage in trafficking with some of those on what I call the wrong side of the veil.

I cannot explain the events that happened around her or why she behaved as she did. I pray for her soul and hope and believe that she is there in the Bright Room with her daughters and family.

Blackie died too young on us. His oldest sons were only teenagers when he passed away. He and I had so much fun during my teen years. For a while, he put up fences with Step-dad and me. Blackie was the first person to take me out to a pub and the first guy I shared a beer with.

He had so many fun stories about his life, which he shared with me during our Saturday night adventures. I met his dad a couple of times, who was also a nice man. So, too, was Blackie's brother, Andy. They are all three reunited now, peaceful and together in the Light of God.

CHAPTER 21
THE DOUBLY SAD NOVEMBER

1960s

1963 provided one of the saddest Novembers for us. If I close my eyes, I can still see my mom in her slippers, wearing her beat-up, black faux-fur coat over a blue housedress.

She stood in the middle of our block 28th Street, between Surf Avenue and the Boardwalk. Her long dark auburn hair was blowing in the cold November afternoon wind as it shrieked across the Coney Island bay, under the boardwalk, and down the street.

I remember that I could hear the surf crashing and that my backside was ice cold as I sat on the concrete curb in my pajamas and socks, wrapped in my winter coat.

I sat breathing the afternoon's ocean air, teeth chattering lightly, and breath steaming. Coney Island was a sweet new puppy in the summer, but a mean snarling bitch come winter. It was almost wintertime, and the frosty old bitch had already begun growling.

Our block had one of the old boardwalk entrance ramps on it, and people were just stumbling down the ramp as though drunk. They weren't. They were all in shock and probably heartbroken.

Mom was holding the neighbor from across the street in her arms. They had never even spoken to each other before, but both ladies were hugging each other tight in the middle of our street and crying like babies.

It's funny that such terrible things are required to bring folks from the same neighborhood together. They stood holding each other in the middle of the street, crying. Everyone was out in the street. Everyone was crying. Our president had been shot.

All the grown-ups came out to the street, be they white, black, brown, or yellow. They were terrified and shared the same haunted look. Different religions were represented, as some were Catholic, some Protestant, and some Jewish. Everyone came outside.

They shared their horror and shock in the middle of the street, crying or just seeking consolation. A few of them raged and cursed aloud. There was a feeling of disbelief in the air, and although very young, I could feel it. The shooting incident occurred in front of people watching a parade in Texas.

It happened after lunch time, and then every television channel was talking about it. I remember running outside to be with my mom after we saw the news.

My sister Diane was only a baby. She was inside the old wooden bungalow with my grandmother, and I could hear her little voice crying as we went outside. She started crying just as mom did. Nanny closed the door to the bungalow as it was too cold to keep it open, and the kitchen stove was only good for so much warmth. Choked voices drifted towards my ears.

My mom and some of the neighbors were already hoarse, wailing *this couldn't have happened; this can't be real,* over and over again. I sat on the curb and listened.

Our president had just been shot, and it was for real. It seemed everybody in Coney Island knew what happened.

I cried while I sat and listened to the grown-ups. Mom liked President Kennedy. She said that he was the first president in a long time that helped us, helped the poor, as much as he could. For some strange reason, I also remember Mom also saying that *Step-dad* never helped us.

I probably sat there shivering and crying, wishing I could help, but not knowing how. I was just sitting on the curb, freezing my butt off.

Nanny told me that the president once cursed on television because of something with Cuba and missiles. Nanny thought he was a hero. Mom said President Kennedy was a real hero to the poor. We were poor. He helped us, and now he was dead. Why would anyone shoot a good man like him? A couple of days later the man who had been arrested for shooting our president was himself shot dead on live television.

These events were a lot for my younger self to identify with, but I recall listening to my mother and grandmother discussing the matter. It was an awful thing that happened to our country.

In the coming days we saw the president's little boy, John F. Kennedy, Jr., as he stood at attention on television with his mother. It was during the funeral procession for his father. He was around my age, standing tall as he saluted. I remember Mom saying he was a brave little boy. It made my mom cry to see him there. I cried because I knew that his father had died. I remember Mom said she was so proud of him, and that he'd grow into a good man. She said we were both going to be good men. We were both born the same year. I know for a fact that John, Jr. did grow up to be a good man.

John F. Kennedy Jr. grew up and went into the publishing business, and started a magazine called *George*. I briefly met JFK, Jr. on a spring day in 1998, just outside the office building where *George* was published, on Broadway and 50th in Manhattan.

Mom had been right: he grew up to be the kind of man any parent could be proud of. He was polite, down to earth, and really thoughtful.

By 1997, my right leg had regained enough function to allow me to drive confidently, so Matt and I drove into Manhattan from Brooklyn and were waiting to take Martha home from work. She was working for Audit & Accounting in the same building as *George*. Whenever I was able, I liked to take Matt with me to get his mom. It was always a thrill for him; he liked going out in the car. I imagine it was a thrill for her, too, since it meant no subway ride home, and special mommy and son time during the car ride.

Matt and I were sitting on the low steps of the building's front area, facing the Winter Garden Theater where *Cats* was playing in apparent perpetuity. It was warm out, so Matt was outside with me, enjoying the weather while we waited. There came JFK, Jr., leaving the building.

He was walking briskly towards the Broadway curb and a shiny black town car. He stopped when he saw my son Matthew and came over to where we were sitting.

He went out of his way to simply look at this little kid and shake hands with him. Although Matt was just three years old, he was a little gentleman. JFK, Jr. shook Matt's hand, then mine. He asked my son for his name and asked how old he was. My little guy answered with his small boy's voice,

"Matthew. I am three years old," and he showed Mr. Kennedy three fingers.

I asked Mr. Kennedy how the publishing business was treating him. He said okay so far. His magazine *George* was still pretty new, just a few years old. He asked me about the cane I was holding. I told him I had ironically gotten injured while working in the publishing industry. He asked how.

I explained that some unfriendly ice had gotten the best of me, but like Bugs Bunny, I was making a comeback. He laughed with me; it was a warm and pleasant laugh. It was amazing to me that he just came over to talk to us like that. He wished both of us well. We said thanks and wished him the same. He left us and walked to the black town car that was waiting for him. He looked back and waved to Matt one more time, which honestly surprised me even more. Matt waved back enthusiastically.

God bless us, I thought. I felt a ray of hope and looked forward to the future of JFK, Jr. and my own son. Nostalgically, I remembered watching him on a little black-and-white TV screen. He made me cry that day in 1963 because he was so brave even though he had lost his dad. He made me cry twice in my life. The second time he'd been flying a plane.

Gratefully, I believe without doubt that he is okay now, celebrating eternity with his mom and dad and other family and friends, as they too wait for the rest of their loved ones to come home. Sometime, and soon enough, we'll meet again. Eternity has a strange way of bringing us all back together.

CHAPTER 22
BULLIES AND TEACHERS REMEMBERED

1960s

Our West 17th Street apartment in Coney Island was located between Neptune and Mermaid Avenues. Along the Mermaid Avenue blocks surrounding our new neighborhood was an Italian deli, French cleaners, a pizzeria, a Chinese take-out, the Salvation Army store, Carolina's Italian Restaurant, and a laundromat.

At the east end of the Avenue sat the big subway station, the last stop for many New York City subway lines, or the first stop from Coney Island (depending on whom you asked). Across from us on

17th was a set of row houses or possibly small multiple apartment dwellings and a small church. It wasn't a Catholic church.

On our side of the street next to the parish house was a little candy store, followed by four row houses with three or four apartments each. Next to the four-family apartment complex we lived in was Public School 80, which I attended from kindergarten to second grade.

Before we were able to move into that apartment, we spent some time in the apartment of one of my mom's longtime friends. Two days after the fire, my mom's friend, Mary Popps, came to the church and collected us. After that buggy fire took our belongings from the basement apartment, my family would've remained homeless for some time, if not for Mary Popp's kindness and intervention, bless her soul.

Mary Popps knew Mom for many years. When I was fifteen years old, I found out how they became friends, but we'll get to that later. Mary Popps took Mom and us kids to the Salvation Army on Mermaid and 15th. She bought us all coats, undergarments, pants, shirts, socks, and shoes.

During our years in Coney Island, we did quite a bit of clothes and furniture shopping at the Salvation Army store. I think my big sister was embarrassed shopping for clothes there. When I got a bit older (around ten), I too became embarrassed, shame on us both.

It's funny that many cynical adults take the service rendered by the Salvation Army so lightly. They were the only source of cost-effective clothes and furniture for many.

I was old enough to be embarrassed and understand the inevitable taunts, but I also knew we had no choice. It was a blessing for us that there was such a store right in our neighborhood. That fire Sal started utterly destroyed the building right down to the basement bricks in our apartment. We lost it all.

The parish priest helped us find the nice apartment we moved into and our blessings were counted when we attended mass at OLS. The church was one of my favorite places to go. It was always peaceful and comfortingly quiet. It always smelled of incense and candles, wood polish and flowers. I felt safe there.

Our family attended mass on Sundays, Nanny took me there at least once a week to do her Stations of the Cross, usually after she did confession. When she did the stations, I asked a few times what she was doing, but the explanation of it was over my head. She was the only grandparent I ever knew, so I took pleasure in being with her.

I had such an easy commute when I attended P.S. 80, whether for the pre-kindergarten summer classes or the full school year, as it was next door to our home.

The school was nice. The steps were really big (or maybe I was really small). To this day, I still remember Ms. Tepper, my second-grade teacher, with her red hair and glasses.

She was the very bright and inspiring teacher that started me on my love of books and reading. It's my feeling that teachers should be given much more respect and consideration than what they have been over the last few decades. They affect the lives of so many of us. They can alter our entire future.

I've had a few teachers and professors that greatly influenced me. School is really important, and it pains me to think that so much of my immediate family didn't finish their education. My first full- time foray into school was kindergarten started in September of 1965.

The lunch hour was interesting for me at P.S. 80, because sometimes during lunch Mom would pass a peanut butter and jelly sandwich to me through the tall metal fence.

I would then sit and eat lunch with the other little kids. During my elementary years, a number of friends were made, like Jesse, William, Freddy, and Vinny. Jesse and I are still somewhat in touch, over fifty years later (thank you, Facebook).

School was nice, and I liked going because it felt *normal*. However, as the summer approached, I became nervous. Although I made a few friends, of course, not everyone wanted to be friends. There were a few Italian boys from our block that didn't like me. They made fun of my mother and said bad things about her. Those boys got into trouble all the time at school. I remember the teachers and principal spending plenty of time chastising them.

Two of the boys were eight years old and one was the same age as me. The eight-year olds were Salvatore and Vinny. The boy my age was Maurice. Every chance they could they would run up and punch, push, or kick me. They had no reason; they just enjoyed doing it because nobody helped me.

Mom complained so loudly that the principal successfully stopped the troubles within the school. Outside school, the problem was not so easily halted because those boys also lived on the same block as us.

Mom tried to speak to their parents. They told my mom that she should let me fight my own battles, even if I was smaller. She made an effort to teach me to fight.

Those bullies knew I had no father or big brother, and I guess they figured nobody would help me, so why not pick on me. Let's face it: I was the perfect target for a group of bullies, a skinny poor kid with only sisters. My little brother Patrick was born in the autumn of 1965 (more about that little escape artist later).

The bullies though, they really made my life miserable, and I was very lonely after school and during the summer. It was a poor choice: to be either lonely or abused. Mom's newest friend at the time, Uncle Andy, wanted me to take karate lessons. I took some in a Jerome Mackey karate school on King's Highway in Brooklyn.

For the record, I took lessons whenever funds were available but to no avail. I was just not able to defend myself until I was a little older and hardened by work and life. As a result of these experiences, when I reached my teen years I often challenged those that picked on the weaker.

I started hard labor at age twelve. As a teen, physical labor in construction made me strong, while the various street fights I had educated me in self-defense. By age fifteen, I was not the kid you pick on at school. I couldn't choose the bully path because I was someone that had been picked on and bullied. I *did* become a bully to the bullies. I liked sticking up for underdogs and honestly enjoyed beating up the mean ones.

However, none of this mattered for me at ages four through seven because nobody came to fight for me, and I was a little pip squeak.

I mentioned Mary Popps. She was a darling. My mom loved her. Mary knew Mom from Mom's days as a barmaid. My mother had a hard life. Some of her difficulties, if not most, were because of the choices she made. When Mom was pregnant with me, she somehow ended up homeless. It was Mary that took her in and helped her get on her feet. I guess circumstances aside, Mom chose to keep me, so she stayed with Mary till she was ready to give birth. She eventually married Jimmy Knight. But that was how Mary and Mom became close friends. Mary was her guardian angel.

CHAPTER 23
STATIONS OF A SMALL BOY'S CROSS

1960s

Time passed much the same, one day after another. The school season of 1966 was upon me, and I spent many weekend nights at Nanny's house. She lived on 36th Street in Coney Island, also between Mermaid and Neptune. The brisk walks we took from 17th Street to her 36th Street apartment were not always fun, sometimes it was just too darn cold out.

When we could enjoy it, Nanny pointed out seagulls that had odd spots and symbols in the clouds; how the air blew around and which way it went; how certain numbers appeared on license plates or other sources; and how it all connected to a point. At the time, it made no sense to me, but it was amusing, nonetheless.

During the 1966 Memorial Day weekend, I had turned six. I'd gotten a tricycle from Uncle Vinny, my brother's godfather. It was fun to ride, at least until the bullies would push me off the trike and laugh at me. The bullying and a fresh crew cut started just after my birthday, a ritual of summer vacation since we moved to West 17th Street.

The better part of summer was spent at the beach a few blocks away. It was my home away from home. We would set out our blanket in sight of the pier. Since the beach was only two or three blocks away from where we lived, we went often in the summer, pretty much every day except Sunday. Nanny's idea of swimming lessons was a bit on the rough side and not for the fainthearted. She would carry me into water that was up to her neck and over my head, and then drop me in the waves. She showed me how to kick and move my arms and then left me to find my way to shore. In spite of the shocking swim-or-die boot camp, I actually grew to love swimming. Obviously, it beat the alternative.

Whenever my family didn't go to the beach, I was left to my own devices outside the front door. The back yard was off limits due to the neighbor's vicious dog. It once tried to jump the fence to get my little sister and me.

The three bullies started to ride their bikes up and down whenever I did, and they continued to taunt or hit me as they pleased. One afternoon, my tricycle was stolen from the front of the house.

Although they were outside, the three troublemakers swore to my mom that they never saw where the trike went. My mom talked to their moms. Nothing happened. I was heartbroken. Days passed and no trike was found. Crying was useless.

As a child used to disappointment, I remember that quite soon I gave up wondering about the trike and played with a tennis ball I'd found. I'd throw the ball against the stoop and catch the rebounds, the basic play of stoopball. That summer I watched as new neighbors moved into the apartment next door to us. They had kids, both boys and girls.

Every Sunday they went to the same church as us, but we didn't speak to each other much. Both parents had peculiar accents, and I remember hearing that they were Hungarian or something like that. One of the boys, Junior, was a little older than I was. He was ill and never seemed to have much hair.

I liked him a lot because he was always so kind to me. He had a really nice smile. It was a pleasant change from all the other older boys on our block that were just plain mean, at least most of the time.

Summer was ending and I was looking forward to first grade. I had decided I was going to be an altar boy. This made Mom and Nanny really happy. My mom said she was very proud of me for making my own choice in taking an interest in the church. She said this could bring me closer to Heaven. I told her I was happy to be closer to Heaven and that I volunteered in order to say thanks to God.

Nanny took me to do the Stations of the Cross at Our Lady of Solace a number of times and tried to teach me how. She was a very complicated catholic. Nanny told me a story, more than once, about the time I was born. She and Mom used to live near Mary Queen of

Saints in the Fort Green section of Brooklyn. Mary Queen of Saints was the Catholic parish where they attended mass back then.

When I was an infant, Nanny wheeled me in a stroller into that church to do her stations, and an elderly gentleman came over to see the baby she was pushing. He worked in the church doing a number of chores. He and Nanny had been acquaintances. He said I was a very calm baby, and that he felt someday I'd be involved with the church. She thought that was an interesting thing for the man to say, and so she never forgot it and told it to me on a few occasions. Perhaps that influenced my six-year old, altar-boy career choice.

During the last week of my sixth summer on one particularly hot afternoon, I found a dime. It was so hot that I could smell sea gulls roasting in flight. The street was sizzling, and your spit evaporated on contact with the sidewalk. I asked Mom if I could go to Sam's for a chocolate cow with my newfound dime. She said fine but to be alert for trouble and be careful crossing Mermaid Avenue.

My poor Mom, she'd seen me with too many nosebleeds and black eyes that summer. Can you guess from what trio of bullies?

180

After drinking my Chocolate Cow at Sam's, I headed home. Just as I reached the block, I spotted the three terrorists standing in front of their stoop. Salvatore had grown and gained weight. His punches were scary to me because I was a skinny little boy. I remember hoping they didn't see me. Sure enough, they spotted me and immediately ran after me. I had nowhere to run.

Then suddenly, a little voice spoke to me.

"Go into the church."

I didn't hesitate. Once inside Our Lady of Solace, I felt terrified. I was trapped. Then, the little voice whispered to me again. The voice was authoritative, but also soft and calming.

"Do the Stations".

That's all it said. Feeling remarkably calm, I went to the first station knelt down, blessed myself, and said three Our Fathers and two Hail Mary's, then added a special prayer for my family. I really didn't know if that was all there was to it, but it felt right.

As I approached the second painting, I remember feeling a little better. It was as though the images brought me closer to Jesus or maybe they just reminded me of how bad life could be.

I respected and adored Him because He was one person that I knew suffered much more than I ever did or ever could. He kept forgiving and going forward, even after death. I believed in Him as a kid and still do, without a doubt. So, there I was kneeling and praying, and I decided to keep adding special prayers of my own to the litany.

I continued to the next Station. The bullies entered the church. I guess they were concerned that they would get spotted picking on me by one of the nuns or, worse, by the Monsignor. They watched me go to the third station.

I knelt, blessed myself, and began to pray in silence. I ignored them completely. They walked over to me and watched me do the fourth Station. Curious, and quiet, Salvatore asked me what I was doing.

I tried my best to explain what my grandmother had taught me. He asked how many times I said each prayer.

I told them as far as I knew it was three Our Father's, and two Hail Mary's. I further explained that when I finished the rote prayers, I would say my own prayers. Sometimes my prayers reflected on what the painting represented, other times it was to say thanks for how lucky I was not to be horribly crucified like Jesus had been.

The three boys followed me to the next station and knelt beside me in prayer. Each prayed quietly, though I think I remember Maurice mumbling his prayers aloud. We did all the remaining Stations together.

When we were done praying at the last of the Stations, we blessed ourselves with holy water and left the church. Outside, I was shaking I was so scared. I was sure they were going to beat me up again.

Vinny, who was the oldest, put his arm around me, and the boys walked me up the block to Vinny and Maurice's house. The boys asked me to wait in front of the stoop with Jerry, and they asked me to close my eyes.

I was unsure of them but trusted in God. It seemed right, so I closed my eyes. When they asked me to open my eyes, my missing tricycle was there before me.

I thanked them for finding it. In my head, I guessed they had my trike all along.

I told Mom what happened and asked if it was okay for me to go around the block. She said sure.

The boys got their own bikes out, and we rode all the way around the block, pedaling alongside each other.

That last bit of summer I went to their birthday parties and ate at their barbecues. The four of us became altar boys, and we remained friends for the next couple years, after which we moved to different neighborhoods.

The little voice I had heard in the church was a wonderful surprise that I kept reflecting on but never mentioned to anyone except my grandmother.

I vividly remember feeling just plain amazed that an angel or saint spoke out to help me.

That voice was not a sound in my thoughts; or something imagined. Actual words had been spoken aloud in a voice that was serious, authoritative, but friendly, too.

I was too young to fully appreciate the event, but this was a life-changing experience for me.

Something profound and divine had occurred influencing not only me but others as well. It was the first time I had heard that helpful voice, but not the last.

CHAPTER 24
HE SAID NEPHI ONE, SEVEN

1980s

From early spring of 1984 thru the summer of 1986, I was on my own again. Around Christmas of 1984, I moved back in with Grandma A and Frankie G. One night, during late September of 1985, I was all alone in the house. I had been stone cold sober for about a month, having decided enough was enough. It was one heck of a binge - almost eight months of partying due to my divorce from Lauren.

Being friends with a number of bartenders and club owners was quite enabling. Many of them felt sorry for my formerly cheerful, dancing fool of a self. I had become a morose, grumpy version, a shadow of my former self, and it lasted a while.

However, as I said, I had had enough. Surprisingly, during this very messy escapade of my life, I still remembered to pray. I prayed in the morning and at night.

I talked with the Lord as though He was my own Father. I referred to Him as Pop in some of my prayers.

One particular night when I knew Grandma was staying down the road at her daughter's house and Frankie would likely be out all night long working and partying, I planned for some quiet time with HBO and MTV. I expected to eat some pizza muffins and take a hot shower, hopefully to be followed by a good night's sleep - something I was never very good at doing. Since nobody else was home, I thought why not try.

It was fun watching all the movies on HBO or listening to music on MTV. I got a big kick out of the pop culture of the eighties. I loved the video for *Take on Me* by the group Aha.

I watched television that night, ate some snacks, then finally took that hot shower. The house was locked up, and really empty, as I was the only one home. Around midnight, I did lie down to sleep on my side of the room.

When I was in that halfway into sleep stage I heard a noise outside that woke me right up and gave me goose bumps. Growing up the way I did in Brooklyn, any noise that was remotely outside the norm would wake me completely to a fully-alert state, but there were some things that woke me that were just not right. This was one of those things.

Outside the window, I heard a scary sound: a terribly frightening, hair-on-the-arms and back-of-the-neck lifting, sound. It was a laugh, a deep nerve-grating laugh - the kind we only hear in horror movies. It sounded as though it was made by a demon with sulfuric rocks for vocal cords.

I yelled at the closed window and challenged whoever it was, even though my goosebumps were running all over me looking for cover. I figured it was Frankie or one of our mutual friends coming around to disturb me or coax me into going out.

I went outside in my pajamas and walked around the little house to find the culprit. Nobody was around. It was very chilly out, and far too quiet. It was *creepy* quiet.

I went back inside and locked everything up. Sometimes weird things happened in my life. Some of those things were just warnings, other times a threat or a form of attack. That creepy laugh sounded a lot like a threat.

I prayed for protection and trusted with faith. I knelt down beside the bed and said a prayer to my Heavenly Father. I asked Him to keep my loved ones and me safe.

I knew that the scary voice I heard was real and had experienced similar horrors earlier in my life. I got up for some water. I put my drink of water on the nightstand next to the book Frankie or Grandma always left there, turned off the light and lay down to sleep.

After a little while, I was half asleep and started to drift deeper. Sometime later, possibly around two in the morning, I was wakened again as a man's voice called out to me from right there in the room. Yes, in the room.

It was a male voice and very clear. His was not a scary voice, but it was firm and seriously authoritative. Unfortunately, I still didn't understand what was said.

In my semi-sleepy state, it sounded like knee five one seven. The words were just not familiar enough, and as such made no sense. I was sure the voice had said something like *neef eye one, something seven*. It made no sense to me at all.

I closed my eyes, lay there, and tried to get back to sleep. Then, it happened again while I was still wide awake, laying there.

"NEPHI ONE, SEVEN!"

That male authoritative voice exclaimed rather clearly. I didn't know what the heck He was referring to. I sat up and turned on the bedside lamp. On the nightstand, face down, was that one book. I had never touched the book before other than to dust around it.

I figured that maybe this book was what the fuss was about, so I casually flipped it open. There on the left-hand page right at the top I saw the very words that were just brought to my attention by some pushy, important-sounding person I didn't know.

The guy sounded serious though, so I read it.

The page I was looking at began at the top with "1 NEPHI 3:6-20, " and just below that was a paragraph clearly marked number "7". Therefore, I read 1 Nephi, the 7th paragraph, aloud to myself. What was written was the following:

"And it came to pass that I, Nephi, said unto my father: I will go and do the things which the Lord hath commanded, for I know that the Lord giveth no commandments unto the children of men, save He shall prepare a way for them that they may accomplish the thing which He commandeth them."

It made absolutely no sense to me. Later, after some conversations with Grandma A and a few nice Elders, or missionaries, from the Church of Jesus Christ, Latter Day Saints, I had a clue. They felt that the Lord was saying there is something I will have to do, and He wanted me to be prepared for it. There was something He might command me to do or He was commanding me to do. I was not sure which.

To this day, I'm still not sure, except maybe I was to write this missive about a message. This was a message delivered in first order, straight from Heaven to my very ears. The voice I heard had been in the room with me - not outside or in my head.

That voice was the same voice that later in life said *you have to go home now*, and allowed me to save Lisa's life from the fire. Ultimately, I don't need to know what it all meant, as long as He knew. That was good enough for me.

CHAPTER 25
THE RAINY-DAY SALES CALL

1980s

During the latter part of 1986, I worked for NYNEX and Donnelley Directory selling Yellow Page advertising all over Fairfield County, Connecticut.

This was also the year that I was trying to wear the mantle of Aaronic priesthood, as a novice member of the Church of Jesus Christ and the Latter Day Saints, or Mormons.

Religious exercises aside, I was pretty good at sales. It was greatly interesting to my peers that I wouldn't drink alcohol, coffee, or other things like Coca Cola. My faith was again to be tested but not by soft drinks.

While selling yellow page advertising my faith was tested by two individuals working in a jewelry story in Westport, Connecticut. I "cold called" on their store since it was part of my assigned territory. The two gents in the store were well spoken enough but they were not very welcoming. Actually, they were a little mean.

Turned out the two gents were a father and son team, owners of the jewelry store. After a few minutes of polite introduction and conversation on my part, they decided to exert their rude behavior. It had begun to rain outside. It was the proverbial cats-and-dogs downpour, the kind that soaks clothes in three seconds.

Although I was being polite, they abruptly dismissed me. I realized it was pouring out, so I thanked them and stood inside by the door, waiting for the rain to subside. Then they got nasty. The younger one was snickering and said I had to leave immediately, as they needed to lock the doors for their lunch break.

I asked if they could give me a few minutes to let the rain subside since my car was across the parking lot. I knew my suit and tie would get soaked if I left just then. The father spoke in a serious tone,

"You have to go now. We are locking the doors."

I turned to face them, no longer smiling. They looked a bit nervous, partly because I'm not a small guy, and I probably looked ready to throw a punch.

I approached them with deliberation, and I bet they thought I was going to become violent. I did not. I told them that they should be ashamed of themselves and that they are upon the Earth under the eyes of God. I told them that they lacked faith, and they scoffed at that. I said that faith is much greater than most think, and it is respective of how all creatures treat one another in this very connected universe. The son just laughed in my face and said get out.

I turned and walked back to the door, saying a prayer under my breath. As I was walking, they were both behind me. I stopped and turned and told them that I would leave their store and go out into the pouring rain, but they both better watch me. Then I said to them,

"The moment I leave the store the rain will stop, and when my car door closes, the rain will start back up. I prayed for this and believe it will be so."

They laughed and spoke derisively. I walked briskly to the door, opened it, and stepped out into dry air. No rain. I walked a good hundred paces in no real hurry, opened the car door, and looked back at the two of them. They stood staring at me and I closed my car door. The deluge broke again. It rained like the first days of Noah.

I thanked my Heavenly Father for his kindness and drove directly to the office. I told the story to a few colleagues, but most of them were skeptical. This was fact: pure and simple.

The job was not long-lived, even though I was good at it. The company sent me to Pennsylvania for a spell after it became apparent the Fairfield County, Connecticut office was going to close. The day that the NYNEX/Donnelley Directory management started the layoffs all the sales reps were asked to come in and surrender the keys to their company cars. It was a couple of weeks into August. I was still owed commissions and not thrilled about leaving without the pay I felt was due.

Sitting there with the group was depressing. A short line of employees would go in the big office, not to be seen again, as they were made to walk down to the rear office elevators and leave the building. One person sneaked back up the stairs and told us they were taking the keys and giving out pink slips, then sending the terminated out the back door. I got up and left.

I drove my company car to Misquamicut Beach, Rhode Island. The management team tried to find me over the next few days and called Grandma A's house where they threatened to have me arrested for stealing their property. Eventually, they agreed that my returning the car was acceptable, and they would pay me my outstanding commissions. They did pay me, but it took over a year to reconcile the last of what was owed me. It was hard to say goodbye to the band of brothers I had worked with. I hope they all did well. I fondly remember Al and Ron, two of the guys I enjoyed working with.

During the year after that, I did a stint living in Clearwater, Florida. It was nice, but things got real hot, real fast. I decided to head back to Brooklyn to see my little brother Patrick, and our mom.

On my way back to Brooklyn, I stopped at Bush Gardens in Tampa. At a game where you throw quarters and try to cover the red spot in the middle, I covered the red spot in entirety on one lucky toss out of three tries. I won this really huge, stuffed white tiger, which didn't fit in my old 1979 Rabbit.

Unless I threw away my clothes and belongings, I had to sell the prize. I sold the tiger in the parking lot for fifty dollars. It had cost me seventy-five cents. This was quite fortuitous, as I needed the fifty bucks for gas, so I was happy to have it.

By late Spring of 1987, I was back in Brooklyn. I stayed with Mom and Patrick for a number of months. When I got home, I went looking for a job, found something fun to do in the human resource arena, and eventually found an apartment of my own. Life was okay for a while. My brother and I had a lot of fun then, all the way to 1990. With some effort and hard work, I seemed to get my groove back on.

CHAPTER 26

THE NIGHT DELLA GOT HER GROOVE ON

1960s

In October of 1964, Halloween was rolling back around. For trick or treating, I dressed as a bum (again), Loretta as a princess, and Diane a baby. Cindy couldn't go out for trick or treating just yet; she was only a couple of months old.

I pushed Diane in the stroller as we went up and down the block and around the corner to get candy.

Nanny threw most of it away. She said it was poisoned and we would die if we ate it. I didn't think we would've died. Luckily,

Loretta hid some, and we ate it later in secret. Mom was trying to get a job. She was skinny again, probably because we had little to no food except when Nanny was feeling slightly generous and would buy food for us. Sometimes she'd bring in a quart of milk and a loaf of bread.

Another Christmas was coming. I remember thinking it was going to be another bone-dry Christmas with no toys and no tree, just like the year before when my *step-dad* ran away. Mom got hired part-time at a local restaurant, and she was able to bring home food after work.

Loretta had no choice but to watch us younger kids, although sometimes Nanny watched us. They didn't like each other, and eventually I found out why.

I remember that Loretta and Mom were sitting in the kitchen of our new apartment two weeks before Thanksgiving. Mom lost the part-time job. She was told it was because the holidays were a slow time for the restaurant. She had asked her mother for a loan and was told no.

Thanksgiving the year before had been bad enough. One of the neighbors invited us to their house. They didn't let us eat there; they just gave my mother some food in a bag.

We ate that food for Thanksgiving dinner, but their kids teased us about it for weeks. Perhaps that experience was on her mind as Mom sat at the kitchen table, smoking furiously. She cursed aloud and cried a bit. She knew another Thanksgiving was coming, and we were basically in the same boat as the year before. She got up from the table and said she was leaving Loretta in charge and going out. She got dressed up as best as she could - a pink sweater and white pants, with make-up, too.

When my mom dressed up, she looked exactly like a movie star named Ava Gardner. The resemblance was eerie. I saw a picture of Ava Gardner later in life, and I'll be darned, but it could have been my mother. Mom put on her jacket, put her cigarettes in her purse, and went out. We went to the front window to watch her leave, and I heard a guy on the block whistle and call out to her.

"Della, do you have a date tonight?"

She told him to go f#@k himself and kept walking. I had heard her and Nanny using cuss words before, but this sounded different: more humorous and conversational in tone.

Mom was really happy for the next few weeks. We had a new uncle named Big Pat. He was a big friendly Italian guy with blue eyes. He kind of looked like Frank Sinatra with more wrinkles and much bigger shoulders. He smoked Camels and worked for New York City's sanitation department. He and my mother were going on dates.

Mom went food shopping with him, and we had the biggest Thanksgiving dinner ever. A huge turkey was brought home along with the other traditional treats.

I remember the smells and flavors because it was all so delicious. It was a huge improvement from the year before.

We had sweet potatoes, stuffing, cranberry jelly and pumpkin pie - just amazing. I was four-plus years old, but man do I remember that feast. I also remember that the turkey seemed to be with us for so many weeks, and we may have had some of it on Christmas Eve. We had a pretty good Christmas that year also.

We had our first real tree with a ton of silver tinsel, candy canes, and Christmas balls. The tree looked good and smelled like fresh pine from the forest - at least it did until Mom and Nanny buried it with too much tinsel.

They loved that shiny, ugly tinsel. I didn't think tinsel was needed at all. Just some lights or a few ornaments would have worked for me. That Christmas I remember getting a cowboy set and a fire truck. The girls got gifts, too, but nothing I would remember.

A few weeks after New Year's Day, Mom became pregnant again, and Big Pat didn't come back anymore. By March, it was really clear that Mom was going to have another baby, and Nanny was absolutely furious with her. I didn't get it. I heard my Nanny saying things to Mom like,

"How could you not know he was married? He's a f#@king loan shark. He didn't give you the food and money for nothing."

She said other things that were worse than that. After a while, I stopped listening to her words. In a fast nine months I had something I really liked: a little brother.

I have fond memories of my little brother Patrick's arrival in 1965. He was squirmy and active. His father, Big Pat, did come around to see the baby once in a while. My brother looked just like his father, the spitting image.

Mom's friend Vinny, who lived near Sea-Gate at the end of Mermaid Avenue, became Patrick's godfather. He knew my mother from back in the days when she was the barmaid for the Townhouse Downtown Café.

I was thrilled to have a little brother, especially after having so many sisters. Patrick had his father's big blue eyes and wry smile. He always had a look of mischief, even when he was doing nothing.

We were still living in the apartment next to P.S. 80 in Coney Island when Patrick was born. For me, the beach, the church, and the library were the places I enjoyed most when I was a young boy. Each was a short walk away.

My early life involved Our Lady of Solace church or "OLS" in various ways. It's hard to explain, but I remember being naively grateful for everything and anything. If it happened and wasn't painful, I was happy.

I still feel that way, although not as innocently. There were times when I would go inside OLS and sit there, listening to the quiet and have a conversation with Him. On the beach as a teen, I also sat on the furthest rocks to converse with God. It never seemed strange to me to sit there and think to myself or say out loud,

"Hi, Pop. How are you today?"

It always felt as though He was sitting there near me, kind of smiling at me. Every once in a while I would get a hug, not the type of hug we normally associate as such. What I felt was amazing - like warm chills and tingles from the center of my being, up and down my whole self. As an adult, those *hugs* are still amazing.

CHAPTER 27
CHILD WELFARE MAN TO THE RESCUE

1960s

Step-dad showed up again for a very short time in the summer of 1965. He found us in our new apartment on 17th Street, the church block. He brought a kitten that he gave to us. It was a weird looking little thing with strange pointy ears. I called it Simba, after the lion in the Tarzan movies. The last time he visited us he had hit my mother when she was carrying my little sister Cindy inside her belly.

Perhaps *Step-dad* came to visit because he was curious about the new baby that was soon to arrive. It didn't prevent that flat-faced redneck from drinking like a fool and getting violent again. Things got out of hand, but it didn't work out for my *step-dad*.

One night in one of his drunken fits, *Step-dad* kicked the door in, and then he tried to beat my mom up again. I remember seeing her suddenly throw up. She screamed at him to stop hitting her stomach, which was swollen with child. Enraged, I screamed at him and actually hit him in the head with a glass jar of jam. He punched me in the face and kicked me across the room and then kicked my mother again.

Diane and baby Cindy were in their crib screeching at the top of their lungs. The adults screaming at each other were scaring them terribly. Loretta ran to the neighbor's house and they called the cops. The police came fast and handcuffed *Step-dad*. One big cop picked him up by the scruff of his neck and punched him really hard in the gut, asking him how he liked it. He did that a few times, right in front of us.

He was throttling him for hitting a pregnant woman. I was cheering for the cop. Mom went to the hospital and came back in a number of hours with the baby still inside, and no problems except visible bruises.

Step-dad was the natural father of my two sisters Diane and Cindy, respectively (more on that to come). Mom told me that he was a fugitive from a failed bank robbery down south, and that he had broken out of jail twice before he met my mom. When he left with the police, he didn't come back into our lives again until 1972, seven years later.

Patrick was born in 1965. If you consider their birthdates, Diane, Cindy, and Patrick were like blue-eyed triplets: 1963, 1964, and 1965 - a new kid each year. Patrick crawled and walked faster than any kid I ever heard of. He climbed out of his crib before age one. This was one kid that could not stay still. He was the baby brother I hoped for: fun to play with and pretty smart.

In late 1966, he had an accident that involved scalding hot water in the bathtub. Patrick lost almost all the skin on his feet. It took years for him to heal, and he would never be able to wear hard shoes until his adult life. The night he got burned, I was with Nanny. If I had been home, I wonder if this accident would have happened at all.

When I came home from Nanny's the next morning and heard what happened, my heart was broken. My baby brother was in the hospital. Seeing that tiny little boy suffer as he healed was awful. He came home from the hospital close to my seventh birthday.

He was, and is, pretty tough. No matter what he felt, he kept climbing out of his crib or out of his playpen. Bandages and bloody feet, he was obsessed with moving about and loved to crawl. He always crawled near the bathroom, back to the scene of the crime. After that incident with Patrick's feet, Mom had to keep the bathroom door locked on the outside with a hook lock placed above any kid's reach, a habit she took to heart for years to come.

A couple of months after Patrick's accident, a man from the Bureau of Child Welfare came to visit my mom to see how her youngest son was doing. He came back again and again. He told my mother that she was in a bad situation and that she may not be able to keep Patrick or any of her children.

He was sure that she or one of her kids had hurt Patrick in the bathtub. She said nobody did it to him. Patrick did it himself.

On one visit while the man was arguing with my mom, from the corner of his eye he watched Patrick in his playpen. He explained to Mom that because of her financial state, Patrick would be better off with another family. That notion caused me to cry hysterically. I didn't want him to leave. My mother cried too, because she had been forced to leave one daughter at an orphanage earlier in her life. In 1955, Mom had another daughter named Mary Ann that was put up for adoption. I didn't meet Mary Ann until 1999, two years after my mom had passed.

I guess the child welfare man wasn't totally bad. He picked me up and tried to comfort me. He was saying that maybe Patrick and I could be together after all. For some reason the guy was twisting his neck, craning his head around to look at the playpen, when he suddenly put me down and jumped up from the kitchen chair to run into the hallway.

Mom was screaming at him saying he should leave her kids alone. When the guy turned on the bathroom light, everybody just gasped. There was Patrick, bandaged feet all bloody, as he held himself up by the tub. The imp had the hot water running full blast and was filling the tub up. Laughing, the kid tried to climb into the tub again. The man turned off the water, picked up Patrick, and held him up to the light. He was shaking his head, and saying,

"If I hadn't seen it for myself…"

Then he looked at me, took some tissue, and wiped my eyes. Patrick had actually climbed out of his playpen, and because someone had left the bathroom door unlocked, he crawled into the bathroom and climbed up along the tub to turn on the faucet closest to him - the hot water faucet. The man told my mom that it was too bad the hot water faucet was on the outside.

If it had been reversed with the cold-water faucet on the outside, things might have turned out better. He looked at Patrick's bandages and suggested mom clean them.

"Keep the little guy," he said. "…and lock him up tight during the night."

Mom took Patrick in her arms. She said thanks to the man.

He said,

"Don't thank me yet. You need to keep an eye on this one, I am sure that this boy will always be in some hot water."

He left our apartment, and mom changed Patrick's diaper and bandages. We called my little brother Patty-Boy for years, but when he grew up, he was just Patrick. As I mentioned earlier, my little brother and I had much fun during our years. I love the kid.

CHAPTER 28
THE SPELL AND THE WILDCAT

1960s

Another year passed, and Thanksgiving of 1967 was closing in on us. Nanny and Mom set forth to put a harmful spell on Big Pat, for not providing any child support for Patrick. It was a few days before the holiday.

In our kitchen there was a park-sized picnic table, stove, fridge, and sink. Over the table was an alcove, where sat a statue of the Sacred Heart of Mary, displaying only her hands, shoulders, and face. The statue's hands were held in supplication, and she seemed to be praying for us. Her eyes looked at us while we ate.

The Blessed Mother was a presence of goodness, and I always loved Her. She never turned her back on us. That night, my mom and grandmother invoked evil spirits right in front of her statue. The alcove in which Mary's statue sat was near the ceiling and no adult could reach it without standing on a ladder. Mom borrowed a ladder from a neighbor to put the statue there in the first place. This fact is very important.

The two spell casters had a shirt that belonged to Big Pat. They cut it up and squeezed a fresh lemon over one of the largest pieces. They wrapped that material around a photo of him and added some feathers from a dead sparrow, then lit some religious candles, and poured melted wax on the concoction.

I was young but witnessing these kinds of events leaves an indelible impression. There was no doubt in my young mind that what they were doing was wrong. Nanny said some spooky stuff, and there was a gust of air that suddenly blew through the kitchen. She burned part of the shirt. The lights were off.

The only light was from the candles which, when she burned the shirt, the candles suddenly blew out. Scary, but not too surprising as the windows were old and drafty.

Nanny put the concoction in the freezer. Then, she told Mom to make sure no kids touched it. I was the only kid aware of their little hocus pocus, as I was peeking and listening from the other room. No way on Earth would *I* touch it. After they went into the forward bedrooms, I sneaked a peek in the freezer, got goosebumps, then ran quietly back to my room and jumped into bed.

The next morning Mom was livid. She was cursing a blue streak into the morning air. She wanted to know who turned the Blessed Mother's statue around and faced her to the wall. She was really ticked and cursed and raved like a lunatic.

We little kids were innocent, and way too short to have touched the statue at all. My mom stopped carrying on and sat down at the picnic table we used in the kitchen. She was smoking and blankly looking up at the statue which was no longer looking back into the kitchen. She started to cry or at least sniffle.

Mom got up and pushed the table closer to the alcove. She stood on it, but she was still too short. She climbed down and put a milk crate on top of the table (the one where she stored laundry detergent). She climbed up - cigarette hanging from her lips and turned the statue around to face the room again. When the table was fixed and all was back in place, Mom really began to cry.

It took a while before she calmed down. The Blessed Mother's face looked sad as well. Her bright colors seemed faded, and the statue looked much older than the day before.

I recall it was the next day or so when we found out that Big Pat had been in a bad car crash. He was still alive but lost some front teeth, hurt his arm, and maybe needed some stitches on his head. He'd been driving home from the bar when his car crashed. We didn't see Big Pat again for months.

On another note, just before *Step-dad* was on his way back to jail the year Patrick was born, he showed up and dropped off that strange cat we named Simba. Simba grew pretty big. He was as big as a medium sized dog, like a cocker spaniel. The neighbor's German shepherd hated Simba and would howl, growl, and bark at Simba whenever the cat sat in the window.

Simba got out of the house a few times and always came back with a pigeon, rat, or mouse as a trophy. The cat had the biggest pointy ears and never seemed very friendly. He did like me though, as I could pet him without too many scratches or bites. As a matter of fact, all of our pets over the course of our lifetime seemed to like me, and most of them did not like my poor brother Patrick, for reasons unknown.

Pat was not mean to them, and I was not especially nice to them.

One particular dog gave both brothers equal servings of apathy, but he was Mom's favorite dog (Oh, and Bingo was his name). Over the years, we had many pets, but Simba was the strangest. Those really harsh looking gray eyes of his always made you feel like he was looking at his next meal. Perhaps for Simba, food was wearing our clothes.

The German shepherd next door really freaked out whenever the cat got outside. It was wild to see that dog trying to jump the fence. We kids just screamed and ran inside. The dog almost made it over, but the owner prevented it each time.

Simba was kept inside most of the time, and he would sit at the window and make this awful crying sound.

It was not a house-cat sound, but something more haunting. Another day came when we kids were in the back yard and the neighbor's German shepherd tried to hop the fence, as somebody had let the cat out. It was the last straw: the dog finally jumped the fence. We all froze in terror.

The dog chased after the cat, not us. Simba didn't turn and run away. He snarled a nasty little hissing sound, and all the hair stood straight up on his back.

The dog charged and Simba jumped on top of it. That big cat held on and shredded the dog's back and neck with its hind claws. Contrary to what we all thought would happen, the dog had no chance. Simba was too fast and too mean, and by the time the owner hosed the cat away from his pet, the dog had nearly bled to death.

The owner took his dog to the vet, and it had to be put to sleep. The vet called the police and they came to look for Simba but he was gone.

Simba stayed out of sight for a couple of days, but we knew he'd show up. The cops told my mom to call them when the cat came back. It proved unnecessary for the cops to come back since our neighbor was out to get that cat for what it did. He put a bowl of chopped meat in his back yard. It was filled with rat poison, and Simba couldn't have known the difference. He must have eaten it all because he was stone dead on the back stairs one morning.

The cops came and took his body. They fined mom for housing a wild animal, and she had to pay or go to court. We hadn't known that Simba, the cat that *Step-dad* left for us during his *visit* from North Carolina, was actually a bobcat.

He did seem a bit more feral, but how would we know? At the time, we were cat uneducated Brooklyn folks. So, Mom had to pay the fine, but it took her over a year to do so. We did get a new cat, red in color, and named it Lucky. It was a normal cat. We all liked Lucky, as he was lazy and affectionate. From their brazen daylight raids, it appeared the mice also liked him.

CHAPTER 29

A NIGHT OUT OF CONEY ISLAND HISTORY

1960s

We continued to live on 17th Street until 1968. One warm April night that year an event occurred that scared everybody pretty badly and drove my mom to look for higher ground. A race riot had started (again) because some depraved individual (James Earl Ray) shot Dr. Martin Luther King, Jr. for reasons I won't pretend to know or understand. It made no sense.

Unfortunately, pressure had been building since the big riot in Newark, New Jersey that took place in 1967, following the arrest and death of a black man named John Weerd Smith. It was believed he had been killed by white Newark policemen, after they arrested him in Newark for a traffic infraction.

News broke of Mr. Weerd's death and caused a riot to erupt that lasted for six days in July 1967. Coney Island suffered from that riot, as folks living in the projects of Coney Island took to the streets in a frustrated rage. From the late sixties on, Coney Island was evermore considered rough place to live, but I believe it was at its most dangerous during the riot of 1968.

Following the assassination of Martin Luther King, Jr., New York City put an 8:30 pm curfew on Coney Island's amusement area. Not long after that curfew was placed, angry park patrons, most of whom were black folks, rioted against the curfew, and stormed into the neighboring streets.

Fires were started, and all kinds of destruction and looting took place. Iconic establishments like Nathan's Famous were looted, and parked automobiles were vandalized. I think that night was the end of the Cinderella ride on the boardwalk. It was one of my little sister's favorite rides.

Rioters spilled into the Stillwell Avenue Subway Terminal, and trapped bystanders were assaulted. Six separate subway cars were damaged to the point where they were taken out of commission.

The violence flowed into the Coney Island residential areas. Rioting was underway in many places, and our street had its share. People were screaming and shooting literally in our back yard. We were terrified. Raving maniacs threw stuff at our windows, breaking glass. Gunshots rang out every few minutes.

I remember Mom and us kids trying to escape to the next-door neighbor's house by climbing over the back-porch rail. Our neighbor's father was in the house, and he had a gun. He protected his family with fierce devotion.

We were really lucky to be invited in that night because our apartment was completely wrecked after we left. While we were climbing over the back-porch rail and into our neighbor's house, some people ran up to the backyard fence yelling obscenities. Gunshots flashed brightly outside. Inside our neighbor's apartment, the windows were boarded up. We stayed there till morning.

God blessed us that night, as we survived. Mom was heartbroken to find all our furniture torn up and broken the next day. Again, we had lost much, but the statue of the Blessed Mother had not been broken and remained vigilant.

Mom went looking for a different apartment the next week. She wanted one above street level, where the troubles from the street could not easily reach her and her family. She looked for an apartment for about a month, insistent that we would not be on a first floor or in another basement. She wanted to stay in the neighborhood. She finally got what she wanted: a third-floor apartment only two blocks away.

Mom found the apartment in a somewhat historic brick building. It came with problems of its own since some of the new neighbors would turn out to be pretty restless.

As for me, the move proved to be a good move. I made a bunch of friends on the new block. The friends I made were from all walks of life: African, Hispanic, Italian, German, Irish, and a couple of unknowns. We played together for years, all the time never considering the different colors of our skin.

We just played. Fun was fun, and kids were kids. Too bad that couldn't be true all the time - like when adults get involved. Perhaps being a kid at heart is a good thing.

In spite of the troubles we occasionally experienced, there was nothing as naturally intoxicating as a Coney Island summer. Blue skies, light fluffy clouds, and bright yellow sunshine were often delicately painted over a glistening sandy beach and the sparkling waters of the Atlantic Ocean. Even when it rained it was nice. The summer rain was usually a quick thunderstorm or a sprinkle during the afternoon. I loved thunderstorms as a kid.

When we lived in that third-floor apartment on 15th Street, I would sit on the fire escape with an umbrella and watch the lightning hit the ocean. It drove my mother nuts.

The Coney Island air was filled with some great smells: the soothing breath of the ocean, Nathan's hot dogs and fries, neighborhood pizzerias, and fresh coffee. Synchronized with the olfactory pleasures were the constant cry of seagulls and the rumble of subway trains and roller coasters. During the season, you could hear people cheering and yelling as they enjoyed all the thrilling rides.

You'd also hear music from car radios and sometimes music from the rides themselves, especially the Super Himalaya. Of course, there was a variety of sirens, such as police, fire, and ambulance. All these things mixed together to create the melody of a Coney Island day. Night was similar with the added lullaby of the ocean. The sounds, smells, and sights were a comfort to me in those days. The ambiance of summer near the beach never ceased to tickle me. It wasn't as much fun in the winter, but playing in snow on the beach was kind of cool. Did I mention that we lived near Nathans? Best fries ever!

Coney Island is rich with history and fantasy. It was filled with peoples from all over the world. Nanny had visited Coney Island in the 1920s when she was a teenager.

According to her account and the historic information available, the turn of the twentieth century found Coney Island as the resort spot of the east coast. It was an adult version of Disneyland. Some of the older apartment buildings were in fact hotels (or flophouses), from back in the day - the kind of places where gamblers fought, booze was sloshed, and people died.

The videos I have seen of Coney Island in the 1920s provided an impression that it really was an adult play-land. It was nothing like the Coney Island I knew, circa 1968 and later.

At present, a revival has occurred in Coney Island, highlighted by a baseball stadium, a well-known Hot Dog eating contest, and a parade of mermaids. The thrill goes on.

Before school started in 1968, we had finished moving from West 17th Street to West 15th Street, between Neptune Avenue and Hart Place. After the Blessed Mother's bust had turned away from the room, the riots, and so much of our stuff got trashed, Mom was determined to find an apartment on the top floor in the tallest building on whatever block we moved to. She succeeded, and we moved into the tallest building on 15th Street.

There were at least three doorways to the outer hallway from our apartment, though they were all sealed off except the main door. The number of doors lent well to the idea that the apartment house could have been one of those old flop-house hotels when it was built. It was built in 1920, the very start of the roaring twenties.

The main door provided ingress and egress to the communal staircase. The apartment itself was railroad style with no doors between the rooms. Up on the third floor, ours was the right-hand apartment. We were up above the streets with a nice view of the Wonder Wheel and the Parachute Jump. The views were even better from the roof, and a lot of us went up there, especially on Tuesday nights in the Summer when we would watch the fireworks from the roof.

The girls in the building would sometimes go up there covered in baby oil, to lie in the sun on folding lounge chairs or big towels and bake like lobsters in an oven. Sometimes strangers went up there to hide out, or they slept in the hallways during the cold or rainy weather. When he found them there the super would chase them out.

The building certainly felt old enough, and the walls were thin. Fortunately, the neighbors were interesting and mostly friendly. Augie was the building super. He was a big shouldered, tall, and likeable Italian fellow. His wife and daughters were always very nice. I think they were the same age as Loretta.

They lived on the second floor, directly below us, and it was comforting having such a nice family there. The apartment to our right was rented by a couple with kids; We didn't interact with their kids much, though Mom was neighborly with them.

Donald and Bernadette lived on the second floor next to Augie. Bernadette was another one of my mom's favorite friends. She and Donald had kids, too, and later our families became in-laws for a short time (well, kind of).

On the first floor lived Tessie, her daughter and her three sons. Another family lived next to Tessie on the first floor, but their last name escapes me. They had a son named Raymond, and daughters, Noreen and Claire. Noreen was good friends with Loretta. Clair sometimes babysat us for my mother.

Our new apartment had three bedrooms. They were all small rooms, but one was smaller still, so we dubbed it the *little room*. The apartment was shaped a bit like a slanted letter "y" turned upside-down. You entered the front door and found yourself facing straight down a short hallway that led to the kitchen.

Halfway down, before the kitchen, was the door to the bathroom. It was the only functional door to a room within the apartment (besides the front door that is). The eat-in kitchen was followed by a bedroom, which was probably intended as a dining room at some point since it had no closets.

Alternatively, upon entry, you could make a sharp right and walk into the living room, followed by a bedroom, and to the right of that bedroom was the *little room*.

The summer of 68' we spent painting the apartment and getting familiar with the neighborhood. It took everyone a couple of weeks to get used to walking up the three flights of stairs, but we got used to it. Taking the dog out helped, though Duke walked himself once outside.

On one corner of our block was Jimmy the Butcher's meat store, and on the opposite corner was Weisberg's, Grocery and Deli. If you wanted a great hero sandwich, Weisberg's main deli guy Sal was the man to see. Bernard's Candy Store was on Neptune, close to Stillwell Avenue. I bought and read comic books there for years. Next to Bernard's was Gerace's, a bakery that mostly made Italian bread.

My brother worked in that bakery for years, from his teens through his twenties. Down the street was Charlie the Barber, where many a crew cut was administered. Charlie cut my hair from 3rd grade through high school.

During the summer, we walked down to the beach on most days. It was a three-block hike from our new apartment. Typically, we'd stay on the bay next to the pier. For the first few months, our 15th Street apartment seemed just right, and nothing strange occurred.

We all made friends with some of the kids on the block and tried our best to fit in. I was eight and going to P.S. 90 in the fall for third grade. This was a new school for me, since the first few years were at P.S. 80. My second-grade teacher, Ms. Tepper, had left a good impression on me. I developed a love for reading and writing in her P.S. 80 class. Teachers are not recognized often enough for the kindness and help they are very willing to provide.

I fondly remember Ms. Tepper, Mrs. Erlich, Mrs. Posin, Mr. Cohen, Mrs. Rubin, and Mrs. Messina. All were memorable and influential teachers. I wasn't always studious. As a kid I loved reading comics, monster stories, and watching monster movies.

Nanny often took me to see them, even Night of the Living Dead when it first came out. At age eight, that flick gave me goosebumps. I think those tingles were a form of training, considering what was to come.

CHAPTER 30
THE TINGLER ON CHILLER THEATER

1960s

This period represents the earliest part of my true-life ghost stories. While we were moving into the 15th Street apartment, or inside it painting and cleaning, we met a couple of the neighbors. Two of them hinted that the building might be haunted, albeit with a wink and a nod. We didn't immediately experience any of the spooky activities our fellow tenants alluded to while we were moving in. Things were quiet.

When those stranger things got started in the apartment, the intensity of it built-up exponentially. Perhaps the delay was a quirky kind of test. Perhaps the ethereal tenants were testing our boundaries and theirs. It definitely tested our ability to absorb, deny, and struggle through difficult times in that apartment. We stayed there for eight years.

At the young age of eight, I knew a little bit about things that go bump in the night. Some of it I learned from Nanny.

Not all. Certainly, I didn't learn the things I know about good and evil spirits from watching scary movies, but I did love scary movies.

I remember that I watched "Chiller Theater" every Saturday night. Okay, I say I watched it, but that was without Mom's knowledge. Sometimes I was hiding under the couch to watch. I was like a movie ninja. Three of us watched: Mom and Loretta on the couch, me under it. Duke would occasionally poke around and sniff at me, but he never ratted me out by accident or otherwise. He didn't even wag a tail or anything. Duke was a good dog. He also sat in the room to watch television with us. I think he just liked the company.

This under-the-couch movie watching lasted for few weeks until Chiller Theater presented a Vincent Price movie called "The Tingler." Not the scariest of beasties, "The Tingler" was a caterpillar-like bug-monster that was discovered by Vincent Price's character. It was no bigger than a large dog, but it was gnarly in its execution of a victim. It had these mean, evil looking pincers for grabbing victims.

The Tingler fed on fear and somehow got into a "movie theater" near the end of the movie. That was a first for me: a movie that showed a theater showing a scary movie within the movie I was watching (I am not saying that three times fast).

In the script, some poor patron was watching a horror flick (within the movie) and the Tingler would grab them by the leg with its pincers and suck out their life, connected through their fear. It was drawn to the victim's terrors and just fed on their life force (sounds an awful lot like modern day politics, doesn't it?)

On the couch in our apartment, Mom and big sister were cringing as they watched our black and white television. The actors in the movie were watching some other horror flick on a big movie screen, which was apparently a huge part of "The Tingler" story.

The characters in the make-believe theater were scared silly, which excited the Tingler. As the scene's climax approached in the on-screen scary movie, this Tingler thing is about to put the pincers to some audience member, its next victim being a young woman. Just as the pincers grabbed the leg of the woman to suck the life out of her, I grabbed Mom's and Loretta's ankles with my nails and roared.

They both hit the ceiling like two scared cats jumping off an electrified fence. I immediately got my ass kicked. Mom was so mad she beat me like a dusty rug, but I laughed through it and kept laughing for weeks afterward.

Every time I told that story at school and every time my mom gave me a serious look, I laughed. Once I grabbed at her ankle, and she swatted at me, then she laughed too.

I never had to hide under the couch again to watch Chiller Theater because it was safer for Mom to know where I was when it was on. Loretta didn't stay to watch the show most Saturday nights, being a big shot teenager and all, she got to go out. I ultimately replaced her as the scary-movie couch partner for Mom.

I believe there was another spectator, possibly laughing at the hijinks I perpetrated. I think he was getting some prank-playing ideas of his own. Since he was a ghost (probably a poltergeist), playing pranks had to have made sense. I thought it was a *him*, but I was never sure.

Since I was a child of the sixties and seventies, it was a sure bet that *Charlie* was going to be the name I'd ascribe to an unseen enemy. That was the name most of the army movie heroes used for their enemies. Ultimately, one of the ghosts I nicknamed Charlie. I am sure he was there on 15th Street long before we arrived. Charlie was the mischievous unseen prankster.

Living on 15th Street, it was obvious to us that there was more than just Charlie scaring us. We never knew the actual quantity of spectral pests. Sometimes Charlie and the other phantoms were kind of funny, other times they were just plain scary. More on that later.

Apparently, sometime after we moved out of the 15th Street apartment, Mrs. Brown and her family moved into the same part of that multi-family dwelling that my own family had lived in for eight years. She lived there with her daughter Marilyn and her other relatives, at least until a couple of years ago. Mrs. Brown and her family were dear friends of ours during the years we lived on 15th Street. Her daughters and my sisters spent much time together.

Marilyn, her youngest daughter, was very close friends with my younger sisters Diane and Cindy. Marilyn and her sisters were like extended family to us in the old days. I remember Marilyn at the girls' birthday parties and their communion party. All these girls spent a lot of time together. Marilyn had a cool nickname: Boogaloo. I never knew how she got the name. We all loved dancing in those days; maybe that was the reason.

During the summer of 2004, I visited the old neighborhood and went to the building in question. I took my son, my girlfriend Lisa, her sister Sandi, Sandi's husband Joel. We met Marilyn outside the old apartment building, as she and some others were having a barbeque party on the sidewalk.

That was when I learned that her family was living in the very same apartment my family previously lived in. It was great to see her after so many years, though it brought back bittersweet memories.

Marilyn told me her mom was upstairs in the apartment at that moment. Matthew and I went up to see Mrs. Brown. It was a nice visit, but it was weird to see the old apartment. As a kid, I felt that our apartment was huge and spacious. As a grownup, it felt much smaller. When I went back downstairs, in front of Lisa, et al., I asked Marilyn if there were any odd things happening in the apartment. Her reaction to my question shocked my girlfriend and her family. My son was not paying too much attention, as he was still young. Marilyn told us that she and other family members constantly heard noises in the apartment. There was no explanation for any of them.

They heard kitchen utensils and the sink being used at night when nobody was there. It sounded like someone was making a noisy sandwich, she said. Marilyn also stated that they heard furniture and other things moving around in the apartment, and various loud noises or bangs. She said they heard kitchen cabinet doors opening and closing, or the bathroom door opening and closing. She had no explanation for any of it and told us that some of the other tenants in the building also complained about weird noises and odd phenomena, like doors opening and closing.

There was no doubt that the phenomena we experienced as kids in that same apartment were still manifesting. At this point my girlfriend (and future wife), now understood that the things I had shared with her about that place were true. As we drove back to Sandi and Joel's home in Long Island, I shared a bit more about the sounds of moving furniture. I told them about Charlie the ghost, and of the other things that occurred in that old apartment.

I also told them of the old factory on Hart Place where my closest friends and I once played and where a friend and I had used explosives and holy water to exorcise our very first ghost (or perhaps ghosts) and saved one friend from potential harm.

Mrs. Brown was one of the sweetest ladies I ever knew as kid and seeing her as an adult proved she was still the same. Marilyn died at a young age, but she was reunited with a lot of relatives, as some other members of her family also died too young. Mrs. Brown passed in 2018, and I believe she is now reunited with her family and friends, including my mom.

They are all together in Heaven. God bless their souls. I have no doubt that we all see each again, there in His light (knock on wood).

CHAPTER 31
THE THREE KNOCKS

1960s

I think my grandmother requires an explanation of her own. Her name was Irene Leonard, and she told me she was of Irish ancestry, which many years later I proved via DNA testing and heritage research.

She also said that she was born to J. James Leonard and his wife Edith 'Bunny Nana' Graham in New York City. They lived in the East Village of Manhattan from around 1910 to 1932.

Irene was my maternal grandmother, now gone, having lived to be 97 years old. She passed in July 2005. She was super cognizant in her last days, demonstrated when my wife Lisa met her the first time. Her hair was a fluffy snow-white cloud, and her turquoise eyes were clear and bright, the day we went to see Nanny at the hospital. She knew Lisa's name and remembered my age. She explained to Lisa the reason she stayed beautiful for so many years: something called Oil of Olay. Nanny lived out her senior years in a Coney Island project with my youngest sister Cindy.

When I was a toddler to around 7 years of age, my grandmother (or Nanny as we typically called her) would take me to stay in her apartment on weekends and summer nights. She wanted company, and I liked the tranquility of her apartment. There were no screaming little sisters or crying babies and no cigarette smoke. I really enjoyed the Irish tea with milk and honey, and the toasted rye bread with peanut butter we shared. Over time I met some of Nanny's nine brothers and sisters. I fondly remember Uncle Willie Leonard coming to visit us in Coney Island and drinking beer on the boardwalk.

I also recall going to visit Uncle Richie Leonard in or near Perth Amboy, New Jersey. Uncle Richie was nick-named "the Silver Fox", because his hair had turned silver in color. Nanny said he was her handsome brother. I don't recall too much more of them.

Nanny was different from her siblings in certain ways. She had a couple of weird quirks that I observed even in my early years. Did I mention she was a witch? No disrespect intended, since she used that term on herself on a number of occasions in my lifetime.

Nanny was psychic and had frequent talks with spirits, an association that defies any materially grounded person's beliefs. I always thought she was bit looney but overlooked it as she was nice to me when I was little. Well, we all grow up, and later I realized she was a bit looney, perhaps as a result of crossing back and forth between different sides of the veil, though not always to the better places.

Spirits reach out to some of us, and certainly, that happened to me more than once. I guess some of them spoke with her or visited her. She communicated with the other side, but I think she spoke with the wrong ones too often. I remember Mom and Nanny talking about a specific spiritual phenomenon that they cautioned us kids about. It had to do with an old wives' tale or urban legend if you will, regarding the three knocks.

The three knocks on a door when no one is actually there is considered by many cultures to be a visit from an angel of death. According to a Teutonic Myth, the three knocks means someone in the house will die within three days. Other cultures believe that whoever answers the door is meant to perish. My siblings and I were taught that the three knocks were not to be answered and the door not be opened, especially if it comes at an unexpected hour (such as three in the morning). Trust me: growing up with such a strange rule was freaky, especially if someone did visit and knock three times. It would scare the shit out of us kids.

We had a number of visitors to the apartment that did knock three times, but each did so with varied tempos - not a steady, equally spaced set of three knocks, such as we thought a spirit might make. About a year from the night the bust of the Blessed Mother had turned around to face the wall, the three knocks occurred, the equally-spaced-out kind.

It was an eerie thing because I didn't hear anything the night it happened. I was asleep, but that was no excuse as my sleep had become cat-like. From all the trauma, I became hyper-sensitive to changes in the environment, no matter how small.

On that particular night, the only witnesses to the event were my sister Diane and our family watchdog Duke.

Duke was a serious watchdog, a former police dog. He would bark at any sounds in the hallway outside our door and sometimes at noises in the street.

His bark was gruff and loud and immediately woke me. I'd come charging to the front door to protect the family, typically with a baseball bat in hand. I was not a real threat as a little kid, but I had heart when problems arose. However, that night in 1969 the dog didn't bark.

Diane was sleeping in the bed with Mom. Cindy was there also, on the window-facing side of the bed. Diane was resting comfortably when she felt Mom stirring, which woke her. There was a sound at the door. Three knocks. It was just past three in the morning. Diane saw the dog stand up when Mom got up, but he paid no attention to the noise at the door. If he had heard it, according to Diane, he didn't react.

Diane heard it again. Three gentle knocks - evenly spaced - and perfectly applied.

From Diane's account of it, Mom walked to the door, and sort of stood there for a minute in a trance. Diane said she was scared silly and asked Mom to go back to bed, pulling on her pajama sleeve but Mom opened the door.

Diane told me that the three of them were buffeted by a blast of air from the outer hallway. Duke didn't growl or bark.

He whined and put his ears down. Diane said Mom started to walk into the hallway. Nothing seemed real to my sister, and Mom was acting as though she were sleep walking. Mom came back inside, closed, and locked the door and they went back to bed. The dog just lay down somewhere between the bedroom and the front door.

At about 7:30 am in the morning, Diane awoke, feeling soaked. She thought she might have peed the bed or maybe Cindy did, but then she realized she was covered in blood. At six years old, the only response to that was to scream at the top of her lungs. I ran into the bedroom, and there was Mom in a pool of blood and white as a sheet.

Diane and Cindy were in a panic, grabbing at Mom, yelling at her to wake up.

Loretta came into the room and saw all the blood. She ran to get the neighbors to help. Bernadette or Tessie called the police for an ambulance. I don't remember all the adults that came into the apartment, but a lot of them did. Someone ran around the corner to get my grandmother. I remember seeing the mattress soaked with so much blood. I was in shock.

My mother lay there dead or at least she looked dead. She was white as a sheet.

An ambulance came. Mom's eyes were fluttering, and the group of us kids stood there watching the first responders carry Mom out on a stretcher. We were all crying. We prayed together and asked the Blessed Mother not to take her from us.

Prayers and tears were the days' agenda. Nanny stayed with us, and I think it was Tessie that came up later with some sandwiches for everyone.

Diane and I talked about the events of the previous night. When Mom was laying in her bed getting ready for sleep, she swore to us kids that the room was filled with roses. She said she could see them and smell them. We thought she was just tired or maybe coming down with something. She said the Blessed Mother was there for her or was coming for her. I kissed her goodnight and went down the hall to my room. Loretta had begun using the other twin bed in my room, after she came in from work. I was tired, but I heard Loretta come in sometime after four in the morning.

A little while after Mom was taken by ambulance the phone rang in the apartment. It was a call from one of our neighbors. She told my grandmother that a doctor or nurse said that Mom had just died. Nanny hung up the phone and stoically told us that our mom had just died. Then she said we would all be placed in good homes and might be better off anyway.

My reaction was to run to my room, where I knelt down and prayed. I told Jesus that I believed and trusted in Him. I begged Him and the Blessed Mother not to take Mom from us. I prayed to Him, the Blessed Mother, and St. Jude. We needed Mom, and she needed us. I *needed* her! Mom was my best friend. I did not want her to go. Then that little voice spoke to me for the second time.

"Your mom is going to be fine, have faith."

It was a male voice, quiet, familiar, and very comforting. I felt relieved. The phone rang. My grandmother cried out and told us that the doctors resuscitated Mom. She was alive.

They were sending her to another hospital, Kings County, because she needed treatment that Coney Island Hospital couldn't provide. Twice in her life Mom was sent from one hospital to another. We learned later that radiation was going to be used on Mom to treat her for cervical cancer. Nothing personal, but radiation made Godzilla and monsters of all sorts. If not for the little voice, I would have worried much more.

Mom was in the hospital for almost a month. Nanny came to stay with us, and Loretta ran away. She appeared to hate our grandmother, and I think that feeling was mutual. I believe it had to do with how much time Loretta spent with Grandpa, my grandmother's ex-husband.

Nanny was left in charge of Diane, Cindy, Patrick, and me. While Mom was in the hospital, Loretta went into hiding with an old friend of my mother's, a woman named Patricia. Loretta's new life was beginning, and Nanny was glad she was gone. Loretta did come back to grab clothes, only to leave again. I don't think Loretta was ever the same again after this tragic event, but then again, none of us were the same anymore. My relationship with my grandmother was changing and not for the better.

On those and many other nights my little brother and I would sometimes stay in the bottom bunk after prayers and pretend we were in a candy store. We'd drink malted milk shakes and chocolate egg creams. Then we would eat penny fish candies, Yankee Doodles, saltwater taffy, and all kinds of goodies that were ours for the imagining. These were hungry imaginations. A steady diet of powdered eggs, powdered potatoes, and powdered spinach was a solid motivator for goodies to be vividly imagined. We were innocents back then, but our innocence was soon stolen.

CHAPTER 32
WHAT COULD HAVE POSSESSED HER

1960s

While Mom was in the hospital getting radiated, we all watched as Nanny morphed into an evil witch. Some of the things I am writing next I wish I had forgotten, and I am sure my little brother wishes it more than I do. I hope he forgives me for putting this part of our life in the book. It is true, and it was just awful. God bless Patrick for being able to grow up and be as good and cool a man as he is.

The path of his young life was not a kind direction for anyone to have to traverse. I love my brother very much and my heart breaks thinking about all the years that passed us by, having spent so little time together as older adults. Please make time for your loved ones, no matter where they are or where you are and no matter whom you're with.

Patrick was the child that Nanny actually hated most of all. He was a blue-eyed cute little Italian-looking boy. He was three quarters Italian, which apparently was too much for her. He was only three-and-a-half years old during the time my mom was in the hospital, but almost every time Nanny looked at the kid she hit him. She often screamed at him and cursed him.

"You wop, you guinea bastard!" she would growl.

At first, I thought Nanny was just stressed out especially after being told her daughter had died and then came back. As the days passed, her attacks on the little guy and my sister Diane became more and more furious. Pat suffered the most from her rage. She beat Pat with a wooden spoon, a broomstick, and lastly with a dog leash. Every time she attacked him, I would jump in or jump on top of my brother and take as much of the beating as I could for him. I remember screaming at her to stop and asking why it was happening. It was horrifying.

I didn't know what was wrong. I was only eight years old and not experienced enough to understand what was happening. My younger siblings and I lived in state of constant fear. It felt all so dreadful. We were trapped with a demon in our grandmother's skin. She acted as if she was possessed.

The bathroom door was still locked by the hook-lock that was high up on the outside of the door - not so much to keep Patrick out anymore but to prevent the dog from going in there at night and drinking toilet water.

Every night when we were in the back bedroom trying to sleep we could hear the hook lock drop and the door creak open. We had heard this before but not with Nanny in the house every night. All four of us were in our beds, boys in one set, girls in the other set of bunk beds. We never got up, but she would hear the bathroom door and come screaming from the living room or Mom's bedroom.

"Who got up? Who did it?"

She would be frothing at the mouth with anger. Vicious hate filled her face. We all just hid under the covers, but she would still attack my little brother or my younger sister Diane. I'd end up getting whacked at least half the time, protecting my siblings from her rage. Ironically, she almost never hit Cindy, my youngest sister.

In those days, I didn't know why she avoided hitting Cindy, but in 2003 a theory was formed. I believed I finally knew why she had not hit Cindy during those earlier years. I'll tell you about that theory later, I promise. At the time though, Nanny was poking and swatting us with the broom, screaming at us to leave the f#@king bathroom door closed.

"Stay in your f#@king beds!" she screeched.

She was scary, but so was the ghost. Whoever or whatever the ghost was, it apparently didn't mind seeing us kids suffer. Was it done for the sake of poltergeist enjoyment? We never knew. The bathroom door still kept opening, and then the kitchen sink faucet turned on. Then it got even worse. Our bedroom lights flickered on and off, and the bunk beds started bouncing. In spite of the obvious phenomena, Nanny would still hit Patrick and Diane.

They had a big brother who cared and was willing to take some of the punishment, but I wasn't always fast enough. Every time she came at Patrick or Diane, I jumped on top of them to take the hits. When the beatings began, the hits would be awful, especially with the dog leash.

I remember screaming,

"Leave us alone, leave us alone!"

Whenever I would leap to Patrick's defense and catch about fifty percent of the beating, it made Nanny crazier (if that were possible). She hated when I did this, and she would grab me by the hair and yank me off, so she could keep hitting the little guy. I was immovable, and even when she pulled hair literally out of my head, I stayed in place.

Sometimes Duke would come to the rescue. I think he was initially confused as to what was going on, but after a week of this he decided to take our sides and bit Nanny and growled and barked at her. She eventually locked the dog out of the house.

Each night I prayed for Mom to come home, and each day I felt more hate for a grandmother I had once loved very much.

Our friendship was ending, and then she did the most unspeakable thing possible. Something so wrong that I actually wished her dead at the time.

One morning Pat needed to go to the bathroom really bad. Nanny said he couldn't leave the bed until she was ready. She hit him once and made him lay down again. My sisters and I felt sorry for him and argued with the old witch. She hit each of us in turn. Pat was in pain and his stomach issues were very obvious.

"For goodness sake," I yelled. "Nanny he has to go. He's not even four years old yet, and he has to go!"

She ignored my plea.

"Stay in that f#@king room!", she screeched.

Pat couldn't ignore his troubles anymore, so he dropped his little boy pajama bottoms and shit on the floor. He was crying his eyes out, embarrassed and so afraid. We grabbed some tissue from a Kleenex box and helped clean him. We were moving frantically, terrified of what might happen next. Sure enough, she walked into the room and looked as though she would kill each of us. She didn't touch Pat immediately.

She grabbed me by the arm and made my sisters and me go into the bathroom. She closed the door and blocked it shut with a chair. In a couple of seconds, we heard Patrick screaming. She was yelling, her voice rising above his terror. All we could hear from her were words that still make my stomach lurch. Thinking of it breaks my heart. She screeched evilly,

"I should make you eat it, you guinea bastard!"

I was going insane with rage. My sisters were in shock, but I was furious.

Finally, I forced the door open, literally breaking the door frame, and I was thrown into shock. Patrick was tied to one of the wooden chairs in the kitchen.

He had waste product smeared on his face. He looked as though he had thrown up, and indeed, he had. His little face was marked with handprints. She had smacked him and beat him and tried to make him eat his own bowel movement. He had fought back, but how much could a three-year-old really fight an adult while tied to a chair. No child should ever have been put through such an awful torture.

God bless my poor brother. So much innocence was lost because of these awful events. Nanny was literally spitting on herself with evil hatred. I have no idea what could have possessed her to do such a horrible thing. She was still screaming as I untied Pat, took him to the bathroom, and cleaned him up. My sisters were bawling their eyes out and, at that moment, Loretta came home.

Loretta went crazy. She was afraid to hit Nanny, but she pushed the old woman away from us with a fury, and then she took Pat and Diane with her and left. I learned later that they also went to stay with Mom's old friend. I didn't go, because I had to take care of Duke, who had been out in the street too long. Cindy didn't go because Nanny wouldn't let her. She held onto her and scratched at Loretta.

Nanny didn't hit Cindy when they were there, but after Pat and Diane were gone, she did hit her once or twice. She hit Cindy quite a bit lighter than the rest of us. She stopped hitting me after Patrick was gone.

I was not afraid of her, and she knew it. I was so angry by that time; it was all I could do not to try and strike at her.

For some reason, she stayed clear of me and never pushed Duke out of the house again. Something really insane happened in that apartment during those weeks, and I can only say I wouldn't wish those moments on anyone.

CHAPTER 33
FOLLOW THE LIGHT

1970s

Did I mention that Nanny was psychic? If you recall, I said there was a reason she treated Cindy differently. In 2003, Cindy and I were talking about how old Nanny was and how hard it was for Cindy to care for her.

That was when my theory formed. I believed Nanny knew all the way back in 1969 that Cindy was the granddaughter who would take care of her, up to the day of her death. There is no doubt in my mind that this was the reason she treated Cindy better than the rest of us. She saw her last years in her mind's eye and knew Cindy was the one. She treated me swell when I was really small, but we stopped being close for a long time after the incident with my baby brother. I started to tolerate her again in my teens. I'd keep her company every so often, but what she had done plagued my thoughts all through my life. I tried hard to excuse her behavior as maybe some form of mental illness.

Considering the spells and witchery, perhaps the real reason was deeper into the occult. She may have actually been possessed - especially in that old apartment - which had its share of spirits with ill intent. I don't know if Pat ever forgave her or if he just blocked it all out. He was very little when that happened to him. She never relented in her unexplained hatred of him. The saddest part of it was that Pat was actually a good little boy who never did a thing to her.

Eventually, Mom came home from the hospital. When she heard what had happened, heard what Nanny did to her kids, especially to Patrick, she threw her mother out of the house after giving her a black eye and a bloody nose. She was lucky Mom didn't' kill her. I think Nanny got off easy.

Those two, mother and daughter, had quite a few issues between them that didn't end well. They didn't speak to each other again until about 1971. The silent treatment is one of the key lessons one learns in dysfunctional family life.

Even when they stood on line in the same store, there was no talking, no acknowledgment at all. Interesting observation: they both attended the same mass at OLS where the priest talked about forgiveness. Eventually, they did move forward, with some forgiveness in the mix. It happened when a woman in the neighborhood mugged Nanny and beat her up.

Mom found out and went to see her mother in the hospital. Nanny had been badly beaten. She looked awful, like Rocky at the end of the first movie.

Mom found the mugger and beat her to a pulp. For some reason, that incident was catalyst enough for mother and daughter to reconnect. Mom always tried to take care of her mother. It had to be tough on my mom. She tried so hard to be a helpful daughter, but

Nanny only spoke well of Renee, my mom's sister. Nanny was not the best influence for her daughter; she never really showed any love to Mom.

In later years, when Mom was getting sick for the last time, Nanny wished her dead - out loud. She said she hoped Mom died horribly. Mom did.

In spite of how her mother treated her, Mom was still affectionate to us. She was a loving mother, generous with hugs and kisses for all her kids. We didn't have much, but we had some laughs and lots of love in spite of the difficulties. We made it the best it could be under the circumstances. Sometimes the best you can do was just try to be okay. Keeping the house clean helped, and I tried. I was my mother's Felix Unger robot.

In summary, Mom learned a harsh lesson from the infamous lemon curse she and Nanny used on *Big Pat*. The result of using bad magic against another human was to become sick herself. It's true. Mom was so sick, she actually died and had to be resuscitated more than once. The point is this: it never pays to do anything that requires such ill will or evil intent. It is my belief that hatred, bitterness, and frustration can cause cancer. I knew some fools that tried to place curses on other people. Some used the malocchio or so-called "evil eye". Others used Santeria and voodoo. A few unfriendly persons may have tried to jinx or curse me, too.

On your own, I bet you would learn that every time an angry, bitter individual placed a curse on someone else, it was the one that placed the curse that paid the highest price. Hate causes cancer; I believe this to be true. I feel love is far healthier for us, even if we can't like everyone.

A general observation to consider: Keep your heart light and your life will follow lightly. A phrase I often use is:

"Follow the Light, and you'll get where you're going."

I try to. When I do, it always works best. My Mom didn't ascribe to that way of thinking. She struggled through the cervical cancer and treatment from 1969 to 1972. It took over two years of radiation treatments and medications to help her survive. Almost three years later, she was done with the radiation, but it had caused her to blow up, to retain water, and get really fat looking. Eventually, that also passed.

By 1974, she was pronounced to be in remission. Mom was a tough customer, a natural fighter. She danced with me on my tenth birthday in 1970, even though the year before she was nearly dead.

For the record, 1969 wasn't all bad. It was great watching the New York Mets win the World Series that year. I always loved the New York Mets, as they were the first team I ever saw in real life. I was in the Big Brother program, and my Big Brother took his kids and me to see the New York Mets play baseball on a couple of occasions. Afterwards we'd sometimes go eat Chinese food at Lum's on Northern Boulevard. I still follow the team but with a huge dose of humble pie.

CHAPTER 34
HERE COMES MR. BIG NOSE

1960s

Back in 1969 while the Mets were kicking butt I started my first full-time summer job earning $45 a week. I worked with a community theater and puppet show, aptly named the Bread & Puppet Theatre.

It was an adventure that took me all over the city of New York and gave me the first glimpse into what writers and actors might experience.

The Bread & Puppet Theatre was located on Surf Avenue in Coney Island. It was there I began to write, way back in 1969.

I actually got paid to write and act at nine years old. You can believe that was truly a fun summer for me. Mom was home and getting better and I had a job. The theater had a huge and somewhat scary puppet display, with this giant cigar-smoking Saint Peter puppet as the standard. The theatre folk and the puppet show were memorable.

Sometime around May or June, there was an open enrollment for free puppet-making classes after school. It was run by some of the nicest people I ever knew, Bart and Bridgette. They were sweet folks who also lived on my block. Along with some of the other kids from the neighborhood, I was invited to try my hand at papier-mâché' puppet making. It was sticky fun, making a mask and turning it into a puppet. Bart and Bridgette were genuinely helpful and encouraged the children to write stories about their unique puppets.

My puppet had this honking huge nose. He was a bit on the odd side and the kids all got a laugh looking at him. I wrote a story about him, a man with a nose so big that people made fun of him. The Mr. Big Nose story was based on Cyrano, although in a more contemporary and urban setting. The moral of the story was that regardless of how he looked, he still wanted to have friends.

Although most criticized or bullied him, Mr. Big Nose found some nice people to befriend him and he was truly pleased. The story had a happy ending, and it was simple enough for a nine-year-old kid to write. I had no intention of the story becoming useful, but it did. Bart, Bridgette, and a young fellow named Axel, asked me if I would like to tour with the puppet troupe and help with performances. They wanted to add a presentation of Mr. Big Nose, and felt the way I told the story was so nice that others might like to hear it straight from the creative source. I said yes but we had to ask my Mom if it would be okay.

The Bread and Puppet Theater tours were established to bring morally correct, inspiring stories, and entertainment to a variety of urban communities in New York City. The troupe usually performed in playgrounds or open areas within various projects or low-income apartment complexes. Sometimes we performed at parks.

Bridgette asked my mom. Mom said as long as they kept an eye on me, then it was okay. My sister Loretta liked Axel, and they may have dated briefly. He promised my mom that he would watch me personally. Bridgette also promised, which made Mom feel even better. That summer was really interesting and very hot. I got to travel around in a big van, doors open, and 8-Track music blaring, typically with songs by The Mamas and the Papas, Cream, the Yardbirds, or the Animals. It was fun.

At the play site, I'd help load and unload the props. I had a bit part in one or two of the presentations and was thrilled when the team performed Mr. Big Nose, which I read aloud using a microphone as the narrator of the story. They gave me credit as the writer and artist, and I had to take a bow. It was a neat feeling.

At the end of the week, I was paid forty-five dollars.

Mom was absolutely amazed. She let me keep ten. One fine and brutally hot August afternoon as we were driving back from the City, I threw up and passed out. We learned later that it was caused by heat exhaustion. That was my last day on the tour. My summer puppet show sessions had ended. I was sad that it was over.

Over the subsequent years while I was distracted by life, the Bread and Puppet troupe uprooted and eventually disappeared from Coney Island. The puppet show had closed. All in all, it was an adventure I couldn't forget and one I am thankful for. It was a blessing.

My life felt peaceful for a little bit. At least we were all back together in the old 15th Street apartment, Mom, my sisters and brother and me. We stood together by the window or went up to the roof and watched the Tuesday night Coney Island fireworks.

CHAPTER 35

LOUD NOISES AND HOLY WATER

1970s

A couple of years before we moved from Coney Island, my friends and I had a crazy experience. Hart Place was the small block at the north end of 15th Street. On it was an old abandoned factory. It was there, at thirteen years old, that I participated in the first exorcism of my life. Among some of my best friends back then were Ernie, Herbie, and Neil. Herbie and I lived on West 15th, Neil on West 16th, and Ernie on West 17th Street.

Each of our blocks fell between Neptune Avenue and Hart Place. Hart Place was a small street - just three blocks long. It went from West 15th Street to Cropsey Avenue (which was the same as 17th Street).

In 1973 Hart Place was home to a few apartment buildings, a couple of private houses, and an old catering hall, and that deserted factory. Behind the little street was a creek that ran under the Cropsey Avenue Bridge.

The legend goes that the Cropsey creek was so polluted if you fell in you were going to die or turn into a zombie. It certainly smelled true. One kid did fall in and had to get all kinds of shots.

I don't remember what happened to him after that. One time I was dumb enough to get in a leaky rowboat with James and Greg, two other pals I knew from the neighborhood. We were scared silly when we realized the boat was sinking.

We made it to the shore and ran for it. I ran straight home and jumped into the shower to scrub at my feet and legs, which had creek water on them. Even though that abandoned factory by the creek was a hazardous playground for the neighborhood kids, we all hung out there anyway.

Not sure why, but I had cold chills there fairly often. Sometimes gang fights would occur there. A couple of times I remember bodies being left in cars right near the old factory (after being shot by the mob). It was kind of a dead-end street, even though it wasn't really a dead end.

Still, the factory was the cool spot to play hide-and-seek or manhunt. There was easy access to the roof, and we would hang out up there quite a bit. During summer, the guys and I would stay up there at night and wait for the bats to come out. They typically did just a bit past sunset. I'm not sure where the bats were hiding during the day. We thought it was behind the Pathmark on the other side of the creek, but none of us was sure.

When a bunch of bats did come out, it was our signal to go. We would climb down from the roof in a hurry, then race for the exits through the darkness and go running straight to our homes.

There was one particular room in the old warehouse located at the front end. It was blocked by fallen debris from a fire that had occurred years before. There was a way to climb into that room, but it was a bit risky to do so.

We didn't go in there because the room was cramped and smelled like burnt poop. There was an old furnace in that room, and a rumor existed that the bodies of some people who were murdered in the neighboring area may have been stuffed into that furnace with gasoline poured on them, to burn them up and hide the evidence. That may have been a crock of bull, but my friends and I learned that something weird was definitely happening in that furnace.

The start of this observation was when an eerie event happened to one of us, my friend Neil. He became interested in going into that room. Ernie and I didn't like the idea at all.

The room was always cold, even in summer. We were playing manhunt one afternoon, and it was starting to get dark outside.

It wasn't too cold yet because school had just begun. Herbie had to leave, so Ernie and I started climbing down the roof ladder, shouting "see ya later" to Herbie as he left. We got to the bottom and started calling for Neil, who was hiding out, expecting us to hunt for him and Herbie. Neil didn't respond, but he wasn't hiding either.

We found Neil standing in the middle of the warehouse floor, staring in the direction of that smelly furnace room.

We watched him slowly, almost forcibly, walk toward the room. Ernie and I called him a few times, but he ignored us. It was getting dark. We ran up to him and tried to pull him with us towards the back door, which was the closest available exit. He still didn't respond. Suddenly Ernie and I felt a blast of ice-cold air hit us. We were freezing. It was a teeth-chattering, knee-knocking cold blast of air. It put the hair on the back of our necks straight up. The gust was coming directly from the furnace room, a room that had no windows or doors leading outside. It made no sense at all. It was warm outside, and again, there were no windows.

We screamed in Neil's face, but he didn't appear to hear us. Our hair was blowing around and the air got even colder. Ernie and I both heard a strange whispering sound. I still get the creeps thinking about it. We looked at each other and silently acknowledged that we had to get the heck out of there. In a panic, I grabbed Neil up onto my shoulder and we ran toward the back door. As we passed through the door, it slammed behind us and scared the shit out of us.

It took Neil almost three minutes to snap out of it. When he did, we all went home. At home, I said a dozen prayers. I was worried stiff that something bad had occurred and that Neil was in trouble.

The next afternoon I went to the public library on Mermaid Avenue. In the library, I looked up books and news about ghosts, specifically how to get rid of them. I found a couple of books on the subject. One book mentioned that loud noises may chase them, another mentioned bright lights. Yet another said the tones from bells deterred ghosts.

Holy water was also a powerful tool, and sunlight might help. Sometimes these things worked to chase spirits away.

I borrowed two of the books and shared what I learned with Ernie, Herbie, and Neil. One afternoon Ernie and I went to challenge the thing in the factory furnace room; we felt the two of us were enough. Ernie and I were like Starsky and Hutch going after bad guys, minus the cool red car. We stopped at OLS and filled up a bottle with holy water. We also carried a half dozen blockbusters, a couple of M-80s, and a huge box of firecrackers. These fireworks were leftovers from the recent July 4th celebration. Ernie had some lighter fluid and material we could use as a fuse. It took about a half hour for us to muster up the courage to enter the place, ready for battle.

It was starting to get dark again, but we had flashlights. We made our way over the debris and climbed into that perpetually dark room. We were both muttering prayers and keeping our courage up with as much bravado as two teenage boys could muster. The air got cold quite suddenly. Apprehensive, we went into the furnace room. There was an actual furnace in the middle of it. It looked like an old ceramic baking kiln. The metal door was partly open, and as we approached, we both thought we heard whispers in the air. (That could have been our nerves rasping aloud).

I remember I got the chills as we placed the fireworks, still in their brown bag inside the furnace and set the fuse up. We covered it all with lighter fluid. I took out the holy water and blessed Ernie, myself, and the area we were in. Remembering what I read in the book, I declared my intention at the top of my lungs. I told the spirit to get out and to leave all the kids alone from that point on. I prayed in Jesus name and commanded the spirits to leave the place.

We lit the fuse and scrambled out as fast as we could. Neither of us knew what a half dozen blockbusters and some M-80s might do. Just as we cleared the debris, the place exploded.

It was as though thunder boomed inside the building, generously amplified by the acoustics. When we got outside, we just took off and ran home. The next day after catechism at OLS I called on Ernie, and we went back there to see if there were still any creepy signs. To our surprise, there was a new entranceway. The wall to the furnace room had blown apart and daylight filled the whole room.

For almost another year, we played hide and seek, round-up, and manhunt there at the old factory. Occasionally we watched for the bats then ran home. After our so-called exorcism, there was never another cold wind or any funny whispers at the place. All was calm and things looked right for a change. Later, some company bought the property and knocked the building down flat.

I told my grandmother about the factory event and how I often had cold chills when we hung out there. She looked at me funny and said I should be careful about where I go when I have the chills. She said the chills can be a warning signal sent to you from beyond.

CHAPTER 36
AND THEN THERE WAS ME

1970s

After Mom came home from the hospital, and started to heal, we stayed in the old apartment on 15th Street. I shared the back bedroom with my little brother and two sisters. This was the bedroom that was just past the kitchen, with the picnic table and kitchen appliances. Our bedroom had no closets, but it had a window that led to a fire escape, the one where I liked to watch thunderstorms, much to my mother's dismay.

In the room were two sets of bunk beds, one for the boys and one for the girls. There were two small chests for my brother and me to put our clothes in. The girls' things were kept in dressers down the hall in the little room next to my mother's bedroom.

During the early 1970s, we experienced a lot of crazy phenomena in that room and in that apartment. One night the four of us were sitting around either playing games or maybe I was stacking playing cards, which my jinx of a sister Diane would knock down just by saying the word *remarkable*. She picked that silly word up from a Little Rascals episode. I don't know why it worked, but it did. I could stack really high, and Diane would say,

"Remarkable."

Then she'd crack up laughing as my house of cards tumbled to the floor, as though pummeled by an unseen hand. Both my sisters were actually very pretty and had nice personalities when we were young. They still have nice personalities. We still get along.

Back then, we were sitting around either playing or maybe doing homework when suddenly the shade in the window slammed closed, spinning on its clips with great noise.

It sounded like the spring had popped. It startled all of us, but I just got up, took a fork from the kitchen, and rewound the spring. I put the shade back in the window and that seemed to be the end of it, but it was only the beginning of the exodus for my siblings - one at a time.

That night as we were going to sleep, we all heard some peculiar noises coming from the kitchen. I told my siblings to ignore it. I said it was probably the old refrigerator throwing a bolt or choking on Freon. We all tried to go to sleep.

Mom was watching television in the living room and had it low so we could sleep and so she could hear us. Duke was with her. I guess Loretta was out with friends or just "out". She lived home off and on during her later teens.

As I laid down on the bottom bunk, I felt sleepy. I was just about to get to that dream state when a blood curdling scream scared the living daylights out of me, and I jumped up hitting my head on the upper bunk. It was my little sister Cindy who screamed. She was pointing at the ceiling and couldn't breathe. I got her off the bed just as Mom came running in. She grabbed Cindy and looked at me asking if I did something. I shook my head no. Cindy got her breath and said through trembles and tears,

"Ma, it was a man's face. A man's face came down through the ceiling and was staring at me. Ma, he was horrible looking! Like a burnt old man. He came right through the ceiling. I don't want to stay here."

Then she just bawled. Mom took her inside, and Cindy never slept in that room again.

Over the next few nights other quirky events occurred. One was the beds. For some reason, they started bouncing. Not high, but they were definitely bouncing. Pat, Diane and I didn't like it, but we weren't hurt, and it only lasted a minute or so.

Diane said she felt scared in the bedroom, and it was rare when she'd stay alone there. One night she was alone in the room. Patrick and I were watching television, and Cindy was lying down next to mom. In the living room we heard Diane scream. It was so loud and horrifying it scared the pants off of us. Duke jumped up and ran to where Diane was. I followed, but Mom was even faster than the dog and me.

We found Diane curled up in a ball, under the covers of the lower bunk bed, screaming in terror. When she was calmer, Mom took her out of there. I brought her some water. She couldn't talk without freaking out for what felt like an hour. When she was finally able to speak with less panic in her voice, she explained that she had been sitting on the bottom bunk with her back to the window playing with cut outs. She said she heard a hissing sound behind her, like a cat. Then it was a growling sound, and ultimately a low-pitched cackle.

When she had the nerve to turn (thinking it might have been me playing prank), she saw a witch.

Diane described a short, hunched over old woman, with evil black eyes, long gray and black hair, and horrid teeth, all crooked and pointy. The woman (if it was one) had a long, crooked nose. When she reached out to grab Diane, the shock wore off and Diane screamed for help. Well, we went to OLS and filled up a bottle with holy water. We brought it back and blessed the whole apartment.

Mom had me move the girls' bunk beds into her room. It was a bit tight, but over the next weekend, we sorted it out and used the little room to make things fit.

Pat and I went to bed that night after Diane's witch encounter, but the poor kid was so spooked he slept next to me in my bed for three or four days. Finally, he went back to his own bunk. One night during the first week he was back on the top bunk he looked down and asked me to stop kicking his bed. I said I wasn't.

He insisted, so I suggested we switch bunks, and I took the top bunk. After a few minutes, he complained again. I looked down and said I was not doing anything.

I told him to go to sleep. It got quiet and finally I started to doze. I was about twelve and Patrick was about seven. Later in the night, I woke up. I heard Patrick mumbling something, and I looked down and said,

"Go to sleep" and hoped my little brother would do just that.

Suddenly Patrick screamed and ran out of the room, straight into my Mom's crowded bed where Mom and my sisters were. I climbed down and followed after him.

On the kitchen clock, I noticed that it was around three in the morning. Pat was a white as a sheet. He was shaking so hard I thought his teeth would break. He was telling Mom that someone had grabbed him from behind the bed. He said when he pushed it off the hand was cold and felt wrong. It felt really scary. He also never came back to the room. Then, it was just me.

We set up bunk beds in the little room next to my Mom's bedroom. I took apart the remaining bunk bed in my room and made a guest bed on the other side of the room where my sisters' bunk beds used to be. I ended up alone in there, except the rare occasions when Loretta or her friend stayed the night.

Every so often my bed would shake or bounce, but I'd ignore it, especially after I started working in construction. When I had to get up in the morning, I didn't want to be disturbed. I liked the lights out, and I liked it quiet. If Charlie would act up and try to annoy me, I'd tell him off. I remember one time I told him to quit it and go bother someone else as I had work the next day. I was about fourteen then. I snuggled down in the sheets and chuckled as I heard the neighbor through the wall exclaiming something like,

"What was that? What was that!"

Charlie seemed to get the point most of the time. I was not to be bothered, and I was not afraid of him or any of the spooky stuff going on there. He didn't bother me, but he did bother others. In the room where Mom and the kids were sleeping, there was a wind-up Fischer Price television toy that when wound played "Row, Row, Row Your Boat" and "London Bridges Falling Down". It belonged to one of my sisters, but I don't know which one. I think Nanny gave it to Cindy.

Anyway, one night at about two in the morning the darn thing started playing.

I heard it from the other side of the apartment and ran to see which kid got up in the middle of the night to wind it. I found the whole group - Mom, Diane, Cindy, and Patrick - staring at it as if it was a thing alive. I grabbed it and forced the dial in reverse to unwind it, then shook it a bit. It played out. I shook it again and told Mom not to worry. I said it may have been wound up from earlier and a passing train or truck created enough vibration to cause it to play.

Mom accepted my logic, and she got the kids back to sleep. Of course, nobody confessed to winding it up. In about an hour, London Bridges was playing full tilt. I ran inside again. This time Mom was opening the window. Remember, we lived on the third floor. She grabbed the toy and flung it to the sidewalk below, shattering it to pieces. She yelled out,

"Let's you see play now, you piece of shit!"

Over the next couple of years, more weird stuff happened. One night the television went on by itself. Mom got up and turned it off. Just as she turned to go back to bed, it turned back on. That was it for her. She started apartment hunting again.

CHAPTER 37
SOMETIMES TROUBLE FOLLOWS YOU

1970s

It was midnight of an early summer night in 1979. The D train was passing overhead on the Brighton Beach line. After we locked all the doors at the McDonald's where I was working, I decided to run home.

So straight down the ten blocks from Coney Island Avenue to Brighton First Street I ran, feeling like Steve Austin running along Brighton Beach Avenue to get to his home base.

The salty ocean air had rejuvenated me after an exhaustingly busy night shift, and Brighton Beach Avenue became my personal Olympic track. Like a jet plane, I was flying at top speed and headed for a landing above the corner's former pizzeria one block short of Ocean Parkway.

When I got to our apartment building's wire-and-glass front door, my key jumped in and out of the lock. Inside, I locked the door, turned and jumped up to the fifth step, the fifth out of fifteen.

This was a huge first, a real sports milestone, as I was never able to clear more than four steps. As my foot secured its perch on that fifth step, an explosion ripped through the bottom half of the door. Suddenly, glass flew up and all around me. The staircase shuddered. Like a terrified cat, I bolted to the top of the stairs.

My mom heard the explosion and frantically opened the door for me, so I flew into our apartment, shoving my mom out of the way. I double locked the door and grabbed my baseball bat and shoved it between the door and the wall creating an even stronger barrier.

Some guys were yelling into the hallway,

"You'll be dead by Christmas, you piece of shit. We're gonna get you, Jimmy Jorgensen, and drop you at this door in a garbage bag!"

That they screamed my name made it clear it wasn't a case of mistaken identity. My mom called the police. She looked at me with tears.

"Jimmy, trouble just follows you," she said sniffling.

The hoods didn't shoot anymore but they came up the stairs and shouted more threats at me. We waited for the police to show up.

When the cops arrived, we were too nervous to answer the door, so I climbed up on the roof to look down and make sure that it was the police. It was. After they spoke with my mom and the neighbors, a policeman explained that it looked like a twelve-gauge shotgun had been fired point blank at the door, doing a lot of damage downstairs. The shots took out part of the bottom four steps and most of the wired glass door. At the time, my younger sisters were only fourteen and thirteen and my brother was twelve; this event was shocking for them.

Did we know anybody that would be looking to do this? No. Not really, though I did have my suspicions. I had an idea what happened, but it made no sense for it to be true.

At the time of the shooting, I worked as a crew chief and sometime assistant night manager at the McD's on the corner of Coney Island Avenue and Brighton Beach Avenue, but I was also once a crew chief in another golden arches restaurant on Kings Highway (also in Brooklyn).

One night about eight months before the shotgun blasts, three guys were in our upstairs dining room of the Kings Highway McD's after it was closed. That dining room was probably where these "we are gonna kill you" problems began.

On that night, three guys were in the dining upstairs rolling joints from a huge bag of weed. The manager on duty was a woman only one year older than I was.

I was seventeen, and the only so-called "tough guy" working King's Highway that night. My friend Thad was there, but he was younger than I was and certainly not a fighter by street standards.

While I was scraping and cleaning one side of the grill I had shut off, a petite kid named Mary went upstairs to do the final sweep, after which Thad or I would mop. She came running down the stairs, crying and holding her face. Her face had a big red handprint on the right side. I saw Gina, the closing manager, run to the phone and dial 911. Angered, I went up the stairs to tell whomever it was to get out. I'm sure now that I shouldn't have. The three guys were putting away a lot of marijuana. They were sharing two joints and the upstairs reeked of the junk.

As soon as they saw me, the two bigger guys stood up. They both had that bulky look: the kind one expects from a steroid-a-saurus. I told them that the boss had called the police and that they should leave. The smaller of the two big guys, his pals called him Vinny, pushed me towards the big window facing Kings Highway. He had dark wavy hair and was at least thirty pounds heavier than I was. I was maybe a hundred-seventy. I pushed him back, and he took a swing at me and missed.

"I'm gonna smack you harder than that little snot I chased downstairs before."

He sneered, obviously too stoned to know better. He swung again, but I blocked him and punched him in the cheek. He got pissed off that a guy without a steroid-constructed body was holding his own. I jabbed a quick left, and his nose sprayed blood.

I jumped backwards, closer to the window than I should have. "Vinny" jumped right on top of me. I stood upright in reflex and jabbed quick enough to give him a big black eye on top of his bloody nose, and he almost went through the plate glass window. He hit the floor and hit it hard. He didn't get up.

His larger friend (call him Conan) roared and chased me around the room. This guy was at least foot taller and really looked like a Conan the Barbarian clone - if Conan wore a polyester disco suit. No way would I even try it. I ran down the stairs, straight into a uniform. The police arrested the three of them. The owner of the McD's showed up just after the police and the ambulance left. That Vinny dude was pretty hurt, maybe a concussion from hitting his head when he went down.

A week later, some older fellow showed up with Vinny. Apparently, he was Vinny, Sr.

He demanded I come out to see him. I did. His kid was there with a funny-looking face, due to a broken nose, which I didn't remember giving him.

Vinny, Sr. started to make threats at me when Mary came in, and she showed him the hand-shaped bruise that still lingered from the week before. She told him that the guy he was yelling at defended a little girl from his ape son. This embarrassed him. He turned and slapped his son, then looked at me - hard. He didn't say anything. He grabbed his son and scolded him,

"Stay the F out of here."

CHAPTER 38
THERE GOES TROUBLE

1970s

Nothing more occurred for a few months. Mom gave me a quirky black t-shirt that said "Here Comes Trouble" on the front in red and gold lettering, and "There Goes Trouble" on the back with the same color lettering.

At the time it seemed pretty funny, that is, until I foolishly bought a junk car to drive. It was a 1968 lime green Buick, that I called the "Incredible Bulk". It was a bundle of trouble bought for fifty dollars cold cash.

It was 1978, but to me the '68 was a ten-year-old *new* car. It was also a disaster. I had no money for insurance, so I never registered the car. I only had it for three months when the curse on it was revealed. It was a rainy October night and I was going home from the Kings Highway restaurant. I was making a left turn from Avenue P onto Coney Island Avenue when suddenly, I had no more steering control. I think the tie rod went out.

I slammed the brakes and gently touched the bumper of a parked white and tan Caddy.

My head hit the steering wheel. It hurt, and I was shaken up. When I saw who was getting out of the Caddy, my heart leapt into my mouth.

Getting out of the Cadillac was Vinny "Predatori", Conan "Gigantali" and their pal Jerry "Potbrain." I knew I was in some deep shit there. In three minutes, my Buick was left behind as I was being taken for a ride in the Cadillac with multiple gun barrels jabbing me.

They hit me a few times, and my mouth was bloody. They were taking me to an "uncle's back yard" in Bensonhurst.

They laughed at me when I pleaded, explaining my family really needed me. Some other Italian guys were hanging out at the corner of Kings Highway and West Second Street, where Vinny paused to shoot the breeze. From the little I heard they apparently knew my Cadillac *host* might be driving me to his uncle's house to fill a hole that was recently dug for another purpose. I was praying and thinking and talking a mile a minute.

While Vinny stopped to talk to one of the guys, I convinced Jerry to let me go back to the McD's and get them some cash that I knew was in the safe - money for him and his pals to leave me alone. I told him it was around twelve thousand dollars.

Jerry convinced Vinny to take me back to the store. A different night manager, Mike, was still there with another guy that was a crew chief like me. His name was Leon. He was a Caribbean American, or so I recall. I liked him a lot and we always kept people laughing with our constant rank-outs on each other. "Last Dance", a song by Donna Summers was blasting inside the Caddy when Conan got out and *walked me* into the restaurant.

Stevie, another golden arch colleague, looked up from the grill area when Mary said my name. She smiled and spoke to me, apprehensively eyeing the giant next to me.

"I thought you went home earlier tonight, Jimmy."

She then looked seriously at "Gigantali" and her face caught mine with a "what's up?" expression. Before we went inside, I told Conan I had to go back and get the money from the safe. I told him to get the manager's attention and keep it until I came back out with the cash in a bag. He actually started some horse dung argument with Mike over Burger K's being better than McD's. Mike - being loyal to the arches - took up the cause.

In the back, Leon followed me into the office. I took my application out of the file and folded it up. I didn't want to leave a trail. I wrote a note saying I quit and told them to keep my last check. I pocketed my application and gave a quick low-down to Leon. He said he'd explain to Mike later, and he watched me dash out the back door, into the alley where we dumped the trash at night.

I ran to the train station unseen. I jumped the turnstile and when I sat down inside the air-conditioned car, I cried. I cried the whole way home. About a month later, I got a new job as crew chief for another McD's owner in Brighton Beach, nine blocks from my family dwelling.

I never went back for the Buick and, when asked about it, I explained that it had died on the road and was not worth salvaging.

This brings me back to the guys that shot out the door that night in 1979. The cops told me to be careful and promised they would have a radio car pass by. The problem was the cops never passed by when the bad guys did. One time some hoods tried to drag my sister Diane into a brown Lincoln, but some people passing on the street in front of our building stopped them and rescued her, literally pulling her back screaming from the car door. Those kind of problems arose and increasingly worsened.

CHAPTER 39
RUN FROM YOUR LIFE

1970s

Only a few weeks after Diane was nearly taken, I was in the parking garage at the Kings Plaza mall with Tricia, my girlfriend at the time. Somebody took two shots at us from across the garage. The car parked next to us lost a taillight and a rear windshield. Tricia was not really aware of why I reacted the way I did. I grabbed the keys to her mom's car - basically yanking them out of her hand and shoved her into the Plymouth.

We rocketed out of there in her mom's Volare like a Speed Racer cartoon. After that happened, I spoke to Tricia's father. Her father asked me not to see her anymore because I might get her killed. I didn't like it but agreed, as I knew it was safer for her not to see me anymore, in case whoever was shooting at me finally hit something I care about, something important - like her.

Another time, I was sneaking from the subway to my front door and two guys ran out of a car towards me. We scuffled and I got loose and ran inside and locked the repaired glass door. I didn't get hurt, but I was shaken.

After that my mom and grandmother arranged for me to run away to Vermont to live with my mother's sister and her husband. When I was a little boy, my Aunt Renee and Uncle Don lived in Levitt Town, Long Island. They used to take me out to Long Island to give me a break from the Coney Island bullies when I was little. Going to Long Island in those days meant going to the country. I loved it there. When we drove there to Long Island, I'd sit in the back of my aunt's station wagon, facing the way we came from.

Funny thing about my memories of those days has to do with skunks. Once in a while on the drive to Long Island, I'd smell a skunk, probably hit by a car. To this day, the smell of skunks on the road brings back fond memories of riding in my Aunt Renee's station wagon.

Going to Levittown, I remember that I liked to watch the world changing behind me. Go figure. However, this time when I saw Aunt Renee, I was a young adult in real trouble - not a sad little kid. It was a cold, late September day when I left home.

My mother and sisters were crying, and my brother couldn't talk or eat the day before I left. It was one of the most painful goodbyes ever. My seventy-plus-year-old grandmother explained to me that my luck had run out and I had to run from my life. Her pearls of wisdom went like this,

"Things work out a certain way for a reason, Jimmy."

My uncle in Vermont was a retired cop. Officially, he had been Lieutenant Commander of the Malvern, Long Island Police force. He told my mom over the phone not to worry. They had almost a hundred acres of land, and he said that he would shoot any hoodlum that followed me up to Vermont.

My grandmother took me to the Port Authority and put me on the bus to Vermont. I fell asleep crying on the bus. I had to leave, that was the best answer. The other alternative was to find the guys responsible and kill them, but I wasn't able to do anything like that. Leaving my family was never something I wanted to do either. It was the first time I lost my life and lost my home as well. I'm not sure how to compare the feeling, but it hurt so very much.

On the bus I realized there was someone I should have said goodbye to. She was a teacher that I really loved. I often thought the two of us were meant for something more, but the timing was always wrong and never improved. We never had a chance - certainly not in high school, and ultimately not anywhere, a fact that was proven over a span of decades.

But that was then. There I was on the bus, leaving New York, Brooklyn, and family, headed north to the woodlands of Vermont. I had no choice but to disappear. I fell asleep on the bus to Vermont. When I awoke a couple of hours later I saw how some of the world outside Brooklyn looked. I couldn't believe the number of trees. It was amazing. Vermont was beautiful. I was riding on a bus into a forest. I imagined I might end up living like Robin Hood. When I first saw it, I thought Vermont looked like the wilderness adventures I read about in books.

I didn't really know how my relatives would receive me as a young adult. In time, after we reacquainted ourselves, I grew to enjoy my aunt, uncle, and cousins. I didn't see him much there, but my cousin Michael was really easy going.

He didn't live there, but I remember he visited at least once while I was there. The Christmas of 1979 was hard. I was very homesick. I received one card from my family in which my little sister Cindy wrote:

"Please come home because without you there is no Christmas."

I didn't get home that Christmas. I never got back home. I guess it's true when you hear folks say, "You can't go home again." No matter what else happened, after that Christmas I never felt as though I had a home again, and for years to come, I really didn't feel at home anywhere I stayed. I felt comfortable sometimes but not at home. God bless my little sister; she became so lost after that happened to us.

We all had a path to take and it was not easy for any of us. Cindy, I missed you, too. I'm sorry for what happened in your life and for the events that caused such disruption for us all.

In the woods outside my aunt and uncle's place, I asked God to help me find my way home, and a voice answered, saying,

"When you are home, a Christmas Bird will be out in front."

For long years, I searched for that Christmas Bird in front of a potential home, but never found it, not till much, much later.

I tried to make the best of things in Vermont. I enjoyed gathering eggs from the hen house and chopping wood for the fireplace. I hiked a lot. My aunt and uncle had a huge property that led up into the woods. It was sprawling and a solid uphill climb at certain points. At the highest points the view was breath taking.

I was not sure of what to do next. I didn't have a car and couldn't find a local job. It didn't make sense for me to stay there too long, and ultimately, I didn't stay. A week before Christmas, my Vermont relatives talked me into joining the armed services.

I took the Armed Services Vocational Aptitude Battery (ASVAB), the entry exam to the US military. I scored really high on the test and could have learned any trade the USAF had to offer, but I wanted to be an Air Force SWAT cop.

CHAPTER 40
DANCING IN THE DARK

1980s

At the Army Air Force Exchange Service Station (AAFES), I was given a written guarantee that I'd become an EST member if I succeeded in all the training. The acronym E.S.T. stands for Emergency Services Team.

I was shipped off to San Antonio, Texas within a couple of days, to be assigned to a basic training flight.

Flight is the term used to describe a training group in the Air Force, the same way "platoon" is used in the Army.

Our flight was Flight 065 in the 3723rd Squadron and we were kind of an experimental flight, as the team was left on its own quite a bit to see how the program would work with less immediate management from a Training Instructor (TI).

During basic training, the men in my flight elected me as the Dorm Chief, somewhat like an assistant leader under the TI. We had two instructors: Team Leader Staff Sergeant Sutton and Team Instructor Sergeant Earnest. I frequently made them laugh, either at me or with me. Our brother flight 067 was led by a Sergeant Rascussi who truly despised me and with reason.

Our flight was involved in a competition with two other flights in our squadron for the title of *Honor Flight*, which was a recognition of distinguished accomplishment when graduating from basic training. One of our competitors was Flight 067. Obtaining the recognition as an Honor Flight meant the chosen group has the cleanest dorm, does the best on written testing and physical training (PT), and has the tightest marching symmetry, and the most impressive marching cadence presentation.

A cadence presentation can include some razzle-dazzle dance steps, so to speak, and we rocked it. Also involved was an ongoing test of something called *military bearing*.

The concept of military bearing is basically a demonstration that your facade be stoic, your recognition of military chain of command be accurate, and most importantly, in the face of anyone, friend or foe, you do not give in or show weakness. You are a piece of granite.

With military bearing you really needed to keep your cool intact regardless of who addressed you or how they addressed you (loud or soft). Whenever I was addressed, I kept perfect military bearing. I could not be fooled or broken - no matter how often tested. My face was a wall of ice.

When my team members were summoned to his office the TI or TL would change or flip the insignia on the wall to see if we knew whether to salute or not. It was different every time I walked into that office. Sometimes the insignia was an officer, other times a non-com. Other folks that served will likely remember these things.

I hope they remember them as fondly as I do. Some of the best people I ever knew in life I met while in basic training.

To this day, I don't know why they picked me to lead them, but we did well together, and we won the Honor Flight competition. How we won was another matter. It was not easy, since the team leader of Flight 067, Sergeant Rascussi, seemed to be trying his best to make things difficult for us.

I don't think he liked the experiment that our Flight represented, and I further believe he was not happy having to compete with us under the conditions of the experiment.

To keep the dorm clean and up to USAF standards the latrines had to shine, and the dorm floors had to be polished.

The floor polisher was a machine that was supposed to be shared between flights, but the 067 Dorm Chief would not give it to us. We also had very limited access to the necessary tools, including cleaning materials, brushes, towels, and fluids. You were supposed to use what was available, which did not include helpful cleaners like Windex.

I won't say whether or not we smuggled cleaning fluids into our dorm, but we did have the most sparkling latrine in the building (got that from good resources).

An interesting thing happened between Sgt. Rascussi and me. One night, when it was closer to graduation, I did something that was funny, at least for my guys and me (not so much for Sgt. Rascussi). As we were now seniors in basic training, our charge of quarters (CQ) was being provided by another newer flight. The younger airman was placed on duty as our security guard. His job was to keep us safe and out of trouble at night. At one point, he had to use the latrine.

When the airman went to the bathroom, I got up from my bunk and meticulously erased Sgt. Rascussi's name from the access duty board. Basically, that is a chalk board with the names of non-com and commissioned officers allowed into the dorm at any time. I knew from experience that Rascussi was going to come into the dorm around midnight. On my behalf, there was no sign posted by the board that said this action couldn't be performed and I didn't recall a standing order saying that this couldn't be done.

Good old Rascussi would typically come in at odd hours after lights out to wake me up and annoy my flight with some pretense or another. I think he was trying to make us tired and sloppy for the next day's events.

The particular next day following the event of my board wiping included the marching cadence competition between the flights. He was right on cue around 12:30 am. When he came to the door, he ordered the young airman to open it. The poor kid had only one reply he could give without getting in real trouble.

"Sir, no sir."

The shit hit the fan. In a New York heartbeat, Rascussi lost his cool and cussed the poor kid blue in the face. The kid stood his ground though. He was a good airman. When Rascussi finally realized his name was not on the board, he yelled my name, but I feigned sleep, giggling like a little kid at a sleepover. He stormed away and came back with the Senior Master Sergeant Device, who was granted entry immediately. They both stormed over to my bunk and a loud voice told me to get up out of that bed!

I was put on the spot, but my military bearing was literally unshakable. When asked if I had removed Rascussi's name from the board I said "Sir, no Sir" with a straight face and never cracked a smile. Okay, I admit I acted a lot like the incarnation of Bugs Bunny, straight out of Brooklyn. I had a bit of chip on my shoulder when it came to bullies, and Rascussi was a bully, at least to us. I never said I was a saint or an angel while in service or ever for that matter.

Most of my Flight 065 guys were awake thanks to the dressing down I was getting from the senior master sergeant. He turned on the two squadrons that were on my side of the dorm and ordered them to get up and stand at attention. They immediately did. He put them to the question with ferocity.

"Did you men see this here Dorm Chief wipe Sergeant Rascussi's name off the board?"

They answered in unison, and I couldn't have felt prouder to be their friend. They shouted unanimously,

"Sir, No, Sir!"

Then Device wrote Rascussi's name back on the board, and he looked down into my eyes and sneered meanly. He told me that should that name be removed again; my ass would be personally on the line for it. I said

"Sir, Yes, Sir!"

They both left and when they were clearly down the stairs, my whole flight cracked up laughing! It was one of two great memories for us. The other was made the night before the final inspection for cleanest dorm competition.

The next day we had our cadence competition with the other flights. We all marched very well and followed marching orders cleanly. Our brother flights did great too. Then it came down to the creative cadence, something we referred to as "razzle dazzle." I called out our cadence.

When there was a call for razzle dazzle right or razzle dazzle left, the team would break formation and lines of airmen would move in counter directions with perfect synchronicity. We blew everyone else's cadence away.

We were like a pristine dance troop using specific marching maneuvers and gestures with genuinely impressive choreography. We won hands down.

On the night before the final inspection we really needed to buff the floors, because they looked dull compared to the Flight 067 floors. Having dull floors would cost us huge points in the cleanest dorm competition. The problem was we could not get use of the floor buffing machine, probably thanks to my pal Rascussi.

I came up with a plan. Again, our sleep would be interrupted, but it was necessary. I was able to pick the lock on our civilian goods and took two big portable radios out (ghetto blasters, we called them). Lock-picking was a skill I learned in Coney Island. We set the ghetto blasters up in both rooms. Earlier, we had cut up enough buffing cloth to put under the feet of at least twenty guys.

We put the same station on both radios and danced the floors to a bright polish. I fondly remember one song from that night; it was *The Beat Goes On* by The Whispers. We danced and buffed the floor doing the twist, the slide, the bus stop, and more. It was a lot of fun. We were up for hours, and all forty guys took a turn or two with the smoothest dancing slippers on earth. The next day we were inspected.

An absolute fact from that inspection was that Flight 065 set a record for the cleanest dorm that Squadron 3723 ever had. We obtained the title of Honor Flight and graduated from Basic Training with honor and great camaraderie. Basic training in the US Air Force was by far one of my life's favorite episodes. God bless those guys, all of them.

I'd be remiss if I didn't mention my four squad leaders, Butch Pegues, Jimmy Isler, Marlow Cooper, and Mark Newlon. Also remembered from Honor Flight 065, are Bobby Wildrick (Flyboys Forever), Graham Cooper, Jerry Douglas (the Bulldog), Stanley White, the graceful Mr. Chaney, and the fastest man alive, Chowhound Mark Carrington.

When I was in the Air Force, I wrote home (though not often) saying that I liked military life and I really did. Military life had more order to it. My mom always wrote back saying she missed me. She also would write that she wished I was there to help with my brother and the family troubles that they had.

In April 1980, I met another guy from Brooklyn that had joined the Air Force. His name was Leon. He was my Caribbean-American friend from the McDonald's I worked at on Kings Highway. It was really great to see a familiar and friendly face after so many months.

We only had about fifteen minutes together, as he was new to basic training, and I had just graduated and was off to technical training, as a security specialist.

We laughed hard when we saw one another. It was a very happy reunion for two pals from Brooklyn. Leon told me something he had learned, something morbidly fascinating from a few of the supposedly "connected" kids. He said that that Vinny, Conan, and Jerry had all been shot to death in a drug war. Each guy had been murdered in a different place.

After a few more comments about the old crew and the golden arches, Leon left to train with his basic training flight. I was glad to see him. It took time to for me to digest the news he shared. It was kind of shocking. What did this mean to me? Was anyone else going to try and kill me? Was I now safe to go home?

CHAPTER 41
DETOUR ON THE WAY HOME

1980s

Trust me, I wasn't sad for the loss of those three goons if Leon's news proved true, but I still had a number of years to go in the Air Force. I liked being in the service. At least, I thought I did. My Mom and grandmother were always writing letters trying to convince me to find a way to come home. I don't think they understood the implication of military commitment. Looking back, I can't help but wonder if they put a jinx on me - literally. I think they wished me to be home so strongly, well you'll get the gist.

While in tech training for EST, my right knee was really banged up. It was so badly damaged I had to have it casted.

The cast covered from foot to hip to keep the leg immobilized. I was told by the doctor at Wilford Hall after he casted me that it was to be kept dry at all times, not to be on my feet too much, and to take it easy for the next few weeks. He never considered the fact that I was almost twenty years old and not lacking in certain charms and whimsical inspirations.

One night during a rather surprising visit to the apartment of a uniformed girl I danced with (before the knee injury), the cast got soaked in the shower (nothing further needs stating). I went to the hospital and the same captain who treated me the first time re-casted the leg. He warned me not to damage the cast again and said I could be penalized if I did.

A couple of nights later my friends and I went to the Airmen's club. We enjoyed a pitcher of beer for a dollar - then we proceeded to indulge to the tune of about twenty dollars. Dancing ensued. Being a Disco-Danny type showoff on the dance floor, I inadvertently cracked the cast trying to do a split.

The knee hurt. I went back to the hospital. I was told one more incident would result in an Article 15, which in civilian speak is a precursor to a possible court martial.

Three weeks later, the cast was officially removed and on that day the Air Force decided that my damaged knee was the result of an accident I had prior to joining. The doc said the old injury caused something called Osgood-Schlatter disease. They disqualified me from the EST program and from any security services. I was given some new job choices. I could clean the base as a janitor or work in administration. Optionally, I could take an honorable discharge with no veteran benefits.

At age twenty, the idea of toilet cleaner or desk jockey was unappealing. I wanted to be an Air Force EST cop. I didn't have much of a choice then and hindsight doesn't help now. Subsequently on May 7, 1980 I was given an honorable discharge, mandated due to a combination of written guarantees, circumstances, and injuries. I took the honorable in lieu of cleaning toilet bowls or typing at a desk all day.

My mother got her wish for me to come home and rescue my teenage brother from the hoods he was playing cards with. I didn't go straight home though. Before I went home to Brooklyn, there was a girl I wanted to see again. Her name was Sara and she and her friends, and a couple of guys I knew had been shipped off to the military's Defense Language Institute in Monterey, California.

It was a long detour I was willing to make on my way back to Brooklyn. I took a bus from San Antonio, Texas to Monterey, California to go see her, never considering that I had little money and no place to stay when I got there. Although I did manage to get some meals on base, I didn't eat enough to maintain my output of calories due to a lack of funds. Over a few weeks, I lost more than twenty pounds. It was one heck of a loopy diet.

The adventure of it all was pretty neat. I managed to stay there, sleeping on the beach or wherever, and enjoyed the whole experience. I felt free. One weird thing happened while I was on the beach by myself. About one hundred yards away I saw a black dog run into the water.

It struck me as strange, as nobody was there with the dog. Nobody else noticed. I walked down to where the dog went in and looked around. No dog.

It bummed me out. Later, I told Sara and her friends about it, and they said they would show me where the dog probably went. We drove down to the Fisherman's Wharf to have dinner together, for what was to be my second-to-last night in Monterey. At the end of the dock, my friend TJ laughed at me and said,

"Hey, Brooklyn. Look in the water. There's your dog!"

I looked and there were about five black seals cavorting in the water.

Okay, I never saw a seal outside the Coney Island Aquarium. Easy mistake to make for a city kid from the east coast. I felt better knowing a dog hadn't committed suicide by drowning in front of me.

On my last day there Sara's jealous boyfriend caught wind of my being in the area. I guess someone said they saw us dancing together the night before. She didn't tell me she had a boyfriend when we met in basic training.

He looked all over for me, getting angrier by the second, so I was told. When he found me, I stood my ground, but he was over six feet tall and all solid muscle. He beat me like an enemy flag.

In a number of hours, after I partially recovered from the beating, I was sent home with a first-class airplane ticket. It was paid for by some of the girls, TJ, and a few of his new friends. My stop off on the way home was over. It was time to fly back to Brooklyn in style.

CHAPTER 42
DOES SHE GET A PHONE CALL OR NOT

1980s

After I got home from the service in 1980, I took a job working as a bank teller, and found a small apartment within walking distance. I didn't want to live in the Brighton Beach apartment anymore, as I had developed a real need for privacy and quiet. I would visit my mother and siblings in Brighton almost three times a week.

It wasn't a long subway ride, but I had to change from the N train in Coney Island to the D train, and then go a couple of stops to Ocean Parkway. Twenty minutes max.

During this time in my life, I dated a young woman named Diane. She was petite and had a nice personality. My mother liked her more than she liked anyone else I dated up to that point.

Over the year or so that we dated, Diane grew close to my younger sisters, which was nice for her and them but not always good for me. That proved especially true when I decided that the relationship had gone far enough.

I wasn't ready for anything serious and wanted time to hang out with some of the guys or see other people without having to feel guilty for it. Diane wasn't the cause of that guilty feeling, I was. She was sweet, but I wasn't willing to commit.

Diane stayed close with Mom and the siblings for months after we were no longer a couple. There may have been a fortuitous reason for that.

You see, one afternoon Diane was in the apartment hanging out with my sister Cindy and watching daytime soap operas and sorting out laundry for Mom. While putting the clothes away, they both heard a groan and a loud crash from the kitchen.

They ran into the kitchen to find Mom on the floor, eyes fluttering and incoherent. Diane called an ambulance while Cindy held onto Mom.

Mom was first taken to Coney Island Hospital. While there, the hospital staff made a decision that Mom's apparent condition would get better care at Kings County Hospital. When I got home from work, I found out that Mom was taken to Kings County. In those days, there were no cell phones, and nobody knew the name of the bank I was working at (not that I hadn't told them a few times already). Mom had the name and number written on a pad that hung alongside the wall telephone.

By the time I got to Kings County Hospital, Nanny and my Aunt Renee were already there, as was my big sister Loretta. We were waiting to speak to a doctor about Mom's diagnosis and condition. The hospital staff was polite but had no information. We were getting frustrated. Finally, a doctor came forth to speak with us. My aunt took charge, as she was a registered nurse and best understood medical terminology.

The doctor introduced himself as one of the chief neurosurgeons on staff. His name was Dr. Tanaz.

He was very professional in demeanor and quite patient with us. He explained that Mom had experienced a brain aneurysm, and the only solution to prevent her death was surgery. Dr. Tanaz made it clear that most people suffering the same way didn't make it through the night or through the surgery.

Mom was bleeding to death inside her skull. Her brain was swelling and the retention of fluids inside her head was dangerous on its own. Perhaps as is protocol, Dr. Tanaz suggested we put her affairs in order and prepare for the worse.

That was when it happened. That little voice - the person who had been so helpful when I was a kid - he spoke up.

He told me to make sure that Mom had a phone in the recovery room. I shared the idea with Dr. Tanaz and the family. My aunt frowned and said,

"Jimmy, this is very serious."

I knew how serious it was, but I persisted. I wanted to be sure that there would be a phone in the recovery room. Dr. Tanaz said I did not understand the dire circumstances my mother faced. He explained that almost 99% of the time the patient did not immediately recover their ability to speak or even walk for days if ever. I told him I understood, but I was adamant.

"Will there be a telephone in the recovery room, in case Mom needs it?"

I wasn't backing down in spite of grumblings from my family members and the doctor's apparent resistance to provide an answer, which was probably because he felt it may give us false hope.

Dr. Tanaz left us for a few minutes. When he came back, he explained that the surgery was scheduled for the morning and that it might take a very long time, perhaps the whole day. He verified that there was a phone for Mom to use in the recovery room. We all left after visiting hours ended, I remember that was about 8:00 pm.

The next day we all went to the hospital to sit around, pray, and wait while mom was treated. The operation lasted the whole day. Around 8:00 pm we left.

Blackie drove us all back home; Aunt Renee drove Nanny and herself home. At around 10:00 pm, Aunt Renee left the Brighton

Beach apartment, perhaps to go stay with her family in Long Island or Westchester, as her home was all the way up in Vermont.

Nanny was going back to her apartment, and everyone was worried. Then the phone rang. I picked it up and heard my Mom ranting at me for not being there at the hospital.

"Why the hell am I here all alone? Who brought me here? What time are you coming tomorrow?"

Then she shared other colorful pissed-off words.

I told Mom we were there until visiting hours ended and that we'd be there the next day. Nanny spoke with Mom for a minute and then all the kids did.

The next day we all took the journey from Brighton Beach to Kings County Hospital, which was on Clarkson Avenue in Brooklyn. We got there early. We were a little shocked to see Mom all wired up with a lot of bandages on her head.

She looked weak but didn't sound it. Mom made a full recovery and was sent home the end of that week. Within weeks, she was walking, talking, and smoking, as if nothing happened.

She did have to take some kind of medicine for the rest of her life, but she was okay. Mom had no slurred speech, no trouble walking, no headaches, and no loss of appetite, temper, or humor.

On the third day we visited the hospital we saw Dr. Tanaz. I remember he asked me about the phone call thing. He was curious as to why I was so insistent, and I am sure he was impressed by the fact that Mom did want the phone and did use it right after waking from anesthesia.

I told the doctor that I knew Mom would want to use the phone. I explained that I didn't know why I knew, I just knew. I did tell him that it was my belief that God needed him to help Mom, and that the phone call simply verified that fact. He was there for God's purpose. I believed that and still do.

Not much later in life, the story of the phone call would come back and visit the good doctor. Sometimes things just happened for a reason. That reason is up to the Lord to understand, and we mortals can only be grateful when it is to the benefit of our loved ones or us.

CHAPTER 43

THERE WAS ALWAYS THE FALL GUY

1990s

On February 17, 1994, I was working with Thomas Publishing, selling advertising in the company's regional buying guides. These guides were like yellow pages for industrial and manufacturing businesses. This particular day, I had a clear premonition. I was warned not to go outside. The little voice was serious.

One of my bosses, Orlando, who at the time also happened to be the son-in-law of the company CEO, wanted to come out to my home office and observe me in my day-to-day activities. This was important to him, as I was the top sales representative for the New York City region, and number two in the nation.

It was a tough market, but somehow I managed to close one of every three sales presentations for decent-sized ad programs. I don't believe I was anything special; I was just honest. If the advertising program made sense and if the customer liked any of the three the ads I drew for them while at their premises, then it was a no-brainer, especially if the target market was important to them.

I worked from home by telephone most of the time and went out to see customers three or four times a day all over the New York metropolitan area. I did do my own graphic arts on an Apple Computer with MacDraw Pro software. I had no formal training, but the nerd factor in my DNA was pretty high up there. I liked to draw, and I loved tinkering with computers.

Orlando came over early, around 9:30 am. He sat and listened to me on the phone for a couple of hours. Matt was with his mother in the other room. He was about seven months old. After listening to my calls for an hour or so, Orlando was impressed. He liked that I was so natural and conversational with folks on the phone. He also liked that I could do the art.

Then he said he wanted to go out to meet customers with me. I said that was a bad idea. I explained that outside was a world of snow and ice and if we took my car out of its parking spot, I'd lose the spot and have to dig out another spot. He was insistent on it. I told him to wait there in my little office space, as I needed a restroom break. I told Martha what Orlando wanted to do and explained that the little voice said I should not go out today. She argued that I go, as he was the top sales manager and my job was very important to our family.

The problems I faced were daunting. I knew moving the car would cost me a spot on the block, and since Orlando took the subway to come to Carroll Gardens, he would not be driving. I also had a really bad feeling about going out on sales calls. My version of spider-senses was screaming that something awful would happen. I was ready to show Orlando my office and let him hear me on the phone, but I was not inclined to leave for sales calls on such a cold day.

Reluctantly, I agreed with Martha and Orlando to go see customers. I packed the briefcase bag with some of the Thomas

Regional Directories we sold advertising space in and changed my clothes. I was still lobbying to postpone driving and told Orlando that if we move the car and I lose the spot, he would have to help me dig out a new spot. He promised that he would.

I said goodbye to Matt and Martha and headed down the stairs to go dig out the car. My heavy briefcase was in my left hand.

At the top of the stoop, I stepped forward and reached out for the handrail with my right hand, the briefcase in my left swung forward like a pendulum.

Suddenly, my feet went out from under me, and I was literally catapulted into the air. From the top of the stoop to the curb is about a ten-foot drop. My body shot out from under me and flew up in the air. I had slipped on black ice. Jarringly, I was slammed onto the curb, smashing my lower back first, while banging my head really hard. I saw stars.

As I lay there in shock, I watched Orlando clinging to the handrail as he came down to help me. I was in awful pain and really pissed off. He started laughing. I think it was a nervous laugh. I didn't laugh. Believe it or not, I somehow got up, and we dug out the car and saw the two appointments I had made. I closed both sales and also sold an ad to a neighboring company on a cold call.

When I got home later, I felt something was really out of place. My back was really hurting me, and I had pins and needles starting in my left leg, then in my right. I took as hot a shower as I could. The next day was a sales meeting at 5 Penn Plaza, the main office location. I made it into the office. At the meeting, Orlando made light of the incident while complimenting my sales skills and creative talents. I think I may have called him an insensitive asshole. Subsequently, I met with my former sales manager Rochelle. I went home after I explained to Rochelle what happened to me, and how bad I felt since the fall.

When I got home, the pain really kicked in. I was trying to walk up the two flights to the apartment, and then suddenly, no legs. I fell flat on my face and busted my lip. I couldn't get up and was in terrible pain. One of the neighbors helped me up to the apartment and had to leave me lying on the floor. The next day I was taken to Methodist hospital and tests were performed. It looked bad. It felt worse.

I damaged certain lumbar disks and fractured my cervical spine. I found out how serious the cervical fracture was, but not until much later. The pain in my back was an 11 out of 10. I was a nervous wreck but sedated by pain meds. I chose to stay in Methodist Hospital because that was where my son had been born. By the end of the third day I couldn't feel my legs. The pain in my back was incredible. It was shockingly painful.

CHAPTER 44
A ROLEX WATCH AND ARMANI SUIT

1990s

God bless all the people on this planet that by injury or disease lose their ambulatory abilities or their sight. These are among the worse conditions I have ever seen human beings subjected to. Thanks to my own experiences, I pray for people that are sick, injured, or in any kind of despair.

I believe prayers help. That made a lot of sense, as I had one resource to cling to: my faith. I prayed hard, day and night, for God to help me find a solution to the problems I faced.

My legs were not working, and my son was a baby. I needed His help. I believed that God can provide answers in quirky ways, so I was willing to accept His answer, no matter what it was.

Martha wanted me to leave Methodist Hospital and go to one of the top New York City hospitals. She had only recently begun a job working for Wunder Bank and couldn't take a lot of time off. I'm sure the events and circumstances were really stressful. I stubbornly did not want to leave Methodist Hospital. I had a feeling that I needed to stay there.

One evening I spoke with Martha on the phone. She again asked if I would consider going to the Hospital for Special Surgery. I told her I knew I had to stay where I was - I just didn't know why I knew.

After we spoke, a resident physician came to see me. He explained that a specialist was interested in my case and wanted to discuss a new surgical procedure that was being used to treat my type of injury. I said sure, why not. The resident said the specialist would be in the next day. He assured me that the doctor coming to visit was among the top neurosurgeons in New York City and was in fact a chief consultant to all the major hospitals. I said thanks and prayed myself to sleep. I prayed and trusted that God would provide help.

The next morning after I got back from a round of MRIs and finishing a late breakfast. A gentleman came to the room, dressed in what looked like an Armani suit. He was sporting a really cool-looking watch, which I guessed was a Rolex.

He seemed familiar but looked so dapper I couldn't place it at first. Then he came over to the end of my bed and read my chart. He smiled at me and waited till I finished eating before introducing himself. He had an odd look on his face as though he too felt I was familiar. Then it hit me.

He said good morning and stated that I seemed familiar to him. I smiled and said,

"I was the guy that insisted on a phone for my mom in the recovery room, Dr. Tanaz."

He laughed and said he somewhat recalled the event. He explained the procedure he wanted to try and believed that it would help me get relief from pain and give me back full use of my legs. I agreed, and we planned for surgery.

The surgery took place at the end of March, so you can imagine I'd been in the hospital for weeks. The surgery was performed, and the results were good but not immediate. For two years subsequent to the surgery I struggled with back pain and weak legs.

I did physical therapy, pain management, and then still more physical therapy, including something called work-hardening. In the third year, my right leg came back. It was startling, as it was all pins and needles for a day, then it just seemed to go back to work. The other leg took a little longer.

During the years of healing, Martha and I consulted with some high-level neurologists and neurosurgeons. The top professionals in the field would do tests, look at MRIs, and all with the same result. They said I'd never heal, the injury was too extreme, and the surgery failed. I didn't believe them and said as much. I knew that God would heal my legs, heal all of me.

CHAPTER 45
A LIFE INTERRUPTED

1990s

In 1993 my son was born. Matthew James is one of the greatest joys in my life. Because of him I can always say I did something right, at least once. Being his dad and meeting Lisa after things changed between his mom and I are two of my favorite life chapters. Lisa and Matthew really make my life worth living. I thank God Lisa came into our lives when she did. Becoming a father had matured me.

It increased my respect for the world around and helped me appreciate life in a humbler fashion.

On February 17, 1994, when Matt was about seven months old, I had that awful, painful, accident that also changed my life forever. In spite of the pain and difficulty the accident caused, I am grateful to God for it. It taught me how to be physically and emotionally grateful, to accept things that are not always what they appear to be, and to be patient with faith.

Maybe some reading this will see being grateful for getting hurt as impossible or even nonsense. It's not.

I say, have faith. Look to your heart for the answer and I believe you will see the truth about what really happened. I created the following acronym to help a friend understand my perspective.

Faith (F.A.I.T.H.) is a:

Fundamental

Ability

Inherent

To

Humans

In some way, big or small, we all have it. I have a great deal of faith, which is a constant source of strength for me. On some levels, faith is a source of real magic. Things happen, optimal outcomes manifest, or a new doorway is opened.

From my vantage point, it is faith that makes that all occur because faith invites the Holy Spirit (the true power behind the law of attraction).

Among the various experiences I have had, there were also genuinely accurate visions. Some of the visions and messages I received proved to benefit people I know, and once in a while, it helped people I didn't know (like Joe on the F train).

Sometimes it's a small voice that sporadically provides news about the future, typically not meant for me, and never including lottery numbers, so don't go there. Believe me - I have asked but no lottery numbers were ever forthcoming.

I'm in my late fifties now and trust me: the idea of living this long is a shock to me. I find it hard to believe that this kid from Brooklyn actually made it through all these wacky, weird, and wonderful events. When I was in my late teens, I was in the path of mafia hoods, both Italian and Russian, and still made it through. I have been haunted by fun-loving spooks and really scary ones. At minimum, this has been a life unusual.

For those that live with me there is no avoiding the unusual. For those that know me well, there is no escaping my faith and sheer determination to keep going in spite of all obstacles. *I get knocked down, but I get up again*, is the theme to my life (and occasional ringtone). I'll get up and keep going all the way until I get to that bright cheerful place I know exists. That is the gist of it.

I was allowed to see exactly where people go when they first leave this life. It's beyond amazing and much more than beautiful.

I am compelled to share more about that and will. Before I continue, you should know I had to change a few names in the telling of my life. Some names were changed in order to protect the innocent, and to protect myself and mine.

I still want to live to be an old man, and I am getting there fast. I can feel the clock ticking, sense the motes in the air evaporating. In fact, while sitting here typing this down, I felt three chest hairs turn white and two new wrinkles appear on my face.

They may just be laugh lines. Laughing is good. I laugh a lot, and the people I am closest to also laugh. I love to laugh with them and often.

What I remember most about my mom was the way she laughed. It sounded like a cross between an old air conditioner and a hard-smoking frog. She had a wet laugh, phlegm-ridden and deep, almost always ending in a coughing fit, but infectious, nonetheless.

My mom had a wicked sense of humor. Although times were often tough, most of the time with my Mom was spent with a laugh or a smile. That was not always the case, like when I moved away or when something bad occurred. None of the ghostly stuff was fun for Mom.

Perhaps because I was dead but didn't stay dead is what draws lost souls towards me. For some reason or another, it seems as though the other side likes trying to touch base with me. Sometimes I don't mind, but there have been a few times that it was downright spooky or annoying. I wasn't scared when I was little. When you're a kid, things that go bump in the night tend to be frightening, but they didn't frighten me then. They did later.

My wife Lisa never had such supernatural experiences until we met. When she was much younger, she was given a premonition by a seer. She was told she would meet a man with light eyes and a son further down the road of her life. We met when she was thirty-seven.

Before we met and before I knew of her, Lisa was shown to me in a most wondrous dream or vision. I'll explain in greater detail later, but for now, I can say it was a beautiful, life-altering event - so much so that it dynamically changed my life. It was a straight validation of my faith in God.

Though I live a life often filled with laughter and music there were times when I have been beset by danger and supernatural happenings. Yet, there was always a feeling that another adventure was unfolding. As an adult, the unique experiences I have had, especially at wakes and funerals, made everything clear.

We have a place to go after this, and we don't lose our loved ones. We are just separated from them temporarily from here to there. We all get back together and, yes, there is a reunion of sorts, more like a huge welcome party.

This is probably the greatest miracle of my life, having seen on three occasions where we go when we die. The most powerful knowledge on Earth is knowing that when we leave here we go into the Bright Room. There, all is made right. All love is found, and nothing is lost ever again. In His eternal Light, we celebrate and rejoice.

For now, we have to live the life we have in the mortal realm and make it the best it can be. Sometimes we will like it, other times we may not. It's up to us to choose how we feel.

CHAPTER 46

WHAT IS BLUE AND STOPS THE CLOCK

1990s

On another note, during the time I was home recovering from spinal surgery, I had an eerie episode. I was sleeping on quilts on the floor with my knees raised, listening to music.

Suddenly I was awake, looking down at myself sleeping. It freaked me out. Just as suddenly I fell back into myself and physically jolted my body up to a kneeling position. I had an out of body experience, and I have no doubt this occurred.

There were a number of strange experiences I had, which I attributed to the supernatural. One such event occurred just before New Year's Day of 1974. I was thirteen then, and my friends and I agreed to meet at the Trump Village movie theater, to see a new scary movie that was just out. It was called "The Exorcist".

After dinner, I dressed warmly and walked to the theater to meet my friends. It was raining out and I was getting wet. The walk was about three quarters of mile. When I got to the theater, my friends were nowhere in sight.

I went to the box office window and told the ticket lady that my parents were supposed to meet me. I explained that I thought they were inside and asked if I could go look. She let me go in.

The theater was cold and being wet didn't help. I found a seat and watched the movie minus my friends. I didn't like it. I thought it was blasphemous and not scary at all, just gross. I watched to the end, which was around 9:00 pm. On the way home it was still raining out. As I walked along Neptune Avenue, I noticed something peculiar. I couldn't hear anything.

I snapped my fingers and heard that but didn't hear the raindrops. I noticed there were no cars around. I got to the corner of 15th Street on the far side of Neptune Avenue.

Everything was eerily quiet. My eyes got a little fuzzy. For some reason, as I watched the light turn from red to green, the color blue began draping over everything I was looking at. Then all of the sudden, there was nothing but the color blue. It was kind of a sky blue. I had no idea what was happening. I still don't. Then next thing I knew, I was putting one foot on the steps of our apartment building. The blue-colored light faded. I stopped for a second and shook my head. I realized the rain had stopped, and I wasn't soaked.

I went upstairs expecting everyone to be in the kitchen or living room. They weren't. Only Mom was up, and she was angry with me. She was upset that I got home so late on a school night. I was confused. Then I saw the clock over the picnic table on the kitchen wall. It said 3:00. It was three o'clock in the morning! How in the world was that possible? The movie let out at 9:00 pm, and I walked straight home. I apologized and told Mom I must have lost track of time. Turned out she wasn't mad - just worried.

I went to bed and slept well. Over the next few days, I stopped using my glasses in the classroom. For some reason, I didn't need them anymore. I know this chapter is not like the others and makes no sense in that it has no basis for spiritual or scientific consideration that I am aware of, but I can say that this actually happened, whatever this episode was.

There had to be a reason, since so many other quirky things had happened, but I have no idea what <u>really</u> happened or why. I definitely don't know what the color blue was about. I do know that I lost at least five hours of time that night.

CHAPTER 47
MIKEY DIDN'T LIKE IT

1990s

Living in Carroll Gardens provided some delightful experiences, most of which were food oriented. There were bakeries all over the place, so we never lacked for fresh Italian bread or pastries. Around the corner on Union Street was Nino's pizza, and not more than two blocks away was the famous House of Pizza & Calzone, also on Union Street. I loved their calzones! Although we walked around the block and ate more pizza from Nino's, whenever we ordered for delivery (as rare as that was) it was from House of Pizza & Calzone.

During that time when I was recovering from my greatest physical injury, I was fortunate enough to have for company two guys that to this day I consider my little brothers: Tito and Hamlet. Tito, whose real name was Hector, was Martha's little brother, and Hamlet was a close friend of his. We were all three kindred spirits and became very close friends, but more like brothers.

Another person that was very close to me during that time was my nephew Michael. He was my sister Diane's oldest son. Mike was big kid back in those days and very strong. He helped me carrying things around, including his cousin Matthew who was about a year old when Mike came to stay with us.

It was the summer of 1995 and, although I was in "recovery mode," my injuries from the year before had been serious enough that I still couldn't walk properly. My left leg was still partly numb, but my right leg was stronger, which meant I was able to drive again. The right leg was awake. My lower back was still an unfriendly and painful reminder of the accident.

It was great to have Mike around to help out, and it didn't hurt that he was also a great video game partner and opponent. We would *cheese* each other in Mortal Combat, or team-up with Killer Instinct, or sometimes play Primal Rage or Sonic the Hedgehog. We had fun. We liked the same stuff and the same kind of action-and-comedy-based movies. That was also true of Hamlet and Tito, as well, but they had lives to live, and Mike stayed with us for most of the summer that year.

One night when Martha and I had to take Matthew to see Dr. Attanasi, the baby's pediatrician, Mike said he'd like to stay in the apartment and play video games on his own.

He was almost fourteen, so I didn't see a problem with that. We took Matt to the doctor for his shots and checkup. Matt was doing great by the Grace of God and he was a happy little boy with a big appetite. After the doctor visit, we went to the supermarket. I wasn't much help, but I did keep Matthew company while the real shopping was accomplished. By the time we headed back, it had already been dark outside for a while.

Once the car was parked for the night and Matthew tucked into his stroller, we made our way up the block to our apartment building we lived in, which was 195 President Street in the Carrol Gardens section of Brooklyn. I moved slowly but could carry some of the groceries. We were surprised to see Mike sitting on the stoop in front of the apartment building with Brownie the family Chihuahua, in tow. He appeared to be dismayed, so we asked him what was wrong.

Mike explained that when he was in the living room playing Sonic, he thought he saw someone peek around from the master bedroom and then jump back.

He said he ignored it at first, thinking it might have been flickering car lights going down the block.

Our railroad-style apartment was on the third floor, so it was possible for car lights coming down the block to flicker in through the bedroom window. Mike said he got up to check if someone was there and felt his arm hairs stand up as he passed through the Matthew's bedroom into the master bedroom. He didn't find anyone and went back to the couch.

He waited a few minutes and then continued playing the game, figuring it was his imagination. He said that from his peripheral point of view a dark figure with red eyes suddenly stood in the opening between the two bedrooms. When he put his full attention on the spot, it was empty, but the hair on the back of his neck and arms were straight up. He grabbed Brownie and ran outside to wait for us on the stoop. I asked him if he heard anything and he said no. Obviously shaken, he repeated that he just saw something.

We made our way up to the apartment - an effort of no small consequence for me at the time - but I was able and quite determined. We went into the apartment and put the little guy into his crib, and Martha put the groceries away. I hobbled around the apartment with Mike, but we found nothing amiss.

I told him it was probably his imagination going wild, maybe as a result of the two scary movies we watched a few nights before. We had a light supper, and everyone got ready to hit the hay. Mike had been sleeping on the futon sofa, which was a very comfy place to sleep, whether opened or not. Mike always slept with the futon in the sofa position - not fully opened. He liked having the cushion behind him to rest against. Later that night while we were all sleeping, something occurred that changed the dynamics of the apartment for good. Around two in the morning, Mike began yelling for help.

I scrambled up and grabbed the crutches and got quickly into the living room. Matthew was awake and crying, probably from being so startled by Mike's yelling. Martha beat me into the living room, and when I joined her a moment later, I saw a very pale-faced young man sitting on the couch: eyes wide with shock, tears falling slowly. His hands and arms were trembling, and his foot was tapping on its own, a reaction of seriously jangled nerves. He just sat there, shaking and trembling.

After a few minutes, a second drink of water, a quick visit to the bathroom, and a bunch of reassuring hugs from his uncle, Mike was able to explain why he was in the shape he was and what made him scream for help. He told Martha and me that he was sound asleep and suddenly couldn't breathe.

He said he opened his eyes and saw two hideous red eyes staring into his face and that the rest of the thing holding him was all in black (like a deep shadow) and it had a pointed head or hood. It didn't speak; it just pressed down on his face with one hand and his chest with another hand. Mike said he tried to move but couldn't.

Remember when I said Mike was a big kid. At age fourteen, Mike was about five foot eleven and weighed over two hundred pounds. He was very strong. Whatever held Mike down had to be a whole lot stronger since panic provides a huge adrenaline rush in any average person, and Mike was a bit stronger than most average teens. He was in shock.

"Uncle Jimmy, I could not move a muscle, and it was holding my face. Something happened and the thing loosened its grip just enough, so I pushed up screaming. Then, it was just not there anymore. It was just gone."

I believed Mike was telling the truth, but Martha thought he was having nightmares. She was not happy about her sleep getting interrupted since she still had a job to go to.

The next morning, Martha took Matt along with her to drop him off at the Children's Center, which was Wunder Bank's own day care service. It was very secure, and the staff was really nice. When she left, she was not that happy and said we would have to talk about Mike later.

What she didn't know was that there would be no reason to talk about Mike later on. He had had more than his share of terror the night before and really wanted to get out of our apartment before nightfall.

Mike pleaded with me to take him back to my Mom's apartment in Coney Island, where he lived during school days. He said he felt bad because he knew I needed help, but he was not willing to stay there one more night.

He said that was the scariest thing he ever felt in his whole life. He promised me that what he described was exactly what happened. I didn't doubt him.

He packed up his stuff, and we left for Coney Island. My mother was happy to see Mike and gave him a big hug.

She plopped a huge glass of milk and some Entenmann's donuts in front of hm. He dug into them with gusto. I had one or two with some milk. After a nice visit and some quality time with Mom, Mike, and my brother Pat, I prepared to leave for Carrol Gardens.

Mom asked me if I had holy water in the house, and I said I did. I kept some in a vial right by my bed. I would often pray and, once in a while, I blessed the baby, my wife, and myself with the holy water.

The last time I refilled the bottle it was at Our Lady of Solace in Coney Island. I always liked that church.

I made it home before Martha and Matt got back and cleaned up a little. The place was in order when they arrived. Matt got a bath, and I made some dinner for us. Nothing else happened that night.

CHAPTER 48
CATCHING THE RED EYE

1990s

Martha asked where Mike was, and I explained that the kid was too terrified to stay in the apartment anymore. She said it was probably a ruse to get back to my Mom's place and play with his friends from the block. Mike's mom (my sister Diane) lived right around the corner from my mother.

Retrospectively, I don't think Martha was right about Mike wanting to leave. I think Mike would've loved to live with us full time, and back then I welcomed the idea, because he had been in my life since he was a baby. I loved him and all the kids (which at the time were eight nephews and a niece).

My spinal injury and subsequent circumstances pulled me away from my niece and nephews, and we saw each other less and less as years passed. I had little power to do anything about their lives, but I have always prayed for them. That may sound like nothing much, but it is my belief that prayer is the greatest gift one can give to another.

Regardless of my thoughts on the matter Mike would not stay in our Carroll Gardens apartment anymore.

He swore that what he saw and felt was real and told me that I needed to watch over Matthew and bless the house a few times. He was genuinely frightened by the event. I did bless the house. Nothing seemed amiss.

Everything was quiet in our apartment for a couple of months. Hamlet and Tito visited me every so often, and we'd play video games or role-playing board games, including one they invented. Most often, we'd watch movies together. Matt was growing, and he was very smart. Before he was a year old, he knew the alphabet.

Overall, things were okay given my limits at the time. Martha and I never spoke about Mike's incident, and so it went by the wayside until another incident occurred. About two months after Mike moved back to my mom's apartment, Martha and I were working out the logistics of Matthew's next day care arrangements so I could try to attend university. I was planning on going back to school to reinvent myself on a professional level. We stayed up late discussing things and then watched some television.

The next day was a Saturday so Martha didn't have to get up for work. After taking turns showering, brushing teeth, and other ablutions, we went to bed to get some sleep. I was feeling back and leg pain and took a muscle relaxer to help stop the spasms. When the medicine kicked in I fell asleep quickly and deeply.

I don't recall what time it was when I fell asleep, but I was in a deep sleep. The bed we shared was queen-sized, so if either person was in motion it was definitely noticeable, sometimes interrupting sleep. I didn't feel a thing that night, but Martha did. She explained later that while she was sleeping, she felt a hand cover her mouth and another hand press down on her chest to hold her still.

Martha said she was absolutely paralyzed with terror for the first few seconds, but as her eyes adjusted to the light she saw two hideous crimson eyes glaring into her own. She told me the sight of the eyes and the black pointed head shocked her enough to make her thrash about. She hoped that her moving and struggling would wake me up, but it didn't.

She fought against the thing holding her and tried to get it to release her face so she could breathe.

The fight between Martha and the red-eyed demon may have lasted a minute or three, and then she got her mouth free. Martha screamed at the top of her lungs. I awoke with a start, fully conscious, and turned on the light by the bed.

She looked white as a sheet, and her eyes were wild with fear. She grabbed me and looked around the room. Then she let go and ran to the baby's crib, but Matthew was fine, although he was awake and fussing - most likely because his mom just screamed so loud. I didn't see anything in the room that looked remotely out of place. I realized I was still a little groggy and said we should go back to sleep, that she probably had a nightmare. That didn't go over well, as she took her frustration out on me for not waking up fast enough.

When she calmed a bit, she explained the whole event, and clearly she believed this was the thing that grabbed my nephew and held him down. I didn't doubt her, but I also didn't know what to make of it. First, Mike had the experience he described, and then Martha had the same type of scary episode.

Thank God, Matthew was okay, and he didn't appear to be touched or harmed, although it is important to point out the area the crib was in is surrounded by religious images and blessed often with holy water and prayer.

I comforted Martha as much as I could, but she was stressed to the max. Nothing I could say would help her relax after her ordeal. I think she took a couple of baby aspirin or Tylenol. Gradually, she was able to calm down enough to go back to sleep.

Why would something like this happen, and what had invited it into our home? I couldn't figure it out, but I did have a suspicion. It reminded me of something my grandmother had experienced.

My grandmother had gone to Vermont to visit her daughter, Renee, and spend time with her other family. This visit was a couple of years before my eventual and mandatory move to Vermont. Nanny spent most of her time with us in Coney Island and then Brighton Beach, but she did go visit her other daughter, or more to the fact hopped in Renee's car and was taken to Vermont for a visit.

On one particular occasion during the time we all lived in Coney Island, along with our spooky friend "Charlie", my aunt and grandmother took a ride through the Vermont countryside to check out some of the old churches. They were doing some spiritually-uplifting kind of sightseeing. One specific church was not like the others or so I recall Nanny saying. It was dark and had black crosses - all of them hung upside down. She also saw a monk or someone she thought was a monk. He was all in black and had a pointy hat. Nanny said his eyes looked a bit red and that maybe he was a drug fiend. She called out to him and tried to get his attention. At that time, her daughter (my Aunt Renee) found her inside the weird church and pulled her out, saying she didn't like the place. Nanny left willingly but was confused as to whom the man was and why he wouldn't show himself clearly.

When she got back from her trip and was telling these events to my mother, I felt goosebumps. By the way, I was not eavesdropping I was just there. At my age, I didn't have far to go, especially when it was time for dinner. Nanny explained that the monk seemed to follow her around the building, and she thought she glimpsed him at her daughter's house. I'm not sure why my aunt didn't driver her back, but Nanny came home by bus from that trip. I was never sure if it was her or something clinging to her, but there was something weird with Nanny, something sinister.

After Martha's incident with the red-eyed monster, I kept a bottle of holy water right within reach on the nightstand next to the bed. Subsequent to that event, I blessed Matthew and Martha with holy water more often. I was not sure as to the origin of the problem but did find other references to something like it on the internet in later years.

One web author described the entity as a shadow man. Another website had an article, which explained there could be at least four different types of shadow men, and the most interesting article painted one of these entities as something really scary.

"Definitely the most dangerous of the types of Shadow People, demonic shadows should be avoided at all costs. Among Shadow People, these are one of the few types that you can sometimes see the eyes. Many accounts of them talk of glowing red eyes, which is a particularly bad sign," the article went on as follows,

"Demonic forms vary widely, but usually retain a humanoid shape, but are often exaggerated in height, have wings or horns or elongated fingers. They do not give the impression of being a normal ghost or sentient entity. Luckily these demonic Shadow People are typically tied to one location." (ParaRational.com, Cliff, 2016)

Retrospectively, it would appear that it was some sort of shadow entity that had shown itself and then attacked my nephew Michael, then later in the same year returned and attacked Martha. I was really worried that something might happen to my son, but thank God nothing ever did, at least regarding this red-eyed shadow phenomenon. I wasn't sure when it would return or if it would. I prayed for strength and healing. This and other events made me more conscious of the fact that I really wanted to walk normally again.

CHAPTER 49
YOU ARE NOT WELCOME HERE

1990s

A couple of months passed without incident. My right leg had strengthened with most credit given to the Lord. The physical therapy group I was attending gets some credit, too. We were doing a combination of pain management and work-hardening therapies. Having the right leg back on the team was helpful in a big way: I could drive again with confidence.

The year 1996 was closing in, and I began making plans as to what my next steps would be. I began to apply to colleges all of which were within a subway ride from home. I thought it would be a good idea to reinvent myself somehow, as I was not going to sit in the house and waste away. That was out of the question and would be a sin in my opinion, especially after I heard that fellow at the church with his eyes damaged say how grateful he was.

It's funny but hobbling about doing chores filled me with greater optimism about the future. I believed the Lord had a guiding light on my path, and as long as I kept my gaze upon it I wouldn't get lost. I had a tough time convincing Martha to keep her optimism and be strong. Her boss in the Wunder Bank IT department was giving her a really hard time. She complained about it a lot and was hoping to find a new job within the firm outside of the IT office. I was praying for her to get some help.

It was around this time when it happened again. It was me the red-eyed shadow man came after. I was lying down in bed, sound asleep, when I felt cold chills. I remember reaching for the blanket with my left hand but realized I couldn't move it. Something was pressing down on my chest and left arm and a hand or a rag covered my mouth and nose.

I opened my eyes and looked directly into a pair of hateful crimson nightmares. I looked directly at them and began struggling. My right arm was free and instinctively I reached out to grasp something on the night table next to my side of the bed.

I gripped it tightly and flipped it open, then pushed mightily, splashing holy water forward. The holy water hit the red-eyed shadow in the face, and it bounded back from the bed as though struck by lightning.

I was up in a flash and attacking it with the holy water, shouting for it to get out of our home in the name of Jesus Christ our Savior.

"In the name of Jesus Christ, you are compelled to leave this place. Get out! You are not welcome! In the name of God, you are not welcome!"

I repeated myself over and again, saying you are not welcome here and cannot return here, in the name of Jesus Christ. The hairs on my arms and neck were standing straight out.

I chased it through the small apartment and watched it literally slither under our front door and out into the hallway. Without hesitation, I continued after it bounding awkwardly down the stairs, voice raised, throwing holy water at it. It disappeared under the exit doors, and was out of the apartment building altogether. I blessed the entryway, transom, and the entire doorway. I blessed the entrance hall and all the stairs on my way back up to the apartment. Martha was really shook up, and Matthew was crying.

I calmed the little guy right down, and then spoke with his mom. I told Martha that that thing could not get back into our building uninvited. We were safe to go back to sleep. The following months led Martha to the job at Audit & Accounting, then within a year she was back at Wunder Bank in a much better role. Her little brother Tito and our pal Hamlet kept me company most often.

We watched movies, played video games, and either cooked or ordered food, which Martha shared when she got home from work. The shadow thing didn't come back for a long time, but it did try once during a particular night when the guys and I ordered pizza and the order came with a surprise.

The pizza order was called in to Nino's Pizzeria, which was around the corner and made deliveries. It usually took twenty or so minutes to get a pie made and delivered. I don't remember what we put on the pizza, but it was not a plain cheese pie. Five minutes after the order was placed, the doorbell rang. We normally had to run down two flights of stairs to answer the bell. Tito was ready to fly downstairs with the money to pay for the pies, when my hair stood up. I yelled at him to stop where he was. He listened. I leaned over the bannister rail outside our third-floor apartment, and yelled out,

"Who's there?"

All three of us felt the hair on our arms and neck stand up, and chills run down our spines when the reply came back,

"*Pizzzzzaaa ...*"

The deep grating voice that said *pizza* sounded horrifically sibilant and truly demonic - not at all like a bona fide Brooklyn pizza delivery professional.

I had a flashback to my friend's grandmother's house in Bethel, Connecticut, on a night when I heard a terrifying, demonic sounding laugh. This voice matched that laugh. I asked Hamlet to run to the front of the apartment and look down on the stoop to see who was standing there.

Hamlet was at the window in a second, and when he opened it and looked outside, he saw nobody on the stoop. There were no cars or bikes for the delivery of pizza anywhere. Whatever was down there, it was clearly not the pizza guy. Hamlet ran back after closing the window, looking ashen and confused. He asked me what was going on. In reply, I went back into the hallway and yelled down the stairs:

"In the name of Jesus Christ, you are compelled from here, and in the Lord's name you are banned from here. Be gone spirit or demon! You are not welcome."

I grabbed some holy water and blessed all three of us, then blessed Matthew in his playpen. I blessed the doorway and every corner of the room (again). Matt was so young he was oblivious to the incident.

Ten minutes later, the pizza was really delivered, and when we asked who it was, an Italian accent answered,

"Nino's Pizza."

That manifestation in the apartment was final. We did not see or feel anything like that again while we lived there. Over the next few years, I went to school and we put together a plan to move away from

Brooklyn. If I knew then what I know now regarding the incredible value of Brooklyn real estate, I might have thought better about leaving our Carroll Gardens neighborhood. It's true that hindsight is 20/20.

In 1999, Martha, Matthew, and I moved to the Borough of Ringwood, New Jersey.

We found a place in the Cupsaw Lake section of the Borough of Ringwood. It was a nice place right near the lake and the clubhouse.

Finding that place was another experience that required Divine intervention and even though I had strong faith, having my call for help answered so expediently was something I still needed to get used to.

CHAPTER 50
A QUIRKY CONNECTION TO WALDRON

1990s

Martha and I started looking for a house or cooperative apartment in 1998, not long after I received a worker's compensation settlement for the on-the-job injury. This injury was discussed earlier, but the consequences of it were far reaching and long lasting.

The hunt for a house took us all over the place. We looked in Brooklyn at some old pre-war cooperative that would have cost a half-million to fix properly. Another day we were in Westchester, searching through Katonah, Ardsley, and the White Plains area. On another

Saturday, we found a house in New Jersey that Martha thought was a gem.

We invested a lot of time on that house, which was located in Glen Rock. The address was a house on Waldron Road, and it was a pretty place. Regarding that house, the problems for us were twofold: it was a bit over our budget in the asking price, and there was already a deposit on the home with contract pending. Someone else had the same idea we did. It was a great looking home, but the other people already had dibs on it.

One afternoon of weekend house hunting, we drove to Tuxedo, New York, located in Orange County, just outside of New Jersey. On the way home from Tuxedo, our discussion turned into a bad argument. Martha was getting depressed, and I was frustrated that we couldn't compromise on a house. Matthew was hungry and thirsty. We had run out of milk for him, and there was none left in the travel cooler. Feeling stressed out, I took a few wrong turns and got lost. We found a store, a little deli market in this cute lake community in New Jersey.

Outside the deli, we sat in the car while Matthew drank a cup of milk and ate part of a sandwich. He would turn six in a few months but ate like a ten-year-old. Martha and I were hungry too, we shared a sandwich and a ginger ale. After we ate and calmed down, I had an epiphany. I told Martha the problem was not in the houses we saw: it was with us.

I explained that we were trying to do this on our own, which was insufficient. I told her to close her eyes, bless herself and listen. I prayed. I asked our Heavenly Father for His intervention in Jesus name. I prayed and said Lord we need an answer today - not tomorrow or the next day, but today. I pleaded with Him to help us find a home and closed the prayer in His name. We sat quietly.

I started the car and we drove away from the deli, headed down the small winding road along the lake. It was a serenely rustic and naturally pretty road we drove on - a picture of early springtime. As we drove along, we saw a beach club on the lake that looked inviting. About a block further along, I spotted something in my periphery. It was a sign that said, *"for sale by owner"*. It was just off the lake road. On a hunch, I turned us around and went back to look.

The house was a split-level or bi-level, home. The vinyl siding was white. It looked bigger than we thought we could afford. The wooden "for sale" signpost looked brand new. On the sign were flyers in a basket. I asked Martha if she liked the look of the house. She said yes, but thought I was being ridiculous. I told her I had a feeling about it, to please grab a flyer. I was too sore from driving so much and didn't want to drag my lazy leg around. She got out and picked up a flyer.

We read it together. The amenities described were everything we had hoped for. The asking price was amazingly within range.

I told Martha I wanted to park the car and go ring the bell. She agreed. We parked and looked around the area, then walked to the house. Matt held his mother's hand, and we walked to the front door and rang the bell.

It opened instantly. A young woman answered and inside was a man sitting on the staircase, looking enthusiastic. From what we were told, the couple had just put up the signpost about a half hour before we rang the bell. They were thrilled to show us the place. It seemed that they were motivated to sell because they had a deposit on another home closer to the husband's job with an easier commute to New York when necessary for work or entertainment.

We understood that. We looked around at the rooms, they were lovely and decent sized, and the kitchen was big, but needed some updates. The basement or lower level was finished nicely and had sliding doors that led to a big backyard.

The place had more than one bathroom! It was amazing to find something so nice and spacious, within our range.

Martha's eyes were sparkling with delight. We discussed her potential workday commute by bus to New York City. It was a possible ninety minutes one-way. She was okay with it, as she really liked the house. We offered the couple a price that matched their asking.

We already lost out for offering too low on other nice homes. The couple, Michael and Heather, accepted on the spot!

We signed an agreement, giving them a two-thousand-dollar check as a deposit. We agreed to close by the end of April, which was about one month away. We would need the month of May to finish our current lease and would use that month to clean and prep the new house. We moved into the Kraft Place home the day before my birthday in 1999.

On my birthday, I went out and cut my own grass for the first time in my life. It was a delightful experience. The smell of the cut grass, the air quality and the peaceful feeling that permeated the moment is etched in my memory.

Michael and Heather left some furniture at the house which we really didn't need. After calling them, I agreed to bring the furniture to them. There was a little more to it than that but no need to cast aspersions here. Hamlet helped me load the furniture in my Dodge Caravan, and we drove to the address Michael had supplied.

The house they had moved into was that same Waldron Road home Martha and I had seen months ago, which Martha really liked. I didn't like it as much as Kraft Place and was happy not to have it. There I was bringing furniture with Hamlet's help to that very same place.

To me, this was a clear sign that the Lord had heard my prayer. What were the odds that Michael and Heather would be the ones that had a hold on the same house in Glen Rock that Martha liked?

It was in a town a few miles away from where we bought. No coincidence here. We found our home on the day we prayed. It was a same day delivery.

I am sure that our Heavenly Father had plans for us there, but humanity has freedom of choice which can create challenges, even for the omnipotent. Due to the wonderful times I had with my son at Cupsaw Lake, and the friends I made, Kraft Place will always hold some of my lifetime's most cherished memories.

At that time, in 1999 a prayer was answered the same day. We bought the house. There was a Christmas Bird or Cardinal on a flag across the street on a neighbor's house which I took for a sign.

Later, I learned the message from years before was about a real cardinal - not a picture on a flag. We lived happily together in that house for about three years. By 1999, my legs were getting better, my back rarely hurt, and I was definitely ready to go back to work. Unfortunately, we didn't know whom to trust with our son if we both worked in the city which was over an hour away from the Borough of Ringwood where we lived. We did find some nice folks to help but only part of the time.

We decided that I would work from home, fixing computers designing and implementing websites. It allowed me to continue enjoying the quality father and son time I had with Matthew. I love my son, and it was just awesome to be there with him through the start of elementary school all the way into middle school.

I volunteered at Matt's elementary school to help teach computer lab and gave a special class on writing for second graders and for a couple of years I was Santa Clause for the borough's two elementary schools. That was great fun.

The years Matt and I spent in Cupsaw Lake were some of the most fun-filled days I had being a father. Matthew and I had a blast at the lake, in the backyard playing catch, going snow sledding, watching movies, or playing video games, and sometimes cooking dinner together.

Unbeknownst to me at the time, Martha was feeling left out. She wasn't excluded. The job kept her away from much of it and on weekends she didn't want to snow-sled or go to the lake. When she eventually asked for the divorce, she implied that she had been jealous of the relationship Matthew and I had.

We lived very near Cupsaw Lake. I made friends there with some truly decent people. Woody and Louise, Tony and Dottie, Andy, Paul, Denise, Danny, and too many others to list. Woody and I would meet after our kids got on the school bus and then walk around the lake together. Tony and I would go swimming in the evenings of summer. It was a refreshing and relaxing life for me, especially because I worked from home.

Some days I was not physically up to the walk or the swim, but most days I could do it. I gradually got stronger, and when my legs were sound, Matthew and I began taking karate classes together. There was a Japanese-style dojo at the Erskine Lakes Volunteer Fire Company building.

It was there that we befriended Pedro, the teacher or sensei. I had experience in martial arts and excelled quickly. He was a good teacher. In time, I helped Pedro with some of the training, particularly little kids. Then, Martha decided she wanted to try karate.

Around that time, my neck began to hurt. The C-5 level fracture I was living with began to manifest itself painfully.

Bolts of pain lanced down from my neck and through my shoulders. I would sporadically lose feeling in my hands and right arm. This was a heartbreaking experience for me, as I just got my legs back not long before. I took a break from karate and never went back. Perhaps things do happen for a reason.

Almost a year before my neck started to go awry, I began sleeping in the guestroom downstairs. Why? Because my legs twitched in my sleep which disturbed Martha, who had to get up at 6:00 to get ready for work. She had to make the 7:15 bus to the Port Authority.

Her commute to Wunder Bank was about 75 minutes one way, so I moved downstairs during the Spring of 2001, only a couple of months after I had my first annual vision. It was incredibly vivid and definitely scary.

CHAPTER 51
THE FIRST OF THE UNWANTED VISIONS

2000s

The beginning of 2001 was somewhat uneventful, especially since the Y2K bug the year before proved genuinely anti-climactic. People scared the crap out each other, regarding computers, Social Security, airplane control towers failing, and all kinds of nonsense.

I knew Y2K would be nothing, and I was right. Part of my astute estimation had to do with my recent education at the esteemed New York University, where I earned an Associate's Degree in Business, concentrated on computer applications.

I graduated at age 40 and was the first person in my immediate family (at least those I grew up with) to actually go to college and finish a degree.

I realized then that nobody is too old to learn, and you're never too old to go to school. As a matter of fact, I subsequently earned a Bachelor's of Science Degree in Organizational Leadership at age 50, and a Master's of Science in Management at age 57. Let me reiterate: you are never too old to learn, given the opportunity.

As I mentioned, in 2001 I moved to the basement to help Martha sleep better. With me downstairs, she avoided my two hundred plus pounds of bouncing the bed during muscle spasms and leg twitches. I was still functionally doing a lot around the house; as I said, I felt stronger. Both legs were working fully by the summer of 2000. I was grateful to God for His kindness.

About 1997, subsequent to the man in the church that had lost his sight, I began a practice to demonstrate my gratitude to the Lord and to offer some penance.

Once a month for 24 hours, I would not eat any solid food. During that period, I would pray often and reflect on my life. This idea of service to God was not novel nor was it new in any way. I still maintain, and once a month I fast in prayer and penance.

My friends from the Church of Jesus Christ and the Latter Day Saints (or Mormons), explained that the Church had a practice of no food or water from one day to the next on the first Sunday of the month. I remembered that. I did this type of fasting with my Mormon friends in Connecticut back in the 1980s. In fact, for a short period I did join their Church though my participation was short-lived.

Some of the rules were not compatible with my life experiences and cultural beliefs. I was probably the worst example of a twenty-something male to associate with marriage-ready young Mormon women.

There was one person that I really liked; she was genuine, and her soul glowed through big brown eyes. I was a wild thing in my twenties and already a divorcé. No amount of faith could shock the wildness from me at that time: we are sinners born. My prayers are there for that young lady and all those whose life I touched at that time. Sadly, that wildness in me was matched with a volatile temper, which led to many a violent altercation.

I enjoyed fighting, especially against bullies. I was not a calm young man, but I was not an evil one either. I believe now I'm a good man, the way I always thought I should be, but still not a saint.

It's always been my belief that the Lord picked me up and slammed me on a curb to force me to see the light and behave with more care and consideration for others. It took a little time, but I do believe His plan eventually worked, outside of certain problems.

Sadly, in 2001, the problems of my marriage were beginning, and I didn't know how bad they would get. What I did know was that there was something coming, something horrifying. I saw the whole incident as clear as day. The event unfolded in front of my eyes during early January of 2001. It was a vision like none before. I was sitting on the bed and folding clothes when it occurred.

It was surreal, as though the entire scene was unfolding in the air before me. What I saw in the vision was a thing that looked like a missile or jet crashing into a tall building. It unfolded a little more, and I realized it was one of the Twin Towers at the World Trade Center. The scene was frightening enough when not a moment later another impact occurred on the second building.

Flames filled my eyes. Subsequently, the vision pulled me to a different vantage point, and I saw both buildings fall to the ground.

The entire premonition may have occurred over the course of seconds, but it felt like hours had passed. I immediately called Martha who was at work in downtown Manhattan and told her what I saw.

I told her I wasn't sure if it was meteors, rockets, or planes. The more I thought about it, the more I realized it wasn't meteors. I explained that I strongly felt the entire thing was planned - not accidental - and that there were most likely terrorists involved. She said that nothing was going on outside her office windows which were up pretty high. Nothing happened that day or that week, and we both forgot about the entire thing until one sad day in September.

On the morning of September 11, 2001, Woody and I were beginning our walk around Cupsaw Lake. The kids had gotten on the 8:30 a.m. bus to school. Woody was a firefighter and always carried a Plectron communication device and his cell phone in case an emergency occurred. As we began walking, two things occurred simultaneously, Woody's Plectron began sounding off and the firehouse alarm began ringing. Woody excused himself and jogged back to his house to get his car and go to the firehouse.

Less than a minute later my cell phone rang. It was Martha, and she was frantic.

"Jimmy, do you remember when you said something was going to crash into the World Trade Center? Oh my God, it happened!"

I asked what hit the building, and she said it was a plane. I had to digest the words for a second, and then the vision came back. I told Martha that there would be another one very soon and that she better not leave her building.

She hung up, as her colleagues were all getting a little noisy. As we now know, the second plane did hit. Martha called me back.

She was terrified. Again, I told her to stay in the building. I explained as calmly as I could that both of those buildings were going to fall down. I knew when the buildings fell the streets would not be safe. From the high floor she was on, the entire office could clearly see the buildings and the fire and smoke. I told her I was coming to New York to get her. I begged her to stay put.

Matthew was in school, and the schools in our town chose not to upset the children with news of the event. I climbed into my Jeep Liberty and prayed to God for safe travel to get Martha and bring her home.

I was not sure what to make of it all. Why did I see this tragic tableau ahead of today, and what was I supposed to do with that? I drove off and headed to I-287, to drive towards the Tappan Zee Bridge. I heard on the news that the George Washington Bridge was being closed off and figured I'd never be able to pass either of the tunnels to get into New York City.

I was listening to the news in the car as I headed south on I-287 towards Nyack, New York. Law enforcement officers were stopping cars, sending people back home. I prayed and begged God to let me get to Martha, but I couldn't get there. I had to turn around and head back and could no longer reach her by mobile phone. I drove upset.

To make things worse, this odd sedan swerved in front of me and slowed down. The driver was pissing me off, as he seemed to be intentionally blocking me. I was really upset and thought aloud that God had ignored me. I felt helpless and worried.

My hope for Martha's safety was diminishing as I could not make a phone call and had no idea what was going on. I was so worried. The news on the radio was providing updates about the response to the two planes and the evacuation process.

My knowing for sure that they were going to fall down made the news feel even worse.

I prayed aloud but stopped in frustration as the driver of the sedan was still blocking me. The sedan and its intentional swerving were becoming quite annoying. I didn't know why the driver was doing the things he or she was, but it had to be on purpose as there were only a few cars on the road.

I thought about what I should do while trying not to get further pissed at the nuisance driver in front of me. I don't tailgate as a practice and policy, but this fool was putting his car so close in front of me I was forced to tailgate. I cleared my thoughts and finally prayed.

"Father, I'm sorry for doubting you. I need to get calm, as I am worried about my wife. I have to trust you and so, I ask in Jesus name, for you to help Martha get home safe and give me guidance."

The sedan in front suddenly sped up and, as it raced away I saw the license plate clearly for the first time. It spelled out the word *skeptic*.

The exit for Airmont, New York was looming, so with nothing else to do I got off and headed to the Airmont Barber shop, where my son and I had gone a few times for haircuts. Two good barbers worked there, Sal and Giuseppe.

I parked the car and still couldn't get cell service to call Martha back. Inside the barbershop was a pay phone, so I tried that and got through.

Martha was stressed. She was saying in a panicked low voice that I had been right. Two planes had crashed into the Twin Towers. She was in a mild state of shock, but as we talked, she calmed down. I admonished her not to leave the office building. I explained the two towers were going to fall, and when they did, it would make a dangerous mess on the streets, so she should stay put. As I was saying this, a voice in my head said to tell her to follow the money. Follow the leaders.

I asked her if the CEO or the big bosses had left the building. She said they had not. I told her when they leave you can leave. I said keep your faith and follow the big money people when they leave. God will provide you a safe path home; I have no doubt of this. Then the phone died.

With nothing else to do, I sat in Sal's chair and got a haircut while watching the news. The news showed people jumping out of the building to escape the heat and flame. There in the barber shop it all seemed surreal. We couldn't imagine their terror. It had to be horrible to watch in person because it was horrible to watch on the news. We all prayed for them.

The barbershop was quiet: none of the usual camaraderie and cheer was being shared. The television station zoomed in on the people jumping out of the flames. It was heartbreaking and gut-wrenching. Then the buildings began to fall.

There is no way to express the look of horror on the faces in the barbershop or the faces of all the people filmed by reporters that were daring enough to remain close in the moments the buildings began to collapse. God bless the poor souls that died that day, all of them.

The loss was tremendous. The impact and ramifications of that horrendous day unfolded over the years that followed. It was an awful thing.

I left the barbershop after the second building came down. I didn't want to watch the news anymore. I drove home in tears, praying for those that could survive and for all those that were taken. When I got home, I tried the land line in the house and got through again.

Martha was not able to come to the phone. I hung up and got dinner prepped, and then got ready to meet the school bus, as Matthew would be headed home soon. At the bus stop with some other parents, stories were shared of people trying to get home.

The ninety-minute commute from New York City to Ringwood was taking as much as six hours for some of the commuters trying to escape from New York. The troubles created were exponential.

When Matt and I walked into the house, I was hoping Martha was still at Wunder Bank, so I tried to call again. No good. I made a snack for Matthew and helped him with his homework, waiting for any news. The phone rang and it was Martha.

She explained that the CEO and CFO, and other bosses were leaving. She mentioned that a high-level executive, the director of wellness, or something like that, had stopped in and asked Martha if she wanted to follow her to a ferry that was nearby.

She asked me what she should do. It was clear in my mind. I told her to follow the woman, to stick closely to her. The story Martha told me later was that they quickly walked to a ferry that was docked by a health or sports club within a few blocks of the building she worked in, away from Ground Zero.

Just as soon as they boarded, the ferry left the pier. When they got off the ferry, they had to walk fast and made it onto a bus that was just closing its doors to go from Hoboken to Secaucus. They got to Secaucus and ran to a train that was getting ready to leave. Again, the doors shut behind them as they boarded.

They took that train to Waldwick in Bergen County, New Jersey. The husband of the woman Martha was traveling with was a limo driver, and he met them in Waldwick. He was kind enough to drive Martha straight home to Ringwood.

Here is where I explain why I believe divine intervention happened that day. Some people took as much as eight hours to get home from the city on September 11th. Martha's commute from our house in Ringwood, New Jersey, to downtown New York City, normally took ninety minutes one way. On September 11, 2001, from the time she left Wunder Bank with the Wellness Director to the time she walked in the door, approximately forty-five minutes had lapsed. It was the fastest she ever got home, a miracle in my opinion.

Martha was the only actual witness to my having this vision and the correlated insights of the day. It may have saved her life. It was a miracle to be sure. We were terribly sad for all the people that lost loved ones and for those that perished. In the aftermath, we came together as one nation. It took a horrible tragedy to bring us together, but we were united, all walks of life, all political views, everyone.

As time passed and influences changed, too many people seem to have forgotten that feeling of unification, forgotten the patriotic tears that were shed by all of us. I pray that we never forsake those that were taken that day. If we do, we fail as a nation, and as Americans.

Not Forsaken

Fallen heroes and victims lost,

their bravery given, at terrible cost.

Let none forget this, our nation's pain,

for each was touched, by all those slain.

The Twins have fallen, many years have gone,

together we pray, their memory lives on,

those fallen heroes, and victims taken,

loved ones are here, you are not forsaken.

~ JJJ

CHAPTER 52

SUBMERGING THE CAR IN MY PAJAMAS

2000s

Subsequent to the events of 2001, I experienced other visions in some form or another, often near the beginning of the year, but not limited to any particular day or month. Some visions were related to disasters. Others were simpler, reflecting job circumstances, health issues, or deaths in the family.

My interpretation of each vision was often close but sometimes inaccurate. The inaccuracy was caused by my discernment of the images as they appeared. Each was initially defined by my own peculiar world view. After the actual event happened, the clues would fall in place and the vision would make better sense.

I believe this occasional insight was some kind of precognitive phenomenon. Perhaps it was connected to the other side of the veil, but I wasn't really sure.

My visions often occurred like daydreams. It was like being able to see something or some event, through a fog. While observing, the fog would lift here and there, and certain aspects would be made quite clear. Other visions took on physical manifestation. This occurred around Thanksgiving week in 2004.

Lisa was staying with me in my Forest Hills apartment. We had gotten engaged and planned to get married in June of 2005. That wedding event also had quirky phenomenon tied to it.

However, during this particular November evening in 2004, I had a vision that became quite physical. I was just going to sleep after a long day. Nothing was on my mind, and I was relaxed.

I recall we did go to the gym that afternoon, and I had a good workout, which was probably why I was tired enough to sleep. My sleep was restless, as usual.

I was dreaming. Something unfamiliar was going on in the dream. I was sitting in a small sedan parked by a building. The building had a low roof, probably no more than two stories tall. I realized all the buildings around me were similar in size though some were more colorful. I looked at the rearview mirror of the car. This was a very vivid dream. In the rearview, I saw a wall of water coming at the car.

Within seconds, the car was engulfed by water; and the inside was filling up. I couldn't get out. My legs became soaking wet; I felt I was going to drown.

I yelled and jumped up out of bed. My pajama legs were soaked. Lisa asked me why I was out of bed. I couldn't reply. The moment was still stuck in my head. I put the light on, and we both looked at my pants. They were stone dry. No moisture was found anywhere on my person.

I described the dream to Lisa and expressed how vivid it was. I was totally freaked out, as I never dreamt like that (although I did have one dream that was startlingly vivid and affected me even minutes after I was awake. I called that dream "The miracle of the causeway").

This event was nothing like that one. I woke with soaking wet pants on. I know the pajamas were wet, and I know they were suddenly dry. Outside of that, I had no idea why that dream occurred or what it meant, but I found out after Christmas.

On December 26, 2004, a terrible earthquake occurred near Indonesia, off the coast of Northern Sumatra. The earthquake was powerful. At 9.2, it was the third largest earthquake recorded on the seismograph, and it hit with the power of 23,000 atomic bombs going off at once. According to available data, it was scientifically called an undersea megathrust earthquake. The tsunami it caused was devastating and took the lives of approximately 228,000 people in numerous regions of the Indian Ocean.

Countries that felt the painful impact included Thailand, Indonesia, Sri Lanka, India, Malaysia, Bangladesh, and South Africa, and still others. I didn't understand the portent of the dream I had. If I had, how would I tell people that something awful was about to happen. Who would believe me?

Would anyone have believed me if I told them I saw big flying saucers? In January of 2005, I had another vision.

It was a powerful and utterly confusing vision. I was washing dishes in my Forest Hills apartment when I had a profound image pop into my head. It was like a collage of photos and some video. I saw people gathered in various places, cities, and even on beaches. They were looking up in the air, and their faces held sheer terror.

As they were looking skyward, I looked up and saw this giant white flying saucer, then two more. It was scary as heck because it looked so real. I was afraid we were about to get invaded or something like that.

It was a swirling, misty spaceship, bigger than most towns. The whole vision took a few seconds and then passed. What the heck was that, I thought! I walked over to the apartment terrace and looked out over the neighboring schoolyard and down Queen's Boulevard. I looked up into the sky. There were some puffy clouds, a lot of blue, a few birds flying about in the cold air, but no flying saucer of any kind. I didn't know what to make of it.

I told Lisa about the vision, and we wrote it down in the notebook she suggested I start using. I referred to it as the Book of Weird.

Later that year, in August, we were watching the news in the living room of our new home. People were boarding up their homes and preparing to evacuate parts of Louisiana and other Gulf Coast areas as a big hurricane was coming, a potential category 5 named Katrina.

More than one person interviewed by news reporters looked up at the sky with fear on their faces. They knew something bad was coming. During the news report, I left the room, got something to drink, and walked back into the living room. I gasped when I saw what was on the television screen.

"Lisa the big flying saucer I saw, that's it."

I took a drink and drew a deep breath. "That is the big, white, misty, and very scary flying saucer I saw in the vision!"

Lisa agreed. We grabbed the book of weird and read the notes. The description was accurate to the point of amazement. On the television, was a radar shot of the biggest storm ever seen in years, Hurricane Katrina.

The swirling white cloud that was depicted via radar looked enormous and did look like a great big flying saucer.

We were both stunned by the revelation. Then we both prayed for the people that this monster would fall upon. Two more Category 5 hurricanes formed in 2005, Rita and Wilma. I remember asking the question,

"Why am I getting this information, if it cannot be used for any good?"

I realize now that I'm not meant to know why. So, yes, I get messages, but not all of them can be delivered.

CHAPTER 53
THE MIRACLE OF THE CAUSEWAY

2000s

Some visions did get delivered, but one of the most important in my life was the vision of Lisa and the miracle of the causeway. I believe Lisa and I were spiritually introduced. During the months I lived in my own guest room while married to my son's mother, I felt terribly lonely and had begun to despair.

It was clear that Martha and I would no longer remain married. Things had to change, but I was not sure how to handle it all. I couldn't see my way around the sadness I felt, or the lingering feeling of dread regarding the changes that were forthcoming. I was depressed. During the long months of my living in the guest room, I wandered around Cupsaw Lake, sometimes in the rain, to hide my tears. I'm no saint, but I am human, and the thought of having a broken family, of losing time with my son, was just heart wrenching. I spent a lot of time praying. I asked the Lord for guidance. I didn't want to be alone but didn't know what steps to take.

Based on the changes we had been through, and the time we spent apart (for over a year, albeit in the same house), it was clearly over for Martha and me. She was apparently moving on and made it known. I was lost.

I prayed and asked my Heavenly Father if it was meant for me to be alone, to be without hearth and home. I was confused because there had been a flag with a red cardinal across the street from the house we bought.

You see, almost twenty years earlier the little voice said that I'd know I was home because the Christmas bird would be out front. The Christmas bird for me was a red cardinal.

One night in particular, a few days after a really upsetting Halloween party, I fell asleep with a very heavy heart. I prayed my way to sleep, but it took a while.

Finally, I slept, and I dreamt. In the dream, I came upon a causeway strewn with rock. It was high in the air, nestled between two mountains.

On one side of the causeway that I stood upon was a park or forested area, with a stream, healthy trees, and beautiful birds flittering about. On the other side was just stone.

Music was playing the whole time. It was unearthly, angelic, and impossible not to be moved by. I had no idea where the music was coming from. On the other end of the bridge was a tall, regal woman dressed in blue. Her colors were vibrant. Her face shone like sunlight. She smiled at me when She caught my eyes fixed upon Her face.

I realized that I was in the presence of the Blessed Mother or at least that was what I believed and still do.

The Blessed Mother glanced down, and I followed Her gaze to the person kneeling at Her side. Her right hand rested upon that person's head. I heard and felt the angelic music playing all through me.

As I watched, the person kneeling changed in form many times. It was a young woman, at once a red head, then blonde, then brunette, then a Nubian noblewoman, then a starry-eyed Latina, then a Jamaican with deep brown eyes, then a light brown-haired woman with green eyes. It went on for a time like this, and I cannot account for how long.

The transformations finally stopped, and the last visage was a young Asian princess, almost androgynous in form, as she appeared to be young, thin, and delicate.

I looked up at the Holy Mother, in time to see Her push the young lady towards me. This svelte Asian visage leapt at me and, as she did, she transformed into what I thought was a great wolf with a huge maw and her teeth ripped into my core.

No pain was felt. Instead, a feeling of warmth flowed: a wonderful tingling, which filled me to such an extreme that I bolted upright in my bed and shook with amazement.

The hair on my neck, arms, and legs stood straight up. The tingling was still there.

More amazing, the music was still playing, incredibly clear, and hypnotically beautiful. I shed tears out of joy and stumbled to the bathroom. I relieved myself and washed my face, and the whole time the music kept playing.

I couldn't stop crying and smiling, and I knew the dreary weight of sadness had been removed. The music kept playing for a good five minutes as I walked around the basement area of the house. I was absolutely amazed. I had no idea what it all meant, but the memory was so vivid that I believed it was not a dream, but a vision given to me with all the kindness that our loving Blessed Mother has in Her heart. Holy Mother has had such impact on my life, and my own mother loved Her dearly.

What could it all mean, I wondered? Where did that music come from? It was haunting and, although I tried to hold it, the sound of it lingered a while longer, then faded, away from my hearing and out of my thoughts.

I knew there had been some music playing, but after an hour or so, I couldn't recall the sound of it. I ultimately stopped sitting there all googly eyed and moved on with my day.

I had a job interview, and if I landed the job, it would be the first full-time job in a while, thanks to those icy stairs years earlier. I was again my optimistic self, and the world filled my heart with confidence.

I spent the next six or so weeks job hunting and processing the whole divorce thing as it unfolded. Having not worked for so many years, it was a painstaking process of attempt, reject, attempt again.

While this part of my life was proceeding along, my feeling of being lost reared itself up every so often, but faith held me up. I wasn't alone in the house; I had my son there, but he was clearly filled with anxiety over the forthcoming changes.

We tried to discuss it with him together, and I think that helped. Of course, Martha was there in the house, but when she was upstairs, it was not an altogether friendly exchange. We were both running out of patience with the circumstances.

CHAPTER 54

THE ROOM WAS FULL OF PEOPLE

2000s

Once again it sucked to be me. It hit me hard so I prayed. I felt alone and miserable and I didn't like the feeling. I felt trapped in my own life, down in the basement of my own home. Work was trickling in. Some of the work I did have involved doing a website for the Borough of Ringwood. I also sent out a whole lot of resumes. Job hunting is a full-time job.

Weeks passed, and it was close to Thanksgiving. One afternoon I was feeling pretty low. Matthew had gone to karate with his mother. I was looking at the computer screen and my reflection, feeling alone. I prayed again and asked not to be left alone and to help me find peace. I hadn't thought much about that vision, the one with the Blessed Mother, but I did at that moment. On the computer screen, an email popped up.

It was a dating service advertisement for Matchmaker.com. I deleted it and kept working. After a while, I felt that tingling feeling come upon me - the warmth and didn't know why. I prayed and thanked God and Jesus for the kindness. The computer popped again with another email from Matchmaker.com.

I looked at it for a while. I knew I didn't want to get involved with any of the single moms in town, and I was leery of dating at all, especially after the recent turn of events. It had been over fourteen years since I dated. In my head, I prayed and said okay, if this is Your answer, I will give it a try. I registered and created a profile. I figured it wouldn't matter to Martha, since we had basically been apart for nearly two years by then. She was clearly moving on, therefore, I decided to try the dating web service. I gave it a week or so but lost interest and focused on job hunting.

On Thanksgiving, Martha wanted to have a dinner in the house with a specific guest. I put my foot down and said no. It would be just the three of us, and we were going out for dinner. I took us to Boston Market. Matt and I liked the food, but it was weird being the only diners in the restaurant. That was our last Thanksgiving together.

In January, I finally landed a job working for a reputable publishing company, American Lawyer Media (ALM). My start date as an account executive was scheduled for Valentine's Day of 2003, which was a Friday. I recall it was a snowy day when I first showed my face at ALM. Starting on a Friday made sense, in order to get through the basic orientation and information process, before going strong in advertising sales the following week. I was thrilled that I'd be staring a new job in a field where I once excelled. The apartment situation was still a problem, so I had to commute from Ringwood for a while.

The Saturday after I started at ALM, Matthew and I climbed up the snowy sides of Ringwood State Park during an actual snowstorm. We wanted to do something brave and adventurous that day, and we did. We were the only hikers on the high trails. In the park, we saw some cross-country skiers. We spoke to them for a little bit, and they wished us luck. We climbed all the way up to the top of the trail and had a picnic lunch in the snow. While there we saw an Eagle flying near us - it was awesome. It flew really close to us. We took a picture together with our portable camera. Today that's called a selfie.

That picture holds great meaning for me, and I believe for Matthew, too. We didn't know how much we'd have to go through in the coming months and years, but that day showed us we could overcome any obstacle or difficulty and make a picnic out of it.

When I started the job, I kept up the apartment hunt at the same time. My commute from Ringwood, New Jersey to Park Avenue South, New York City, was tough and getting tougher.

From around March 8 thru March 11, 2003, I attended a conference in Washington, DC with the ALM advertising team.

The conference was the Society for Human Resource Management (SHRM) Annual Employment Law and Legislative Conference. The hotel I stayed in was the historic Mayflower, on Connecticut Avenue. It was a beautiful hotel and filled with grand statehood and history and had a gorgeous lobby.

During the few days I was there, I manned the ALM booth, met with potential advertisers, and enjoyed some good company and good food. It was a pleasant first conference experience. Not my first ever, just my first since going back to work.

My hotel room was pretty big. It had a king-sized bed, nice bathroom, and faced Connecticut Avenue. Outside the window, closer to the floor below was a curved streetlight. On one particular night, I came back into the room and found it pretty dark. I glanced outside and saw that the streetlight was out. No worries. I put on lamps, took a hot shower, and read some material for a while. I called and spoke to Matthew. All in all, things were quiet.

As is my habit, I took a book into the bathroom to read before sleeping. I left one lamp on by the bed. Not long after, I washed my hands, brushed my teeth, and went to bed. I lay down on the bed and intertwined my fingers behind my head.

I said a little prayer of thanks and started to get comfy. Then I noticed something odd. Someone was lying next to me. From my right-side periphery, I saw the depression of a head in the pillow, as well as a body shape on the blankets.

My hair stood up.

Slowly, with more courage than I thought I had, I sat up and looked around the room. It was then that I realized I was not alone at all. There were over a dozen people of all walks standing around the room, looking at me.

My reaction was immediate. I knelt down by the bed and prayed. I asked my Heavenly Father to please help the souls in the room to find their way home, back to His love and Light. I prayed for mercy for them and asked for guidance. I closed the prayer in Jesus name and said Amen.

The moment I said Amen, the corner window lit up. I think the streetlight came on. I looked at it, and I spoke to the people in the room.

"That is where you all need to go. That is the way home, and I promise you in Jesus name, that you will find peace and reunite with your loved ones, once you cross. Please go into the light, the one in the window. God bless you all."

One by one, they walked up and into the light as it streamed through the window. The last to go was the man on my bed. He smiled and although he was gossamer, he impressed me as a gentleman. He went into the light, and the room seemed to dim. I laid down on the bed and fell immediately to sleep.

It was one of the most profoundly peaceful sleeps I ever had. The next day we came back home to New York. I took that Thursday off to go look at apartments, as I was still commuting from Ringwood and living downstairs.

I was with ALM for a little over a year. The people I worked with were very nice, including my immediate boss, Mrs. Corrigan, and my colleagues Martin, Isabelle, Michelle, Muhammed, and the others who shared the office. They were key witnesses to my crazy sense of humor and lack of sainthood. I hope I made them smile and laugh once in a while and maybe even inspired them a bit.

While apartment hunting, I looked in on Matchmaker.com again. At first, I looked in New Jersey, for an apartment and for companionship. Not much there for me. I realized I was a native New Yorker, so I changed the profile to the New York City area on both counts. A few weeks before the conference in Washington D.C., I tried Matchmaker.com again. The way Matchmaker.com worked, you input data about yourself, added a picture, and then started a search.

The site populated results that were based on a percentage of match to the information you had in your profile. The first page of results had 60% matches, nothing higher. Nobody there caught my attention, and some looked too high maintenance for my taste. I clicked the next page, also full of 60% matches. One person caught my attention, and in early February we began to communicate. I needed her advice.

CHAPTER 55
THAT'S WHAT STOCKY MEANS

2000s

The person that caught my attention was a pretty Asian woman. Her name on Matchmaker.com was Suki.

What caught my eye was that hers was the only picture that had an angry person in it. I was curious: why would someone post an angry-looking picture, even if she was cute. I read her profile information. Apparently, she had dated a number of people via the online dating service, was really fed up, and filled with disappointment.

One of her comments was that if a person wanted to learn the truth about online dating they should write her. I did. I told her I hadn't dated in over fourteen years and asked what kind of stuff to look out for.

In reply she explained that a lot of people put pictures up that were taken over ten or twenty years prior. She said some folks don't tell the truth about their marital status (whether they have kids), if they are sick, or just out of jail. She kinda freaked me out. Funny thing though, the dialog between us was witty. I think we were both cracking up, on our respective ends of the internet, sitting at our keyboards.

Weeks passed and we would occasionally write each other, sometimes just to ask how things were. We had a good pen-pal thing going.

Before going to conference, I told Suki that I had an appointment to see an apartment not far from her job in Westchester. I explained I was looking to improve my commute to Manhattan, and the apartment happened to be near a Metro North train line. Suki sent me her phone number and said she was at the desk in case I wanted to call and talk. To this day, she swears that she hit the send button and her phone rang simultaneously. Not true! I was just sitting at the desk that afternoon and I dial really fast by sheer habit.

We discussed meeting for lunch on March 13th, the day I was going to see the Westchester apartment. I was scheduled to visit two places that day, one in the morning and one later in the afternoon. I asked Suki if her picture was accurate, and if she was always as grumpy as the picture looked. She laughed. She asked me what I actually looked like. I explained that my picture was recent, that I was not too tall, and that I was stocky. She asked me what stocky meant. I tried to explain.

Then she said,

"Are you fat?"

I laughed. I said I don't think of myself as fat, just kind of big. Suki had no idea what stocky meant, as it wasn't part of her cultural norm. We agreed to meet, talked a little more, and then hung up to continue our respective workdays.

I was interested in meeting her, especially to hear more of the stories she had shared.

Knowing we'd just be back from the DC conference I asked my boss in advance for the day off in order to go see the apartments. It was okay, as I had a couple of days available to use as needed. After the first apartment viewing, Suki and I met for the first time. It was cold out, and I wore a thick leather jacket. I waited in the parking lot at Gannett Publishing in White Plains where Suki worked.

I saw her walking towards me in a parka jacket, the hood framing her cute little face. She looked way too young. I was a nervous wreck. We greeted each other. Her eyes slowly roamed across from shoulder to shoulder and she said,

"So that's what stocky means."

I chuckled. Then I asked her to do me a huge favor. I said,

"Before you get in my car and we go to lunch, could you please show me your driver's license?"

Suki was amused and asked why. I told her she looked way too young for me to have lunch with. I was already forty-two and was not about to go to lunch with an eighteen-year-old.

She laughed hard at that and opened her purse to fish out her license. I was dumbstruck. Suki was thirty-seven years old. My jaw slacked, and I asked how did she look so young. She said it was a good diet. I kidded around and said I'm going to have to eat the food you do.

Her driver's license had the name Lisa. She explained that she was born in New York City, her birth name was Lisa, and that Suki was her Chinese name. She was a native New Yorker of Chinese American descent. We went to lunch, both very nervous. She barely spoke two words, and I couldn't stop talking a mile a minute.

While eating we touched hands for the first time. Lisa said she felt a shock, a warm tingly feeling. She mentioned it but had no idea what it meant.

Lisa said she was using the name Suki for MatchMaker.com, and that meeting me was the very last time she would meet anyone from an online dating service.

She was only trying to find a date for her little sister's wedding in the coming summer. I smiled and hoped at the moment that it would be me she took to the wedding. She reiterated that this was the end of the line for her with online dating, and if this date with me didn't work, it was over in general.

She was ready to go full-on spinster. I was the last guy she would ever date from an online service. Funny thing, Lisa was the first woman I dated from an online service. I took her back to her office building after lunch and we shook gloves. Like I said, it was cold out.

Both of the Westchester apartments I looked at turned out to be too expensive or just too small, so it was a no-go. I started thinking about the possibility of commuting to my job from near the Ringwood house, and as such, staying put in New Jersey. The thought was daunting, mostly due to concerns about my lower back and how my neck had begun troubling me.

On a brighter note, Lisa and I decided to go out on a real date the following Saturday night, an auspicious night indeed.

CHAPTER 56
FUN FILLED TIME IN THE RECOVERY ROOM

2000s

On that Saturday night, I offered to drive to Brooklyn to pick Lisa up at her apartment. She lived in my old stomping grounds, Carroll Gardens. She suggested we dine in the area and that I find parking before getting her.

Earlier that Saturday, Matthew and I made plans for Sunday morning to have breakfast together, then later go to the movies to see Jet Li, and eat at Johnny Rockets.

I promised him I'd be there. I never broke any promises to my son. I don't like to break promises in general.

I drove to Brooklyn and picked Lisa up at her place. We had a really nice night and a great dinner at a Mediterranean place. I was amazed as to how gentrified Smith Street had become. At dinner, we touched hands and this time I felt the shock of warmth and tingling energy. I didn't know what it meant either. Later, we had much fun at a cool coffee shop where we bopped our heads to 80s music.

We walked around the neighborhood, looking at all the new restaurants, coffee shops, and pubs that had opened up, dappling Smith Street with charm from 3rd Street to Atlantic Avenue. It was really an impressive change, and to think I had only been gone from the neighborhood for a few years. I took her back home later on, and we spent time talking in her studio apartment.

Something amazing happened to me while I was with Lisa. During every moment I spent with her, I felt peace. I experienced such a calming sensation that it made me so want to stay with her. We both wanted that, I think. However, I had promised Matthew that I'd be there in the morning when he woke up.

Lisa and I hugged at the downstairs door and I left. While driving home I heard a song on the radio, "If You're Not the One" by Daniel Bedingfield. The words haunted me and made me miss Lisa terribly, so I pulled over on Route 208 and called Lisa to tell her I was sorry that I had to leave. She sounded disappointed. I would never have disappointed her, but I had promised my son, and that promise could not be broken.

We didn't see each other again for a long time. During that gap, I was apartment hunting and trying to find my balance with work, parenthood, and physical issues. Matthew and I had a great time the next day. We roamed the huge Palisades Center Mall in Nyack, NY, and had a lot of fun.

We both loved Jet Li movies, and *Cradle to the Grave* was still playing there. That night I went to sleep feeling enthusiastic that things would work out, and life would end up okay.

My enthusiasm in life ran into an awful obstacle two days later, as quite suddenly the pain in my neck and shoulders could no longer be tolerated. Shocking discomfort ran like a derailed train along my neck, shoulders and down my upper spine. My hands were going numb.

This was horrifying, as I was only weeks into my new job and that after such a long period of unemployment due to spinal injuries. The cause of this newfound difficulty was my C-5 vertebra, which had cracked in half nine years earlier during the incident that damaged my lower spine.

I was doing fine for all that time, but in the last few months (perhaps due to my return to karate training), my hands had begun to feel pins and needles, or just go numb, and excruciating pain sporadically radiated down my neck and into my shoulders. Suddenly, it was all just awful.

In case you're wondering why it took nine years for these problems to manifest with a cracked cervical vertebra, it was all postponed by its downstairs neighbor. The C-6, which lives below the C-5, had a large bone spur on it which tilted upwards like a slanted diving board and that spur had held the cracked C-5 in place for years. Karate and yard work loosened it up and let if pinch a nerve.

On March 29, not quite through month two of my ALM employment, I was scheduled for neurosurgery to repair the broken C-5. It was Dr. John Mangiardi, an amazing neurosurgeon, that performed the surgery at Lenox Hill Hospital in New York City. My great friend Woody drove me from Ringwood all the way to Lenox Hill that morning, God bless him. He's a stand-up guy, through and through.

Dr. Mangiardi put a cadaver bone in place where the fractured vertebrae had been removed and fused it with some titanium and screws. He also trimmed the bone spur off C-6. I was in the hospital for only one night. I had a good rapport with Dr. Mangiardi. We laughed at each other's stories.

He knew I was karateka and told me he was into Judo for many years. He warned me not to do combat sports anymore. He gave me other helpful advice, which I still adhere to. After the surgery, I was taken to the recovery room.

Dr. Mangiardi came to see me when I awoke. He had a great sense of humor, and he proved that I did, too.

He said that the surgery was a success. He explained a small problem occurred after the surgery, as the orderly took me by mistake into another operating room. I shrugged and nodded, kind of asking what happened. He said,

"Well, you've had a sex change."

I grabbed at my nether region, only to confirm the plumbing was still there, and we both cracked up laughing. It was tough to laugh, and it hurt like hell, but it was really a funny joke and I love humor.

I stayed in touch with Dr. Mangiardi for a few years and mentioned him in a magazine article I published with the now defunct *Men's Edge Magazine*.

I think it was Woody that came and drove me home, but I cannot remember the going-home event, because the pain meds affected me tremendously. I had only a couple of days off from work and stayed by myself in the basement guestroom while I healed.

I pushed myself and fought to keep my new job. It was a lot to go through: pain, surgery; the apartment hunt; the inevitable move; a new job, and the heartbreak of not being able to take my son with me.

I found myself at another low point. Although down, I clung tightly to my faith. A spark of hope was burning bright at the other end of a causeway. Before I went into the hospital for surgery, a card came to me at work from Lisa.

She wrote something sweet. She promised to focus all her energy on my neck and my healing and asked me to promise the same. She also said she would be there for me and would wait as long as it took to see me again. I did as she asked, concentrating good energy on my neck, and I prayed all the way there.

I still have her card. It meant a lot to me, and Lisa meant a lot to me. She still does and always will. That vision on the causeway with the Blessed Mother was growing clearer. After the surgery, I finally had to move thanks to the courts. The courts advised that I was not fiscally sound enough to take over the mortgage on the house. While looking for a place to live, I stayed for a little bit with my sisters.

Then Lisa moved out of her studio apartment and back in with her parents. She was planning on renting her place out, because she lost her job at Gannet in Westchester. I asked her if I could rent the apartment for a few weeks, while I looked for a place of my own.

She agreed but wouldn't take any rent from me. Eventually, Matt and I found a place, and I moved to Forest Hills, Queens, to live in "7th Heaven". The apartment number was 7H in one of the famous Parker Towers.

Matthew was going on ten years old, which was still too young to understand all that was going on between his parents. It was a painful time, but we adjusted, Matt and I, as best as we could.

I was happy to have a shorter commute to ALM but really sad about being away from my son. I was glad that Matthew picked the place out with me; he had his own room in the apartment. Funny thing: to get to 7H we had to cross over a stone causeway.

We made it as much fun as we could whenever he was with me. Days passed, and then weeks. We were approaching the summer, and I was getting used to apartment life, building rituals, like going to the gym, and eating at certain restaurants.

Each day I awoke, I knelt by the bed and thanked God for His help getting me as far as I had gotten and through all the difficulties that I had faced. Somehow, I was able to keep the new job with ALM, in spite of all the things I endured. And, yes, Lisa and I grew closer.

CHAPTER 57

OUR SPOOKY NEW ENGLAND ADVENTURE

2000s

Lisa and I planned a road trip together, to celebrate our birthdays, which were about a week apart. The plan was to drive to Maine and go looking for good lobsters and awesome chowders, as Lisa had never been to Maine before.

As Lisa and I got to know each other, I shared with her some of the weird and quirky experiences I had.

I told her about Joe on the train, Rick (the father of Matthew's babysitter Dana), and about Charlie in Coney Island.

I also told her about the voice and the visits, like the night I heard Nephi one, seven. She was curious about it all, but explained she never had any supernatural experiences in her life. She did tell me something interesting though. She said when she was in her twenties a gypsy seer told her she'd meet a man in later years, and he would have light eyes and would not be too tall. The fortune teller also said that the man would have a son. Interesting, huh?

During the first week of June 2004, we headed out on the road to New England, driving along in my 2002 Mazda Tribute. The idea was to have some fun with food stops and explore history on the New England coast. We were headed to Ogunquit, where once in the 1980s I enjoyed an amazing New England clam chowder and a delicious breakfast called a Bucksport Pie. I wasn't sure of the pie's real name, but the memory of enjoying it was with me.

On the journey, we first stopped at a hotel near the Mohegan Sun Casino in Connecticut.

The place we stayed in had a huge hot tub in the room. The two of us thought that might be romantic. We got into the tub later on and both of us just passed out from the heat. Not romantic at all. We woke up, dressed, and went to the casino to seek adventure.

It was Lisa's birthday, and so we celebrated. In the Mohegan Sun, we had dinner in one of the restaurants, and afterward we found a bar to have some drinks. A group of nice people were at the bar, and they bought us Birthday Cake shots.

A whole bunch of folks sang "Happy Birthday" to Lisa. We had a really nice night, good food, fun, dancing, and lots of laughs. We were beat when we got back to the hotel, so we took showers and went right to sleep.

The next day we drove through parts of Rhode Island, including Middletown, Portsmouth, and Jamestown. We looked in awe at some of the majestic coastal homes.

We stopped for a bit and stared out over the Atlantic, mesmerized by the haunting waves that rolled to and fro. The Atlantic's unknowable reach over the horizon was captivating. We had no plan to stay in Rhode Island, so we headed up the coast to Maine, slowly inching along as we stopped to peek at this curiosity or that.

In about three hours, we eventually arrived in Ogunquit at the hotel where we had reservations. I believe it was called the Norseman, which I found cute due to my last name being Scandinavian.

We unpacked and went out to find some place to eat and had some pretty decent New England clam chowder soup and crab cakes at a shack on a nearby dock. I promised Lisa the next day we'd get lobster for dinner. We were pretty tired that night, and again, hit the hay and fell straight to sleep. The next day things got strange, but at the time, we didn't realize just how strange things. We drove around for the day, shopping and finding points of interest. We made an excursion up Route 1 to Freeport and scoured through the LL Bean headquarters store. I think we bought some plaid stuff, pajamas and sweatshirts.

On our way back to our hotel, we ended up in a shoe store. It was late in the afternoon, and I bought a nice pair of golf cleats for cheap. We were starving. I asked the shopkeeper for suggestions on finding a good lobster dinner.

He said go back a little way north to the town of Saco and try the Cascades restaurant. We both recognized the name because we had passed it twice, once on the way to LL Bean and again while driving back to Ogunquit. We thanked him and left.

We pulled into the Cascades parking lot and took in the breadth of the building. It was once a beautiful hotel and restaurant but now looked a bit worn down.

Being hungry, we decided to give it a try, especially as it advertised on the sign 2 one-pound lobsters for $11.99. Seemed like a fair deal, provided the lobster was fresh, and the other food was okay, too. We entered the restaurant. There was no wait, and we were shown to a table. It was busy but not crowded.

The patrons and staff were kind of subdued, as the place felt awkwardly quiet and slightly off, so to speak.

The menus were interesting. They had a newspaper style to them and presented a history of the place on one side. The place was a landmark of sorts, originally opened in 1929.

Noted in the menu was a bit of weird information about a curse on the Saco River, which fed the Cascade Waterfall located on the rear of restaurant's property. The story as stated on the menu was about a family of Native Americans.

Just like a lot of legends and myths, any stories passed down through word of mouth, scribbled notes, and over time, information tends to change, so the legend of the Saco River has multiple versions. One variation that was written into the menu said that a cruel event took place near Limington, Maine, and the victim was a chief's daughter.

She was supposedly kidnapped by three white settlers, who carried her off in a canoe and raped her. The girl supposedly either fell out of the boat, or was thrown out, into the infamous "Limington Rips," and was later found dead.

Her father the chief was notably a man of mystic abilities, perhaps he was a tribal shaman. In vengeful anger, he placed a curse on the Saco River and with it, he promised that every year thereafter three people would drown in the river (New England.com, Hansen, 2018).

The menu held more important things for us, such as the price of soup and lobster. Personally, I don't like lobster, but Lisa wanted to have some, so we ordered it for her. I think I ordered a sandwich.

We both decided to wash up before the food came and took turns going to the washroom. That was the first weird experience of the trip.

The rest rooms were a long walk from the dining area, down a dark hallway, past the old hotel desk area. It was as if the hallway itself felt kind of brooding. The whole way there and back, I felt goosebumps, as if I was being watched or followed. I did my business quickly, washed my hands, and returned.

Then Lisa took her turn at the washroom. When she got back, which was pretty darn quick, she shared a story with me of the very same creepy experience, even though I never mentioned any of what I felt or experienced. Both of us had the heebie-jeebies. Our drinks arrived, and the clam chowder was right behind. We ate quietly.

When the waitress came to collect the appetizer and soup bowls and ask if we'd like another beverage, we engaged her in conversation. Lisa and I were both curious about the hotel and if it had any weird history. The server did say the place gave her the creeps every so often and some parts of the restaurant, especially upstairs, she did not want to visit. We asked her about the waterfalls in the back of the property.

She explained it was a hike of about ten minutes or so and that some people did go back there to take pictures, or just look. She made sure to tell us that she never once went back there, and definitely never would. She didn't say.

Our entrée's came and the waitress hurried off, apparently not wanting to engage us in any more conversation. We ate quietly. The food was okay - not great - but okay. Lisa seemed to enjoy her lobsters, but she said they did not taste too fresh. Perhaps they were in a tank for a while longer than they should have been, but boiling water should kill germs, so she ate them.

After we finished, we had coffee and split a dessert. We paid the bill and then went out the back door to see the forested area and find the path that led to the waterfalls. It would start to get dark in an hour or less, so we didn't have too much time. We started along the trail and we came to an area with a bunch of little cottages that appeared to be in disrepair. Something caused my spider-senses to go off on full-alarm mode. I suddenly found myself moving my wallet and cash to a front pocket with my keys and covering them with my handkerchief.

Lisa asked me what I was doing. I told her I felt that someone was watching us, and it was a strong enough feeling that the hair on my nape rose. She asked if we should just leave, but I was firm in my belief that no stalker in the woods would be able to overcome or surprise me and catch me unawares.

My whole life had been filled with sporadic intuitions that when I listened, proved to be right on point. We hiked along the trail passing the creepy old cottages.

On the way, we caught up with a father and daughter that were also going to see the falls.

The four of us came upon the waterfall together. We let them take pictures first, and then we took some. I hopped over a runoff spot and stood pretty close to the waterfall, and Lisa took a couple of pictures. Dusk was upon us, so I suggested using the flash. Lisa took two or three pictures with the "flash on", and then some with the "flash off". I took some photos of her, and we attempted what is now called *a selfie*. We saw that daylight was diffusing and decided to head back.

We couldn't have been more than three minutes behind the father and daughter that were with us, but they were out of sight. We never saw them again, not even in the restaurant parking lot. Once there, I took a few pictures of the building.

The old hotel was situated above the restaurant, and the visible second floor may have held some guest rooms. We weren't sure. We drove away, and both of us felt relieved. Lisa asked me again about what I was feeling. I told her I felt as though someone or something was following us in the woods, and they were watching us when we left.

We drove back to our hotel in Ogunquit. The weather was crazy for June.

It was cold out, and a dense fog was rolling in. We took turns showering and getting ready for bed. Both of us had a bad stomach after the food we ate, but we made some hot tea and it helped.

Lisa awoke in the middle of the night from a bad dream. She was kicking and carrying on when she awoke, so I held her. She had to get off the bed and walk around for a minute. She explained the dream she was having. In it, there were strangers and a gloom. Then, she was in a space that felt like water but made no sense. She saw beads of light-colored blue-green glass coming down on her, like beads of water hitting her face. They were going straight into her nose and mouth. She was struggling, couldn't breathe, and realized she was drowning in the beads. She woke up, fighting for her life. She felt that the air in the room was suffocating, so we opened the door and stood on the deck outside.

It was eerily foggy out there. We went back in, and she restated the dream experience. What bothered her most was not knowing why she would dream something so horrible in the first place and that it felt very real.

We fell asleep for a few hours, then got up, packed our bags, and went for a walk on the beach. It was so cold we needed coats. The fog was slowly dissipating, and the diffused light from the east was genuinely surreal. We headed back home and talked a little bit about the incidents we had: the dream, the creepy restaurant, and the weird feeling by those little cottages.

We stopped in Connecticut at a shopping outlet, spent a few hours shopping about, and went back to the car with little to show for it. The trip had been okay, but the tail end of it left us both a little disconcerted.

CHAPTER 58
I DIDN'T THINK THEY COULD DO THAT

2000s

We made our way back to Queens, stopping for gas and a bite to eat along the way. We got back to the apartment complex and trudged from garage to apartment with bags in tow. The next day was a Sunday, so we had time for laundry. Laundry was fun for us, because we did our laundry next to a bar where we could share a beer and play scrabble on our little portable game set.

We hadn't uploaded the vacation images from the camera as of yet, and so I promised we would look at them after the laundry was done. When we got back, I turned on my trusty HP and uploaded the photos from the camera to the desktop computer.

The photos proved to be disturbing. Initially, I didn't think anything of what I was seeing, and then I saw something quirky in the photos taken by the Cascades waterfall. The lighting of certain images was peculiar.

The pictures with the "flash on" were obvious. The pictures that must have had the "flash off" were weird, in that they were super-bright - almost like someone shot them with a powerful floodlight to capture the entire scene with great clarity.

There were other pictures still uploading from camera to computer, like the ones we took at LL Bean, and the pics in the fog on the beach.

When all were uploaded, I took a break and went to the kitchen to eat supper with Lisa. The sun was still out, and the sunset in view from the living room terrace of 7H was not bad. Not the mountains and ocean splendor you might see when away from the urban zone but a nice changing of colors over the horizon, framed on the bottom by city buildings with Manhattan in the periphery.

It was a nice sunset. I helped with the dishes, and Lisa started doing something with the dry clothes we brought back from the laundry. When I was done in the kitchen, I sat down at the desk, woke the PC, and started looking at the photos more carefully.

Something seemed off. The hairs on my neck and arms stood straight out. In the images from the front of the hotel, there on the second floor leering out of a window on the right of center was the Grim Reaper. I was looking at a clear though somewhat spectral image of a skeletal being with a wicket grin and holding what looked like a scythe. It had to be a trick of the light, so I zoomed in.

Holy crap, I thought. That was no illusion or trick of light! There was a menacing face and body, staring straight at us while we took pictures of the hotel. I was creeped out to say the least. Then, I started to go through the other images. Things got worse.

In the photos with the waterfalls I saw something ghastly. Not something - more like some<u>things</u>. There were faces leering, grinning or just plain staring insanely. One looked like a human jackal; another had a distorted skeleton face. One was a straight-out screaming demon. I was mesmerized and terrified. What was I looking at?

As I continued to review the photos, another image popped into clear view. It was the face of a man jutting out of the waterfall, screaming in anguish. Although there is no sound in photos, the look on his face was unmistakable. This was a soul being tortured, and his pain was quite apparent. I was horrified just looking at his face.

I zoomed in to try to eliminate the image as just some splashing of water mixed with a trick of the light. It was no trick: this was the soul of a man in torment.

I was unable to stop staring at him, and it must have been minutes that I sat there staring at the screen.

I went back through the photos a few more times. At least five of them from the waterfalls and the hotel were spiritually perverse and epically vivid.

The images were so clear and so haunting that I became worried. I was hoping that none of this potential hate and terror followed us back here to Queens. Lisa had not seen any of this yet.

I called her over to look at the pics but said nothing. I was hoping that it might have been me imagining things. After a few minutes, she began to cry, and she clung to me. She asked me what had happened, how was this possible? I didn't have an answer. Like me, Lisa was mesmerized. The thing that had her attention was the face of the screaming demon. It had a mouth full of teeth, large weird black eyes, and huge pointed ears. It appeared to be screaming or raging at the top of its lungs. Then, she saw the anguished man. That scared the heck out of her.

"What is happening to that man?" she asked innocently.

I had no answer other than to say he appeared to be getting tormented. We zoomed in and stared at the terrifyingly pitiful face. Lastly, we looked again at the front of the hotel. Neither of us could believe the clarity of the skeletal monstrosity that was obviously looking right at us as we photographed the place. We sat in terrified captivation looking at it. The fascination people have with things that scare them is really peculiar but, strangely, kind of normal. After a few minutes, Lisa could not look anymore. I saved all the images to the computer and to a backup CD Rom. I also saved them to a backup hard drive that I installed as secondary storage in the PC. The photos were hard to get out of mind. We prayed and purposely watched some comedy shows on television to distract our thoughts.

A couple of days later Matt was home with us in Queens and his uncle Tito came to visit. We all went out for some food and fun. While eating, we discussed with Matt and Tito the images we saw. At the time, Matt was almost eleven, so I was concerned about him seeing these things, they were pretty disturbing. He promised that he would be fine, especially since we were all together.

I showed them the images. It took a while to overcome the shock of what they were looking at. Then, we reviewed the images with a critical eye, to see if this was a trick of light or just a weird camera glitch. Nothing doing. This was captured evil.

My brother-in-law Joel called to say hello while the boys and I were discussing the strange faces and overall eeriness of the event. I put Joel and Lisa's big sister Sandi on speaker, and we all talked about the whole crazy experience.

To make sense of the discussion, I emailed Joel and Sandi the most frightening images from the collection of photos, about five of them. In a few seconds, they began looking at the pictures. Sandi was skeptical, but then she looked at the screaming demon with the weird bat ears and exclaimed her amazement. When they got to the image of the tormented man, they were dumbstruck.

Joel asked if this was a Photoshop trick or some kind of gag. Tito was in the room, as was Matt, and they confirmed that the images were still on the camera. I uploaded the images onto a CD Rom and the desktop.

We all looked at the CD Rom, then I ejected it, and wrote the word Cascades on it in black magic marker. I told Joel I would bring the CD Rom to Lisa's little sister Debbie's house, as we were getting together there the following weekend. We said goodnight and hung up.

For about an hour, we talked about the images and what they might mean. Then we decided to change the subject and watched a couple of movies. Tito stayed the night and left the next day. That afternoon we drove Matt back to his mother's house in Ringwood, New Jersey. Traffic was awful as usual each and every time we drove Matt back to Ringwood.

A few times we were late getting back - not hours late - just a little late. Once we were over an hour late, also traffic related. Lisa and I talked about it later, and we promised we would move closer to him to make life easier.

In June of 2005, Matthew was my Best Man, and Lisa and I kept our promise.

A week had passed since the day we emailed the images to Joel and Sandi. I took a look at the Cascades CD Rom and those awful pictures were still there. Creepy as all heck it was.

That thing in the hotel was clearly and deliberately looking right at us when we took those photos. That still freaks me out.

The following weekend we picked Matthew up and headed to Kendall Park in central New Jersey, to visit Debbie and her husband, Howard. Theirs was the wedding that Lisa wanted a date for when she was using Matchmaker.com for the very last time, which happened to be my first time. Her sister Debbie was eight years younger than Lisa, and twelve years younger than their oldest sister Sandi. Between Lisa and Debbie, was another sister, Elaine, who was three years younger than Lisa.

My in-laws had four girls. It had to be tough as parents, to have four pretty, independent-thinking young women to raise.

We got to the house and put our stuff down, that stuff being sleeping bags and assorted food goods and beverages. These family gatherings were always full of promise, and much fun and good food were key elements that never went missing. The discussion came up between Joel and me about the spooky photographs from Maine.

I told him I brought the CD Rom with me. He walked me to the spot where my knapsack was and saw me pull the disk, still in its case, out of the bag. It was marked in black magic marker, "Cascades." We took the disk to the kitchen and inserted it into Howard's laptop.

A message came up, asking if we wanted to format the disk. That made no sense, as it was formatted, and the images had been added and the CD-R file closed.

That was done in the company of two guys that knew information technology quite well: Tito and myself. In addition, we verified the images were on the disk a week later. I took the disk out and went up to Howard's office and inserted it into his desktop. Same result.

I turned the disk over to review the burn marks which are made when a disk is closed. The disk looked remarkably new, like nothing had ever been burned on it. No images found, because somehow the disk was not only erased but reverted to a clean blank format, with no standard burn indications to be seen anywhere. It made no sense at all. I was astonished.

We skipped the creepy image conversation, especially as the pictures were no longer on the camera chip, which was cleared to make room for a lot of pictures at *this* family get-together. We had a good time and stayed the night.

After breakfast with the family, Lisa, Matt and I headed to Queens, before driving back to Ringwood later that afternoon. When we got home, it occurred to me to look again at the pictures on my PC hard drives.

There was the main C drive and a backup internal hard drive. The pics had to be there and should be in the email I sent to Joel and Sandi. With Lisa, Matt, and I holding our breath, I pressed the desktop's power button.

To our utter astonishment, the computer blew up. No joke. Flames shot out of the side, and the whole PC went up in smoke. I managed to put the fire out and stood there in shock. My PC was gone. My images - all of them - were gone, with no hope of recovery.

Being that this was the earlier days (for me) concerning the concept of backing up my stuff, it was a harsh lesson learned. I did have the checking account info on a floppy disk but not the pictures. We called Joel and Sandi to ask them if they still had the email. Joel looked but it was not there. He didn't remember deleting the email. They purposely didn't download the images because they were too darn scary to keep.

Retrospectively, we all agreed that this was an absolutely strange occurrence. Seems there was a force at work that did not want those pictures shared with anyone. Didn't matter. What I ultimately wanted to share was beautiful and far more important. Before that could be accomplished, Lisa and I needed to keep our promise to move closer to Matthew.

CHAPTER 59
THE CHRISTMAS BIRD

2000s

There is no doubt in my mind that Lisa became a profound influence in Matthew's life. She helped us get started on a journey that would take us to far away and sometimes fascinating places.

The first place we needed to go was home.

In 2004 we started house-hunting in New Jersey. Matthew's mother still lived in Ringwood, and we wanted to be closer to him, to make his time with us more accessible and comforting.

Lisa had one request, that we stay within a reasonable commute to Queens, so we could get to her parents easily, and in case she or I needed to commute to New York City for work. Made sense to me.

At the time I was working in Roseland, New Jersey for a human resource based trade magazine. I was the advertising director for certain areas of service, such as finance and accounting. The commute from Forest Hills, Queens to Roseland was brutal on its own merits, so moving to Northern New Jersey really made sense. I give Lisa a lot of credit for patience and a great sense of humor. We went through some doozies together. We looked at a place in Fairlawn, that appeared spacious, with some potential. On closer inspection, it was a disaster in the making. The owner was a charming character that said things like,

"What asbestos, don't be silly, just buy the house - you'll be fine".

We knew better and just laughed it off. One of the things I told Lisa about that mattered most to me was a promise that had been made about twenty years earlier.

A heavenly voice told me that I would know I was home because the Christmas Bird would be in front of the house. This was really important to me, as I had already gone through such disappointment in life regarding being able to go home.

We looked at a lot of places, including a couple of available homes in Packanack Lake. One of them was a bungalow, that appeared to be a log cabin style. It needed quite a bit of fixing up. We went there once with Matthew. He was shocked at the implied poor quality and need for improvement. But it was in a great school zone. Lisa and I wanted to make sure there would be kids nearby and good schools, in case things worked out that Matthew could attend school by us.

The real estate fellow we met at the bungalow in Packanack was named George. He was friendly and impressed us as genuine and honest. We took an immediate liking to him. The bungalow in Packanack was the lowest priced house in the market, a market which in 2005 was contaminated by unnaturally inflated housing prices. So, we looked around some more for what seemed like months. None of the other homes we liked seemed affordable, and no Christmas Bird was ever seen.

Eventually Lisa and I met George and went back to the bungalow. We were looking it over again and weighed the work that it needed against the asking price. I excused myself from their company and went over by a window that faced the outside through a screened porch. Standing there I reached out to my Heavenly Father.

"Pop, please help me", I prayed under my breath.

"Please help me know if this is really home. You promised me that the Christmas Bird would be in front, but I can't find it. Please Father, please let me know if this can be home"

I closed the prayer in Jesus name, and just as I said "Amen", the most astounding thing occurred. A bright red cardinal landed on the tree right in front of my eyes. My reaction was spontaneous. I screamed out loud, startling Lisa and George,

"Lisa, Lisa, it's the Christmas Bird! The Christmas Bird is right here!"

She ran over to the window and just as she got there she saw the flash of crimson go by the glass as the bird flew away, probably startled by my yelling.

We married and bought the house all in the same month. We spent our honeymoon time cleaning and fixing it up, which took a lot of doing, but was only a beginning. Eventually we committed to a genuine renovation of the place. It needed it.

You might think that it was only a coincidence seeing the cardinal outside, but I believe it was divine intervention. You see the house we bought was situated on the property in such a way as to have no actual backyard, but instead two front and two side yards. Based on the layout of the lot, the tree that the bird landed in was exactly in the front of the house. Also, the tree itself was a dogwood tree.

There are many legends about the dogwood tree that imply it was used for His cross. It should be stated that research regarding that legend had been done before my own efforts, and there is no written history that shows a dogwood tree ever existed in Israel at the time of Jesus. But, if the legend had any truth to it, then the Christmas Bird could not have chosen a better tree to land on in front of my eyes.

More on the dogwood tree later.

When we first moved into the house, there was a damaged plastic statue of the Blessed Mother situated next to a hickory tree.

We replaced that warm reminder of her love with a stone image, and surrounding shell. She has always been there in my life.

The house has been a blessing to us in many ways. At the end of the year we moved in, I lost my job. It was just near Christmas. In a month or so, I came to new career with the public sector, which was respectively a mile from home.

We have both found new careers near home and have both remained in those careers for over a dozen years.

The land we live on is shared with all kinds of nature. There are fifteen species of trees, numerous plants, shrubs and growth that share color and splendor at varying times of the year.

We are visited by deer, rabbits, racoons, wild turkeys, blue jays, woodpeckers, cardinals, doves, finches, possums, moles, hawks, falcons, squirrels, chipmunks, and red furred foxes (obviously not in that order). We often feel like we live in a Discovery Channel environment.

Most importantly, the home has a gift of warmth. All that enter feel the welcome spirit of the cozy rooms within.

The house was filled with family love before we ever set foot in it, and the magic of comfort and peace that existed before us continues with us and our family and friends.

Last of all, to quell any doubts about the Hand of God in finding this place, during my whole life I had never lived more than eight years in a single dwelling.

I prayed to find a home. I've been here at home going on fifteen years now, with no thought of leaving. In fact, it's here that I am writing this message to you.

As to the legend of the dogwood tree, the legend says that the cross Jesus was nailed to was made from the dogwood. It was believed that the dogwood tree was once mighty, like the oak tree, and it was used to make furniture and the like.

Sadly, the legend says it was also used to make crosses for men to be crucified upon. The dogwood tree has beautiful flower petals that blossom during spring, typically near Easter. In the center of the petals is a cluster of small spikey looking brown leaves, like a thorny crown.

A poem was written about the dogwood tree and its blossoms by an unknown poet.

The Dogwood Tree

In Jesus time, the dogwood grew

to a stately size and a lovely hue.

'Twas strong & firm it's branches interwoven,

for the cross of Christ its timbers were chosen.

Seeing the distress at this use of their wood

Christ made a promise which still holds good:

"Never again shall the dogwood grow

Large enough to be used so

Slender & twisted, it shall be

With blossoms like the cross for all to see.

As blood stains the petals marked in brown

The blossom's center wears a thorny crown.

All who see it will remember me

Crucified on a cross from the dogwood tree.

Cherished and protected this tree shall be

A reminder to all of my agony."

– Unknown

CHAPTER 60
A GENTLEMAN WALKED FORWARD

1990s

From here forward an important part of my message to you is revealed. The experience or phenomenon that I refer to as the *Bright Room* provided me with details and information that I really had no earthly privilege to experience. It was only by His design that I became a spontaneous spiritual escort to certain folks that passed from here to there. Of that I am sure. The information I received had to come from a genuine resource because I had no other way of knowing any of the information I shared.

The Bright Room experience occurred at wakes or funerals. At each respective wake I was able to impart quickly gleaned facts to some of those in mourning, facts that were provided by folks on the other side of the veil. The people I shared them with were amazed, and some were downright freaked out by the accuracy of names and descriptions. One dear friend became very emotional.

Nothing in my life has ever compared to the experience I have had stepping into the Bright Room, albeit so briefly. For all my years and all the experiences, I have not seen anything here on Earth like what awaits us afterward.

I was blessed to enjoy many summer days going through a life that sometimes seemed like an Elvis Presley movie. I thought this life was grand. Sure, it was and is hard as heck, but still grand.

With that said, after having been to the Bright Room, nothing on Earth can compare to the feeling that I experienced therein. It is pure. It is bliss. There is no word known for me to describe the joy or the rejoicing that was on exhibit.

The first time that I was given the inspiring glimpse, it was at the wake of my friend Frank M.'s mom.

The viewing was in Long Island, in or near the town of Malvern. To be honest, when this happened to me the first time, I was shocked, and a little confused.

The first time it occurred I had a feeling that was akin to a massive sense of vertigo, lasting only a second or two. I saw something. I didn't know what it was or how to explain it. Kneeling by the casket, saying a prayer in respect, I was whisked into the Bright Room. It happened so fast that I was disoriented. Suddenly, I was standing in this environment that was beautiful and seriously shiny.

Everything was radiant, and I was amazed at the multitude of people. I realized something was different, as the scene was not where I believed I was standing a moment before.

Then I was suddenly back at the casket and the room seemed incredibly small and dim in comparison to the expanse I had just viewed. I had no idea what had happened, and in this instance had no takeaway from the experience to speak about.

The folks at the wake were somber and seemed as though some didn't have a connection to the others in the room, even though they were all there to pay respects to the same person.

I never expected celebrations at wakes, but knowing what I do, it should be a party.

Interestingly enough, when my own mother passed away, I experienced nothing at the wake or the funeral. No vision, no spirits. That was also true for my oldest brother-in-law and my maternal grandmother. No extraordinary event transpired. It was sad, and I felt disconnected at each wake, funeral, and burial that my immediate family endured.

I gave the eulogy for my brother-in-law, Bernard Fran, Senior, whose nickname was Blackie, due to his dark hair and swarthy skin. I miss him, and I am sure his wife and sons miss him more, but I am comforted by knowing we will see each other again.

The second time I was whisked away to the Bright Room was at the wake of a dear friend's mother. The deceased was named Mary, God rest her soul.

Her daughter, Joanie, was a close friend of Martha and me. Our sons, Matthew and Kevin, were pals who attended Pre-K and kindergarten together. The boys were close, and it was nice to see Matt develop a friendship with a classmate his age. I hope Matt can remember some of those days. They were fun.

Joanie and I once saw an angel - really. The angel we saw was a cloud formation. We were driving on the Belt Parkway in Brooklyn, somewhere near the Verrazano Bridge, when we both spotted it. Joanie was driving her minivan. I think we were coming back from an event that took place before her mother's passing. Joanie and I were both amazed and talked about it a few times, but it seemed others in the car were skeptical.

What we saw was an angel, with hands in supplication, a flowing gown, and huge beautiful wings. The angel had clear features and long hair. It may have been a cloud, perhaps sculpted by nature and shared with simple whimsy, but for Joanie and me that angel was real. People had stopped on the side of the parkway to look up and be amazed.

Joanie had a cousin named Dana and, other than knowing she was Joanie's cousin, and that she lived in the neighborhood, I didn't know much about her.

Turned out Dana was a super nice person who on occasion would babysit Matthew for us. She had a good rapport with him.

Martha and I were happy to have someone to call upon, in addition to Matthew's Godparents, Franny and Donald. Donald was married to Franny's sister Antoinette, and Matthew later called him Uncle Donald; he was a great guy. Franny was married to Dom who was a real sweetheart. Matt called him Uncle Dom. They lived down the block from us, and we were very lucky to have them in our lives.

Both Donald and Dominick have been called Home and have been gone a number of years. It's been a long time since I've seen Franny and the family. God bless them all. I hope life gave them some kindness.

As is customary and respectful, we all attended the wake and the funeral mass for Joanie's mom. At the wake, I was standing behind Joanie, and her cousin, Dana. I had already approached the casket and paid my respects in prayer. Standing behind Joanie, for whatever reason, I put my hand on her shoulder.

Suddenly I was not there but instead, was in the Bright Room. My hand was on Mary's shoulder, and we were both looking out at this vast glorious space, filled with happy smiles.

There were hundreds of people there, apparently all to welcome Mary. The room was beautiful, but that is a human term. I do not have the words to describe the beauty, the music, the feeling of euphoria.

I really do not own an adequate enough vocabulary to express the feeling or the sight of it. I simply call it the Bright Room because, as I stated earlier, everything therein is just brilliant. The people, the air, and the magical surroundings: it was all just brilliant, bright, and wondrous.

There were so very many happy faces. This Bright Room thing happens so fast, and yet so much is impressed upon me, including direct contact by someone there. Someone with a message for me to deliver.

A gentleman stepped cheerfully forward from the throng. He looked happy and confident. I recall he was broad shouldered, somewhat taller than I was, with salt and pepper hair, more dark than light, I think he had a mustache, and he wore such a bright smile on his handsome face. He was waving and speaking. I caught some of it as he said aloud,

"It's me! Rick! Please tell her I'm doing okay! I'll see her…"

Then it was over, and I was still standing with my hand on Joanie's shoulder. I stood amazed for a moment or two, breathing and trying to store the data that was just downloaded into my brain. I walked around and knelt down in front of Joanie and looked her in the eyes.

What I was about to tell Joanie I was sure she would believe, as I had already had a number of amazing experiences, some of which she knew about.

There would be no doubt that the event I witnessed was as real as breathing. I told her about where I went, and that it felt like I was there for a few moments. But that was not accurate.

I was not sure how long I was there because it seems time is not apparent on that side of the veil. I don't believe time has any meaning or application there at all. In real time, I believe I was there just a few moments and that I was standing there with her mother looking into the Bright Room, and it was amazing.

I asked her if she knew a guy named Richard or Rick, and described him: broad-shouldered, sort of salt and pepper hair, with a mustache, and a handsome smiling face. He had called to me to tell me to say Rick or Rich was okay.

I shared all this not knowing the dramatic and shocking effect it would have on Dana. The effect was as though she were thunderstruck. She jumped up from the chair, began crying, and ran out.

She came back in a few minutes, and she and Joanie, though very emotional, explained to me who the man I saw was. It was Dana's father. She was so moved, she had to run outside and breathe.

I honestly didn't know her father or that he had passed away. His passing preceded my getting acquainted with them, and it appeared he had passed before Matthew had been born.

Dana asked me what he said, so I repeated it, and again described him. Dana and Joanie were both sure, it was their Rick. Dana's father was there to greet a beloved family member.

Since the opportunity was presented, he sent Dana a message through the eyes and ears of this quickly passing visitor.

I hope Dana remembers that day and understands the powerful meaning of the message she was given. She would clearly see her father again, and he was doing great in his afterlife, at least as far as I could tell.

The Bright Room

Attending a wake, wherein others might grieve,

for a moment or two, though you may not believe,

I'd see a Bright Room, where loved ones stood wait,

where the deceased, now alive, all come celebrate.

Sometimes I'd hear laughter, or a name called aloud,

as the deceased, now alive, returned with joy to the crowd.

Into the Bright Room, slowly dancing, they'd enter,

with love, join the party, family and friends at its center.

Perhaps all the sadness we feel here while living,

is greatly compensated by the reception we're given.

What I saw in the Bright Room, was a miraculous sight,

Love, peace and joy, all in God's perfect Light!

~ JJJ

CHAPTER 61

DANCING ACROSS THE BEDROOM FLOOR

2000s

One of the more profound experiences I have had with the Bright Room had to do with the death of Lisa's grandfather, or Gung-Gung in Cantonese.

When Gung-Gung passed away, he was in his early nineties. He was frail looking with a wisp of white hair. He had an aged and gaunt looking face. His was a peaceful demeanor, and Lisa had great love and respect for him.

The day he died Lisa came over to my apartment (the one on the seventh floor of the Parker Towers, in Forest Hills Queens). She was understandably emotional, losing her beloved grandfather. She didn't know where to start with all that was swirling in her mind. Her father, Mr. Lum, was away on a trip to Africa, and missed the moment when his own father passed into the next realm.

I believe he would have liked to see his father before that happened, but he missed the chance. I think his being away was also upsetting for Lisa, as she made numerous comments about that. She sat with me on the edge of the bed, steadily crying, albeit oh so softly.

While I held Lisa in my arms, a strange thing occurred. From out of nowhere, I watched as a couple came slow dancing into the bedroom. It was an Asian couple.

The gentleman looked to be in his late fifties or early sixties. He was smartly dressed in a brilliant suit, and his hair was combed neatly to one side. He looked great.

It was Gung-Gung. In his arms was a woman with one of the biggest, happiest smiles I ever saw on a dance partner. She was also dressed beautifully in a gown that shimmered with light.

They stopped directly in front of us, and Gung-Gung looked right at Lisa and smiled. The woman he held also smiled at Lisa. He looked at me warmly. His lips mouthed a name, but I only caught one letter: the letter E. It was the only audible sound.

The two apparent sweethearts then simply danced right out of the room into the ether. Lisa saw and heard none of it.

As I held Lisa, I began to convey what had just happened. She was amazed and had no idea what to make of my observation. I described the woman as being Asian, cherubic, with black hair hanging nearly to her shoulders, and she was about a head shorter than Gung-Gung.

I explained the letter E was the only sound I was able to capture or understand and told her that Gung-Gung and his lovely dance partner had stopped by the bed to look down and smile upon her, glance at me, and then dance away into the other side of the veil.

Lisa was absolutely flabbergasted. I asked her who the woman might be. She thought it was probably her grandmother but had no idea what the letter E meant.

She explained to me that her father's mother had died in China when her father was about ten years old. His early life was pretty darn difficult. At only fourteen, he had to leave his father and family and depart for the United States, hoping to pursue what was a better chance for them all.

Lisa's dad, Mr. Lum, lost his mother and little brother when he was very young. Lisa said he never talked about them. She didn't know his mother's name, probably because the memory was just too painful to be shared.

Clearly, there was a woman with Gung-Gung. They were dancing like a happy couple deeply in love. There was a mystery to be solved.

During the next few days while the arrangements for the funeral were made, I visited with Lisa and her family. Lisa and I discussed the event in the apartment on the day Gung-Gung died.

She found a picture of her father's mom, which had been drawn by her grandfather. It was an ink drawing that looked like a photograph. It was Gung-Gung's dance partner.

Gung-Gung was a talented artist which ran in the blood of his family. Lisa finally asked her father about his mother, especially her name. He said he only knew one name for her, and it was Eng. He said it was spelled with an E.

Lisa looked at me with amazement, as I had no prior knowledge of her grandmother's name and her father had not once spoken of his mother to me or around me. Grandmother is simply called Pau-Pau in Cantonese.

The letter E had been the only sound I was able to make out when Gung-Gung was saying goodbye to Lisa on his way to happiness in a magical dance. It is my firm belief that Gung-Gung and Pau-Pau were joyously reunited, and that the love they shared when they were here on earth, for the little time they had, was a true love. The proof was there in the radiant smiles on both their faces.

I met Gung-Gung once more, at his wake.

The wake for Gung-Gung was held in a long-established Flushing, Queens funeral home. I was driving in from Manhattan, having driven to work that day. I promised Lisa I would attend the service and wanted to be on time.

I knew she needed a friend to be on hand, as her other family members all had someone unique to comfort them. As I was driving, all kinds of obstacles were thrown into my path. An accident happened near me, and it slowed everything down.

The exit I thought I was supposed to take was blocked off, and I had to find another route. After a few more wrong turns, I realized something was trying to prevent me from attending the services. I stopped at a red light on Queens Boulevard and took a moment to ask God for help.

I prayed and noted in the prayer that I believed something was keeping me from getting to the service. I didn't know what it might be or why it was trying to prevent me from getting there, but I felt the resistance - instinctively and spiritually. I prayed in His name to ask for help and guidance.

Almost immediately, I found an exit that led me back towards Northern Boulevard and in a matter of minutes I arrived near the funeral home. I found parking rather quickly, along the side street. I hoped it was legal enough not to end up being towed away. That is a risk when parking in the five boroughs. I fixed my tie, made sure I looked respectable, and then entered the funeral home.

Inside, I found a number of relatives in the main hall. There was a set of stairs that went up to the viewing rooms. I followed the signs and the familiar faces, most of those I met only recently. Within the room, I found Lisa. She was clearly happy to see me, and I was very happy to see her, though the venue was sad unto itself.

She looked forlorn, and so did most of the folks there. I greeted those that I knew and expressed my sorrow to Lisa's father and mother. Mr. Lum, Lisa's dad, looked very serious and distraught.

It was probably a shock to have a parent around for so long, then to see them in their passing state of rest. I went to Lisa and sat with her by her father's brother from Toronto, Uncle Kenny. He and I met the year before at sister Debbie's wedding. I liked him immediately. He's a genuinely warm and expressive fellow.

Lisa told me we should approach the coffin together. She explained that when we did, we were to bow together three times, then light burning sticks that looked like incense sticks, but I don't recall if they had a smell.

I had read in one of my books about joss sticks which were to give good luck to those lighting them, but these were different.

We approached the coffin, walking behind others in the line. They were there with sincere intent to pay final respects to a patriarch who was obviously much loved. Our turn came and we stood in front of the coffin. I didn't remark about it, but Gung-Gung looked much better two days before when he and Eng danced through my apartment. He didn't look bad in the coffin, but he didn't look alive either. In the apartment, he had looked absolutely robust, full of joy and vigor, a happy dance partner.

We bowed for the first time. I looked at Lisa and saw her pain. She had tears welling in her eyes. Lisa is such a sweet soul. I know she didn't see what I saw in the apartment though I wish she had. I really felt sorry for her loss.

We bowed for the second time. Simultaneously, something changed. Of a sudden, I was standing in this brilliant space with my right hand on Gung-Gung's shoulder. His shoulder felt firm and real. He looked amazing. In the space were hundreds of people - maybe a thousand - all looking bright and beautiful.

I didn't know any of the people there, but saying they were happy to see him is ridiculously inadequate to express the joy that was there. It was palpable and filled me with a warm sensation, that same buzzing, tingling, awesome feeling I had when the Blessed Mother pushed the last girl at me, and she bit into me and filled my soul. Everyone looked so bright, but I could make out details. It was remarkable. Amazing.

A gentleman some twenty feet to the left of Gung-Gung raised his hand and waved vigorously. He looked like Gung-Gung but slightly taller. He was holding hands with a woman at his side. She was petite, at least next to him. They both looked very happy. I knew - but don't know why I knew - that he was a blood family member, and that the lady was also related, but not by blood. The man called out,

"Hey! It's me, Robert, and S..."

Then I was straightening up from the second bow, and stood standing in amazement next to Lisa. She knew something had happened to me but didn't understand what it was. The weird part was that it felt like I was there with Gung-Gung for a long time, perhaps a few minutes, but there in the funeral parlor, I was still standing up at the coffin, having finished the second bow. We bowed the third time, then placed our sticks in the glass and lit them. It was a very respectful gesture.

To me, it was like providing more light for the path home. I knew though that Gung-Gung was safe and happy and with loved ones. Before we walked away from the coffin, I told Lisa everything that I experienced. We went to the seats and sat by Uncle Kenny where I reiterated what I shared with Lisa. He had goosebumps sitting next to me.

He said Robert was Gung-Gung's older brother, and he had passed away years before. The letter S made sense because Roberts's wife Suzie had passed only a short time after her husband.

My description of Robert was unnerving to Uncle Kenny. I told him that there was absolutely no doubt about what I had experienced.

Lisa solidly accounted that I never knew any of Gung-Gung's history or his family names or even if he had siblings. There was no resource for me to have secured those salient details other than the truth. I was there. Praise God.

CHAPTER 62
HER HAND WAS HELD WITH LOVE

2010s

Lisa had an aunt from her mother's side named Yue Mei Chiu, or Melinda to some.

We often called her EE Je (pronounced like *ji*, or the beginning of the word *giant*). It means little aunt, according to my wife Lisa. Yue Mei was Lisa's mom's little sister. She had a number of difficulties in life, but Yue Mei enjoyed life and made it worthwhile. She was always active, working in arts and crafts, doing exercise, and staying involved with her church.

Yue Mei was born in Guangzhou, China in 1950. When she was about 8 years old, she had moved to Hong Kong. Not long after, as a teenager, Yue Mei moved to the United States and put down roots in Queens, New York. She worked as a seamstress for over 10 years. Yue Mei married Peter and together they owned and operated a fruit and vegetable store.

Two years into the marriage she became a mother to Karen. Subsequently she helped her daughter in raising three grandchildren that she loved and cherished. They were her life's joy. She loved them dearly, and I am sure she still very much does.

Yue Mei's story has an important connection to this missive on heavenly and other spiritual interactions. You see, in 2015, Yue Mei went into a coma. She lingered in that state for days, until her big sister came back from traveling and had a chance to say goodbye.

Peacefully and faithfully, she departed this part of the journey, though with much pain and sorrow for her daughter and family. I was not there as she finally departed the mortal coil.

I had a vision the day before Yue Mei passed. I was half asleep and sat in the bed staring at a sight I couldn't believe.

I clearly heard Yue Mei's voice. She was calling out as she held the hand of a woman I did not know and whose face I could not see because of a blinding yet cheerful light. I could make out that the person was holding her tightly and patiently by the hand and with great, great love.

I heard Yue Mei say,

"A Ma."

I watched as she turned and looked at me and then smiled. In faith and with my most sincere conviction that I say this is true, she was at peace. Nevertheless, this was a vision not the reality of the moment.

On the night the vision occurred, Yue Mei was still in a coma, and the next day with her big sister back home, there was going to be a very hard decision to make.

She had been attached to a ventilator for days, and there was no sign of brain activity. From the vision, I saw she was being held halfway between here and the other side.

I asked Lisa who A Ma was, as I had not heard of that relative. I explained that I saw Yue Mei in a vision, and it was extremely clear that A Ma was holding her hand, acting as an anchor and friend on the other side of the veil.

Lisa explained that A Ma was not the name of an aunt or relative, she said the words A Ma are the same as saying Mom, or Mommy.

It was Yue Mei's mother that was holding her hand, reassuring her that all would be well.

I never met Yue Mei's mom. Lisa called her Ju Pau.

Ju Pau was Lisa's maternal grandmother. Lisa spoke with great delight about her.

With her daughter by her side, the decision was made to see if Yue Mei could make it without the life support device. They took her off of it.

It was not too long before she quietly expired. Her soul was free, and I already knew she was in the Bright Room. Her dear mother, her A Ma, had taken her by the hand to lead her into the Light of God.

She was at peace, for as John, Chapter 2, verse 25 says: "Jesus said to her I am the resurrection and the life. Whoever believes in me, though he/she die, yet shall they live."

Yue Mei believed in the Lord. She is there in His greatness, sharing in the Light with her A Ma and all her family and friends. I believe this without a single doubt. That's called faith.

EPILOG

Someone asked if I ever doubted my faith. I answered honestly and said of course I did, I'm human. When my son was a baby I asked God why He crippled me. The answer was provided by a man that lost his eyes and was grateful God spared his life. I realized that God did not cripple me - He saved me.

There's another question that comes up fairly often. It's the one about death being too soon. How is God good when my little girl died so young? Why did God take our mother from us before we grew up? Why did my dad die when I was a teen?

I realize we all have such questions, and they are deeply personal and very painful. My answer to these is another question:

"What is too soon?"

Why are we holding onto this life and these experiences as though they were forever? They are not. Sometimes I forget I'm on borrowed time. We all are. Nobody is here for keeps. This physical life is a phase, and when compared to forever it's a blip in time. Think about it! How does one compare thirty years or even a hundred years to thousands of years?

The span of all eternity is unknowable. We can count time in decades, centuries, millennia, mega-annum, and so forth. Still, no matter when it happens, losing our loved ones hurts. The pain and suffering we feel with loss is very real.

Here on the mortal coil we have to live with it. There is no real reason for us feel the pain of loss - except that we miss those that left. We cannot question the why, as it won't matter. Not because the pain one feels isn't real - it very much is. It is because the love that goes with that pain is undying.

I do miss loved ones, especially my mom, and it hurts in spite of what I know. I move through that hurt because of faith. Not a blind faith, but a knowledge-based one. I already shared the good news of what I saw. Loved ones that passed before us are already living in the eternal Light, starting with a wondrous reception in the Bright Room. They are at peace. They do not see time as we do because time does not exist for them.

I know we will be reunited with our loved ones and it will seem as though they never left us. Honor them. Live the best life you can while here. It's all connected in the long run, from here to eternity.

Whether you believe this or not isn't going to change certain truths. The first truth is that you too will no longer have a physical life as you know it. You will be leaving here.

Another truth I've been trying to share is that we are not finished by physical death. Jesus broke the bonds of death for all of us, no matter color of skin, gender, or belief system.

Without a doubt I believe that the Lord gave us His Son, born of Mary. For over two-thousand years the life, death, and re-birth of

Jesus Christ has been celebrated worldwide especially on Christmas and Easter.

Jesus lived a short life as a man, and He sacrificed that life to show us the way home. His death was for the sake of all living souls.

He told His disciples the way to the Father is through Him. Believing in Him is one part, living like Him is another. He was good to those around Him, good to His mother, father, family, and friends. He was kind to strangers, and helped people struggling. He healed, forgave, and He loved. I believe in Jesus. I believe in God the Father, our Heavenly Mother, the Holy Spirit, and the host of angels at the Lord's side.

I also believe in the law of attraction because it is an act of faith guided by the Holy Spirit, based on the idea of believing without doubt. Regardless of the variety of religious beliefs, educations, achievements, politics, hair styles, skin colors, and favorite foods, we are all just human beings, physically born, inevitably to die. Eternal peace is the ultimate goal of our human path.

I have seen the tranquility and beauty of the Bright Room. I know where good souls go. Be good to your families, friends, and yourselves, but also be kind to the helpless, elderly, and disabled. Show respect to all of nature, because He made it.

Random acts of kindness are very much like Jesus. He was the embodiment of an act of kindness. If we try to follow His example I believe humanity will have a chance to evolve. It's on us. We have to have faith. We have to want peace.

I hope that this message has some meaning for you. It has been my belief that He wrote the message throughout my life; I am just sharing it as best I can. If this telling was at all helpful for you, please don't thank the messenger, thank God. I wish peace for you and yours.

Meet Again

Working, playing, fast though time,

changes happen, no reason rhyme,

touching souls, we make a friend,

throughout eternity, and meet again.

Perhaps too quick, we squeeze the lime,

we seem so rushed, the short length of time,

but moments happen, we make a friend,

throughout eternity, then meet again.

Living, loving, clear of mind,

like passing goodness, left behind,

touching souls, we make a friend,

throughout eternity, to meet again.

~ JJJ

"Therefore, I say unto you,

Whatsoever ye desire, when ye pray,

believe that ye receive, and ye shall have."

Mark 11:24

ACKNOWLEDGMENTS

Lisa – The Creator of Beautiful Cover Art

Louise – An Exceptional Proof-Reading Friend

My deepest gratitude for helping me take this from conversational chatter about a very odd life to a published means of sharing a message

Reference

Books

- Aldridge, Faye (2011)
  Real Messages from Heaven
  Destiny Image Publishers Inc., Shippensburg, PA

- Burnham, Sophy (2014)
  A Book of Angels
  Penguin Group (USA), New York, NY

- Capra, Fritjof (2010) *The Tao of Physics*
  Shambala Publications, Inc., Boston, MA

- Holzer, Hans (1977)
  Ghosts, True Encounters with the World Beyond
  Black Dog & Leventhal Publishers, New York, NY

- Olsen, Judy C. (2010)
  Angels Round About
  Covenant Communications, Inc., American Fork, UT

Web

- Redd, Nola Taylor, www.Space.com (July 19, 2019)
  Scientific definition of an astronomic material known as Dark Matter
  https://www.space.com/20930-dark-matter.html

- Wagner, Stephen www.ThoughtCo.com (April 24, 2018)
  Explanations for the "Shadow People" Phenomenon
  https://www.thoughtco.com/shadow-people-2596772

- Hansen, Judith www.NewEngland.com (May 1, 2018)
  The Curse of the Saco River | Yankee Classic
  https://newengland.com/today/living/new-england-history/curse-saco-river/

- Cliff www.Pararational.com (November 4, 2016)
  Types of Shadow People – What They Are And What They Want
  https://pararational.com/types-of-shadow-people/

- Offut, Jason www.mysteriousuniverse.org (March 27, 2012)
  The Lurking Shadow People
  https://mysteriousuniverse.org/2012/03/the-lurking-shadow-people/

- Staff writer www.beyondsciencetv.com (July 25, 2017)
  The Mysterious Shadow People
  https://www.beyondsciencetv.com/2017/07/25/the-mysterious-shadow-peopl

Hope Your Glass Overflows

"Pray without ceasing"

Thessalonians 5:17

www.ingramcontent.com/pod-product-compliance
Lightning Source LLC
Chambersburg PA
CBHW071328080526
44587CB00017B/2761